THE STEP-BY-STEP GUIDE TO

REPAIRS & IMPROVEMENTS

John McGowan & Roger DuBern

In association with  *magazine*

BCA

LONDON · NEW YORK · SYDNEY · TORONTO

This edition published 1992
by BCA by arrangement with
Reed International Books Ltd

CN 2479

Printed in Portugal

Acknowledgements

Managing Editor: Lesley McOwan
Design: Pedro Prá-Lopez
Step-by-step illustrations: Keith Field & David Papworth
Anatomical & Finished Project Illustrations: Ted Williams
Editor: Barbara Horn
Production: Nick Thompson
Typesetting: Kingfisher Design Services / Dorchester Typesetting Group Ltd
DIY Consultant: Mike Trier

CONTENTS

ANATOMY & CONSTRUCTION

REPAIRS & DECORATION

PROJECTS STEP-BY-STEP

MAINTAINING THE HOME

INTRODUCTION

Successful do-it-yourself work is based on knowledge and experience, which combine to produce a growing sense of confidence. Even if you have never before attempted any do-it-yourself jobs, this book will teach you all the basic skills you need in order to maintain and improve the interior of your home.

The first section, **Anatomy and Construction**, shows you how a typical home is built – how the walls, floors and ceilings are constructed, and how the various services are supplied to each room. Although your home may differ in detail, the principles will be the same.

Decoration shows you, with clear illustrations to guide you each step of the way, how to apply a variety of decorative treatments and materials to walls, floors and ceilings.

In **Maintenance and Repairs** you will learn how to cope with the basic electricity and plumbing services in your home. This section also shows you how to insulate your home properly and cope with various other common faults and emergencies. By reading this part of the book **now**, before you have an emergency, you may well quickly prevent it from becoming a major crisis.

The third section, **Projects**, includes useful and attractive items to construct for use in your home, ranging from a two-tier coffee table to built-in wardrobes, as well as ways of enhancing the appearance by concealing unsightly pipes and plumbing, and maximising the space by blocking a doorway or building a room divider.

In **Materials and Techniques** you will find details about the tools and materials you will need to tackle the tasks in the book, and explanations of the basic techniques, including preparing surfaces before decorating.

A handy checklist will remind you about regular maintenance jobs, and there is a glossary of technical terms used in the book. Words in the text that appear in italic are more fully explained in the glossary, Tool Kit and Techniques Sections.

ANATOMY & CONSTRUCTION

Pipes and cables supplying gas, water and electricity are generally run in much the same way, though details will, of course, vary from room to room.

You need to know where these supply routes are so that you won't drill holes or hammer nails into surfaces concealing a pipe or cable.

Although some underfloor supply routes can be established by taking up some floorboards, if you need to pin-point the exact location of a cable or pipe buried in the wall, use a battery-powered detector to trace its path.

THE HIDDEN KITCHEN

The kitchen is by far the most complex room in the house. Whatever its size and shape, it is likely to contain appliances requiring every type of supply pipe and cable.

The sink taps need to be connected to sources of hot and cold water, while washing machines and dishwashers need either cold, or hot and cold water supplies. There must also be waste pipes to carry used water to outside drains. For plumbing convenience, these appliances are usually situated close to each other and as close as possible to the outside drain into which the waste water is discharged. A stopcock, usually found under the sink, enables the cold water supply to be turned off.

If there are gas appliances – boiler, oven or hob – then pipes are run to them from the gas meter. Not all houses have a gas supply; some are all electric. Cables run from the electricity meter, via the consumer unit (or fusebox), to the various electric appliances.

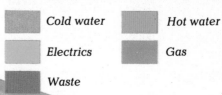

▨ Cold water		▨ Hot water	
▨ Electrics		▨ Gas	
▨ Waste			

THE HIDDEN LOUNGE & DINER

Electricity is likely to dominate these areas whether they are part of an open-plan arrangement or individual rooms. How complex the electricity supply will be is determined by the size and shape of the area, and the number of wall or ceiling lights. The lighting cable may drop down to supply power to a number of wall lights, or may feed pendant lights or a bank of spotlights.

The ring circuit is likely to have a large number of socket outlets on it, positioned at frequent intervals around the room. Whether or not there are sufficient sockets will be determined by the amount of equipment in the room – TV, stereo, table lamps, standard lamps and so on.

The central-heating pipework may run to one or more radiators, and if there is a gas fire, it will need a supply pipe run from the gas meter.

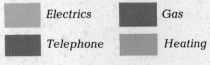

Electrics   Gas

Telephone   Heating

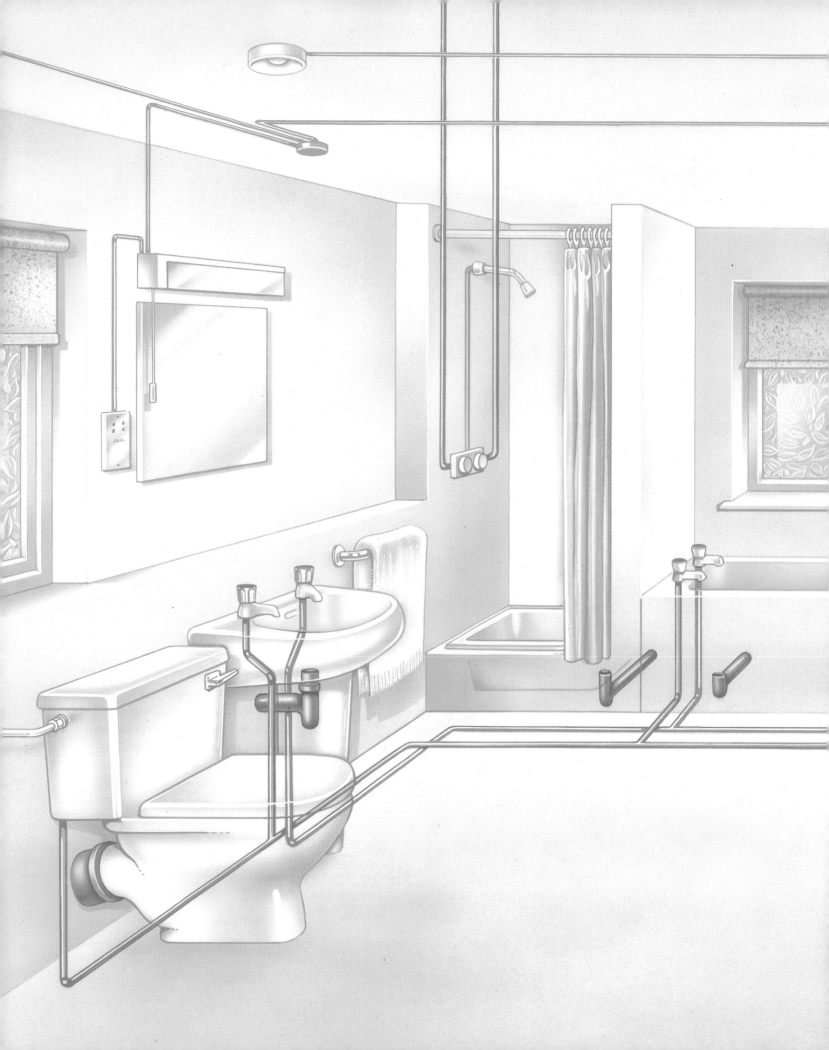

THE HIDDEN BATHROOM

This is the second most complex room, requiring a supply of hot and cold water to individual appliances, with an efficient waste system to carry used water to the house drains. Some bathrooms may contain just a bath and basin, while others also have a separate shower enclosure, bidet and toilet. There may be an airing cupboard, containing the hot-water cylinder, although this can be located in another part of the house.

The electricity supply to the room will be limited, as socket outlets are not allowed. Apart from lighting, electricity may need to be supplied to the immersion heater in the hot-water cylinder, possibly an electric shower, bathroom cabinet with shaver supply unit and light, or a heated towel rail. In a well-planned and fitted bathroom no supply pipes or waste pipes will be visible – they will be run behind appliances and concealed by a simple boxing-in arrangement.

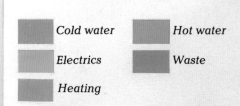

Cold water   Hot water

Electrics   Waste

Heating

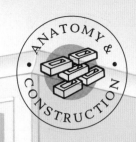

THE HIDDEN BEDROOM

These are likely to be the simplest in the house. A basic room may just have a single central ceiling pendant and one or two socket outlets for portable appliances. However, more sophisticated bedrooms and those being used to double as work or hobby centres will have a more complex electricity arrangement involving numerous socket outlets and flexible and functional lighting. An extra ceiling pendant, perhaps bedside wall spotlights and interior wardrobe lighting may also be installed.

Radiators on the central-heating system will be supplied by underfloor pipework. A single radiator is likely to be sited below the window. In a larger room it could be supplemented by a second radiator.

A useful additional facility in a bedroom is a sink. For convenience in providing a hot and cold water supply to the taps and, more important, drainage, the sink is often sited on a wall adjoining a bathroom.

▨	Cold water	▨	Hot water
▨	Electrics	▨	Waste
▨	Heating	▨	Telephone

TYPES OF WALL

H ere you can see all the different types of internal and external walls that may be found in houses. Your house will have a mixture of two, or possibly three or four, types. It all depends on the age of the house and whether or not it has been altered or extended in some way over the years.

Where straightforward decorating is concerned, for the most part it doesn't matter how a wall is built. The surface will be plaster or plasterboard, and they can be treated the same. Both will accept paint and all wall-coverings from basic wallpaper to vinyl or more unusual finishes, such as hessian. Ceramic tiles, brick tiles, decorative stone and cork can be fixed straight on to them with an adhesive.

You must be careful where screws or nails have to be used, for example, with mirrors, shelving, cupboards or timber cladding. You have to make sure the screws or nails are fixed into a solid background: bricks, blocks or timber uprights, although plasterboard will accept cavity fixings for light loads. If the screws and nails are not properly secured, the fixture will fall off the wall.

Internal Walls

These are the ways that the walls dividing the rooms and hallways of your house can be built.

When tapped with the hand a solid wall will feel and sound solid, whereas a hollow wall sounds hollow. If you drill into a plasterboard wall, the drill will quickly go straight through it and very little dust will emerge. If you drill into a solid wall, you will feel resistance and coloured dust – red, grey or black, for example – will emerge. To locate the timber uprights (studs) behind a partition wall you can drill test holes until you strike wood or you can use a detector.

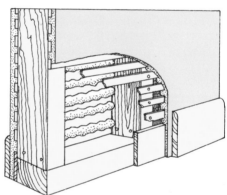

Lath-and-plaster stud partition: Found in houses built before 1920. Plaster layer is fixed to thin timber laths, which, in turn, are nailed to timber uprights.

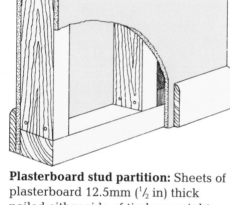

Plasterboard stud partition: Sheets of plasterboard 12.5mm ($\frac{1}{2}$ in) thick nailed either side of timber uprights – usually 75 x 50mm (3 x 2 in) and spaced at 400mm (16 in) centres.

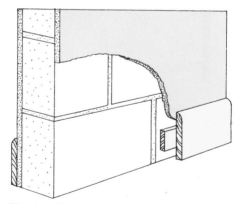

Plastered concrete-block partition: Lightweight building blocks covered with plaster up to 19mm ($\frac{3}{4}$ in) thick. Grey dust emerges when drilled. Special wall-plugs are needed.

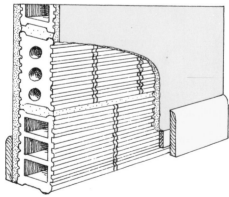

Plastered hollow clay block partition: Lightweight building blocks with a layer of plaster. Red dust emerges when drilled. Special wall-plugs needed.

External Walls

The walls on the outside of the house are always built with bricks or blocks. You can make sound fixings into them any place away from pipes and cables and so on. Cavity walls are found in houses built since the late 1920s. Timber-framed walls are the most modern of all.

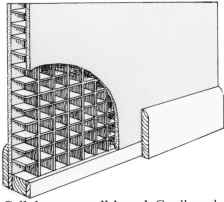

Cellular core wall-board: Cardboard core sandwiched between sheets of 19mm (³/₄ in) plasterboard. Timber uprights, 38mm (1¹/₂ in) wide, are set 400–610mm (16–24 in) apart. Special cavity wall-plugs needed.

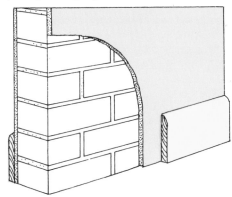

Plastered single skin of brick: Normal bricks covered with a plaster layer about 18mm (³/₄ in) thick. Dust, usually a reddish colour, emerges when drilled.

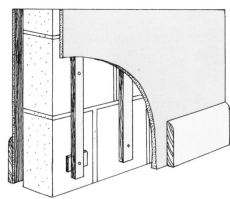

Plasterboard-lined block or brick: Normally only on the inside of an external wall. Sheets of 9.5 or 12mm (³/₈ or ¹/₂ in) thick plasterboard fixed directly to the wall or to 50 x 25mm (2 x 1 in) vertical timber battens.

SOLID WALLS

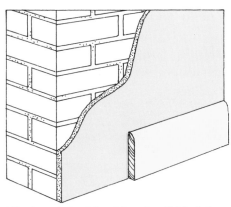

Plastered double skin of solid brick: Normally found only in houses built pre-1920s.

CAVITY WALLS

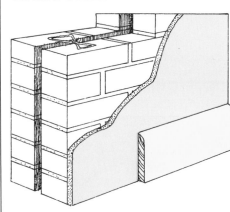

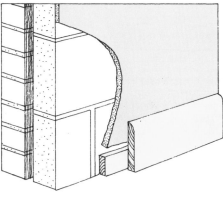

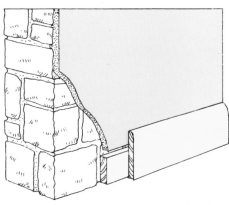

Plastered stone: Normally found only in houses built pre-1920s.

Brick inner leaf plastered (left): Two leaves of brick with a 50mm (2 in) gap between; plastered inner face.

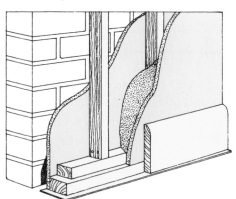

Timber-framed (above): Outer leaf, brick; inner leaf, timber uprights, usually 100 x 50mm (4 x 2 in), set 400mm (16 in) apart. Frame has plywood outside and plasterboard inside.

Block inner leaf plastered (below left): A gap of 50mm (2 in) is between the brick and plastered inner block leaves with 50mm (2 in) gap between.

TYPES OF FLOORS & CEILINGS

Both floors and ceilings tend to be ignored until they give trouble; then making repairs can be a problem unless you know how they are constructed.

Floors fall into two basic types – timber and solid. Solid floors give few problems. They tend to be found at ground floor level in newer houses and in fairly recently built ground floor extensions. They feel solid to walk on and, because of the difficulty of lifting them, they rarely have pipes or cables buried beneath their surface.

Timber floors are very common, particularly in upstairs rooms of houses of all ages and in ground floors of older houses. They may be formed by nailing floorboards or sheets of chipboard over timber beams called floor joists. They are useful because it is easy to run pipes and electric cables under them.

There are only two types of ceiling: the older lath and plaster, and the modern plasterboard. Lath and plaster ceilings tend to crack, sag and generally give more problems than the plasterboard type.

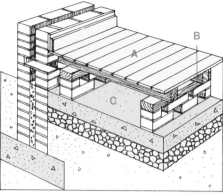

Timber floors: Downstairs, floorboards (A) are nailed to joists (B). The gap (C) under the floor is for air circulation.

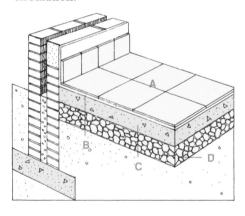

Solid floors: (A) Floor surface tiles over cement. (B) Damp-proof membrane. (C) Concrete. (D) Hardcore. Usually surfaced with a fixed covering.

Floor Types

Solid floors comprise a layer of concrete over hardcore, covered with a sheet of plastic as a dampproof membrane to keep the floor dry and topped with a fine concrete screed.

With timber floors, plain or tongued-and-grooved boards are nailed over joists. These are built into the walls, supported on metal brackets (joist hangers), or built on low walls.

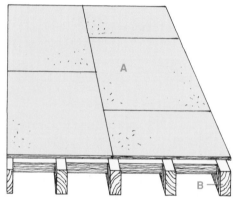

Upper floors: Chipboard panels (A) or floorboards are nailed over the joists (B), which may receive intermediate support from partition walls.

Ceiling Types

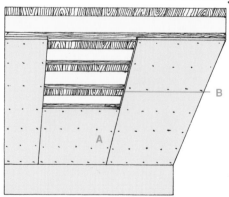

Plasterboard: Sheets of plasterboard (A) are nailed to the undersides of the ceiling joists (B) and the joints between boards smoothed with plaster filler.

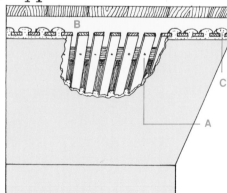

Lath and plaster: Timber strips (laths) (A) nailed to the undersides of the joists (B); plaster (C) containing horse hair is then forced between the laths.

DECORATING

The secret of successful decorating lies in following four golden rules: choose the correct materials, prepare surfaces properly, use the correct tools and equipment and, most important, take the time to do a job to the best of your ability.

All the jobs described in this section can be tackled with confidence by anyone, irrespective of their experience or ability. Follow the rules and you will get first-class results. Before you start, make sure that you have absorbed all the information relating to the specific job, and, where applicable, read and follow any instructions supplied by a manufacturer.

WALLS

Everyone can hang wallpaper correctly if they become aware of the pitfalls in advance and know how to avoid them. There are four stages: first, it is important to work with a wallpaper which is easy to handle. Second, the pattern of the paper should suit the room and individual skill level. Third, the walls must be prepared properly and, last, you should work as slowly as you need to ensure accuracy.

When you buy your wallpaper you will notice that there is a considerably difference between the cheapest and the most expensive. The thinnest wallpaper is usually the least costly but it is really best avoided by the beginner because it tends to tear easily having been pasted. Because of this it can be difficult to avoid problems when positioning it on the wall. So even if it has a very appealing pattern, think twice before buying.

The best bet is a medium-weight paper or a vinyl. Either of these will withstand a fair amount of mishandling without tearing. If you feel a few rolls of paper, you will soon be able to distinguish between thin, medium, and heavy-weight wallpapers; price alone is not an exact guide.

It is also important to buy the correct paste for hanging the paper – see materials section.

PATTERNS

Although pattern and colour are a matter of personal preference, there are points to consider in relation to the room being decorated and, again, to your own ability.

Simply in terms of interior design you would not want to choose a dark, sombre pattern for a small room or one that enjoys very little daylight. It's also true that a pattern with a huge motif would swamp a small room and a tiny motif could sink into insignificance in a spacious room. Also, a large motif or one with a regular, geometric design would be visually disturbing in a room or hallway where there are windows, doors, corners, reveals, nooks and crannies in abundance. This would continually break up the continuity of the pattern and disturb the eye which tends to pick up and follow a pattern repeat.

Apart from being a poor design choice, you would also be creating great difficulties from the practical point of view. Pattern matching is the real skill in hanging wallpaper and the wrong pattern can lead to extremely slow progress, wasted paper, errors and poor results. Should you make mistakes, they may well be obvious.

You must remember that very few rooms, especially in older houses, have true corners, even ceiling lines. Regular patterns, particularly vertical stripes will highlight these faults. A good example is where the ceiling line slopes considerably. Here a row of horizontal flowers would be seen to gradually 'disappear' along the ceiling line from one side of the room to the other. Even a professional could not overcome this situation.

The answer to all these problems is to select a random design so that you won't have to worry about precise pattern matching. This will enable you to work more quickly and enjoy what you are doing. Once you have some experience you will know when to graduate to more complicated levels.

COLOUR SHADING

On the label provided with a roll of paper, you may see the instruction to 'shade before hanging'. This relates to the colour shade in the pattern. The way wallpaper is printed means that the colours can vary from pale to rich – from one roll to the next.

To overcome this, the paper is printed in batches which means that the colours in each batch should be consistent. Usually they are, but there is the odd occasion when they are not.

On the label of the roll is a batch number. Check this against the other rolls – it should be the same. If you take the rolls of paper into a good light, you can check that the colours are the same shade. Should you find one that differs, keep it for a separate wall where the effects of light and shade in the room will disguise the difference.

READY-PASTED

The advantage of using a ready-pasted paper is that you don't have to worry about mixing up a bucket of paste and brushing paste on to the wall-covering before hanging it. The paste is already on the back of the wall-covering in a dried form. To activate it, you immerse it in a trough of water. The wall-covering is then pulled out of the water and brushed straight onto the wall.

In theory this sounds much more convenient, and it can be. However, some people find it difficult to manage. It can be messy in inexperienced hands and, without correct use, the paste may not be completely activated, leaving dry patches which don't stick to the wall. Also, if you work too slowly, the paste can start to dry out which means you have to mix up a small bucket of ordinary paste to reactivate edges. It's one of those things you have to try for yourself.

Novamura is a wall-covering with a difference which, again, some people find easier to use than others. With this, you apply the paste to the wall, not to the wall-covering. The dry length of wall-covering is brushed onto the pasted wall so that it sticks in place.

BUYING

If you refer to the wallpaper calculating chart on p. 237, you will be able to work out the number of rolls needed. Since there is more wastage through matching large motif patterns, add on 10 per cent for these. Because of the problem of possible shading variations and batch numbers mentioned earlier, if you are in doubt about the quantity you need, see if you can order an 'extra' roll on a sale or return basis. This means that if the cellophane wrapper is kept intact and the roll is not needed you can get your money back. The problem with running out and having to go back for an extra roll is that you are unlikely to get one from the same batch and the colour shade could be noticeably different.

Finally, always store rolls of paper on their sides. Standing them upright can damage the all-important edges.

PLANNING & PASTING

Assuming you have got the room ready (*see* 'Repairs and Preparation') and have selected your wall-covering, you can now decide on the best starting point in the room. This depends on the pattern you have chosen.

Normally you would start on the window wall and then work back into the room. The object of this is that should any edges of adjoining lengths be slightly overlapped (they are not supposed to be), then, since you are working away from the light source, a shadow will not be cast on the overlap, making the error evident.

The exception to this is where a large motif is being used and there is a dominant focal point in the room, such as a chimney-breast. Here, for a balanced appearance, the motif would need to be centralized on the breast wall. So, to ensure this happens, you would hang your first length here.

Wallpaper must be hung vertically on the wall. Corners, door frames, the sides of shelf units and similar features cannot be used as a starting point because they are rarely true. The way to establish a true vertical is to use a plumb-line. You pin this to the top of the wall and when it stops swinging it indicates a true vertical. Carefully transfer this mark on to the wall and you have your vertical starting point. The alternative is to use a 1m (3ft), or longer, spirit level.

Every time you take paper on to a new wall – that is, around a corner – you must go through the process of marking a vertical guideline on the wall.

Use a pencil to mark the guideline. Ink or felt pens are not suitable, as they can soak through the paste and stain the paper.

SOAKING THE PAPER

Be thorough when pasting each length of paper. You must cover every bit of it, so work in a systematic way. If you leave a dry patch, it will show as a 'bubble' after the length has been hung on the wall.

Don't splash on the paste so that it is as thick as jam and don't skimp either – this is even worse. You need a smooth overall layer. Work carefully, adjusting the paper on the table so that the edge of paper being pasted is marginally proud of the edge of the table. This prevents paste from getting on to the edge of the table and smearing on to the decorative face of the paper. However careful you are, paste might be left on the table. Have a sponge, bowl of water and towel handy to clean up before the next length is pasted. If any paste gets on to the decorative face of the paper, wipe it off with a clean, wet sponge immediately.

Having pasted and folded the length of paper, you may have to leave it to soak before hanging it. Lightweight papers and vinyl wall-coverings can be hung almost immediately, but other types should be left folded for a while to allow the paste to soak in. Unless the paste has soaked into the paper, it will not stick properly and bubbles may form. In extreme cases, the paper might be almost falling off the wall the following day.

In the absence of any exact guidance on the manufacturer's instruction label, allow medium-weight papers about five minutes to soak and heavyweight and thick-textured papers about ten minutes. You can always tell if a heavyweight paper (the most troublesome) is ready for hanging because it will be soft and floppy.

Try to keep the soaking time the same for each length, otherwise the lengths might stretch irregularly when being brushed on to the wall, making pattern matching difficult. If this should happen, try to match the pattern at eye level, where it will be most noticeable.

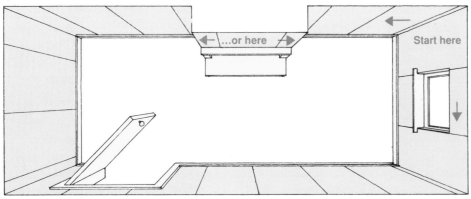

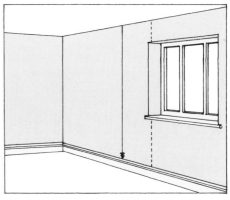

1 Always start to paper beside the main window, then work around the room in the direction shown. Complete the window wall into the corner. The exception is with a large pattern, which must be centred on the chimney-breast or other main focal point.

2 Hang a plumb-line so that the other edge of the paper will overlap the window frame by 12mm ($\frac{1}{2}$ in).

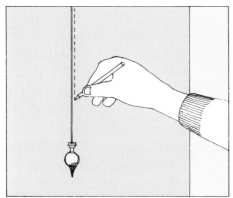

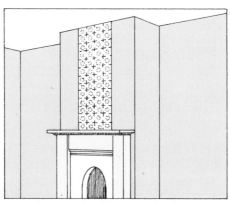

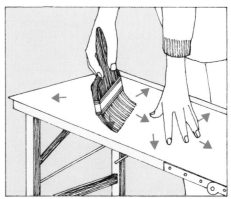

3 When the plumb-line stops swinging, mark its position on the wall in pencil.

4 Centre the first length of a prominent pattern on the middle of the chimney-breast.

5 Let the edge of the paper overlap the table by 12mm ($\frac{1}{2}$ in). Paste from the centre outwards in herringbone fashion. Pay particular attention to edges.

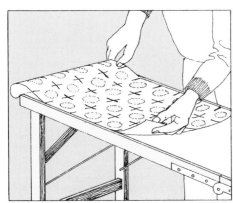

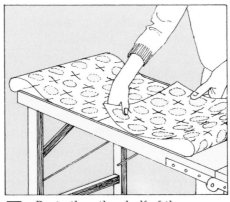

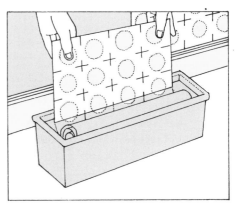

6 Paste half the paper, then take the top edge and turn it over to the middle of the length. Align the edges carefully.

7 Paste the other half of the paper. Turn the other end to the middle to meet the first edge. If necessary leave the paper to soak.

8 Roll up ready-pasted paper loosely, pattern side inwards, and immerse it in water. Pull it out slowly and brush it on to the wall.

HANGING STRAIGHT LENGTHS

Each length of paper must be cut with 50mm (2 in) excess at either end. This is to allow for final trimming at the ceiling and skirting board. When you are using a paper that doesn't need the pattern to be matched, you can just measure the skirting to ceiling height, add 100mm (4 in) and cut out as many full lengths as possible from the roll. It's a good idea to measure each wall separately, and in different places, in case there is a marked difference in height.

If a pattern needs to be matched, it is generally more economical to work from two rolls to save wastage. You can pattern-match the lengths, before cutting them, on the paste table, although at first you may feel it is easier to hang a length before pattern-matching and cutting the next length.

Never assume that the 'free' end of the roll is the top of the pattern. It usually is, but not always. Before pasting a length of paper, write 'top' in pencil on the back of the relevant edge. This will help prevent you from inadvertently hanging a length with the pattern upside down, which is easy to do with some designs.

Before taking the folded paper to the wall, make sure you have your stepladder in the right place to enable you to reach the ceiling comfortably. A decorator's apron with a large pouch pocket for hanging brush and scissors is very useful to wear.

If the top edge of the paper smears the ceiling with paste, turn it over 25mm (1 in) so that only the decorative side brushes the surface. Alternatively, keep a wet sponge handy to wipe away smears since paste stains can be troublesome to wipe clean later. The same applies to the skirting.

PATTERN ALIGNMENT

When using a paper with a pattern, it is usual to see the motif at the top of the wall so position this first before aligning the edge of the paper against the guideline.

Be careful not to let the folded paper drop down suddenly since, being loaded with paste, the weight can cause the paper to stretch or tear making it difficult to match the pattern when hanging the adjoining length.

If you do it properly, brushing out the paper on to the wall should exclude air bubbles underneath it. Should you spot one immediately, then peel back the paper past the bubble and brush it out again.

A bubble that appears the next day can usually be dealt with easily. Use a sharp knife to make a cross cut through the bubble, peel back the resultant flaps of paper, brush paste on to the flaps and smooth them back into place with the brush. If you do it

carefully, you won't be able to see the join.

After you have hung the first length and trimmed it at the top and bottom, hang the second length. Provided that the first length is vertical, all you have to do is butt up the edge of the second length to it, aligning the pattern, of course, before brushing on the top half. You can then release the lower half, which will fall neatly into place butting up to the first length.

Don't vigorously brush a length of paper in order to get a close edge-to-edge contact with the previous length. Vigorous brushing stretches the paper temporarily, but it will shrink on drying and leave a gap at the join, and then there is nothing you can do to conceal it.

Provided you work reasonably quickly, you should be able to hang a length before the paste starts to dry out. If you are not quick enough, you can always 'freshen up' the edges with paste before brushing them on to the wall. The same applies to any edges that 'lift' later.

1 Offer up the first length to the wall and align its edge with the vertical pencil line. Undo the paper, fold by fold.

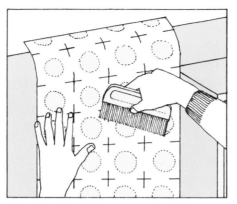

2 Brush out the paper by first smoothing down the middle, then outwards to the edges to remove any air trapped behind the paper.

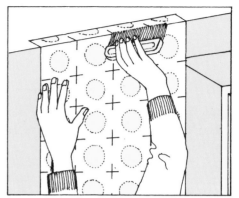

3 Use the brush to press the paper into the angle of ceiling to wall. Then draw the back of the scissors along the angle.

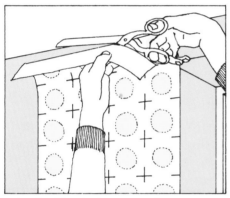

4 Peel back the paper then cut along the crease line carefully. Don't cut below the line or the paper will be short of the ceiling.

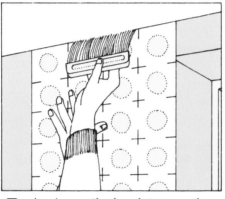

5 Again use the brush to smooth the trimmed edge of the paper back into the ceiling line. It should fit perfectly.

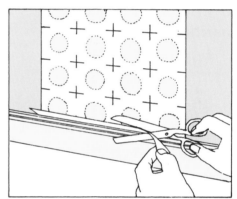

6 Repeat the trimming procedure at the skirting board. If any paste gets on the ceiling or skirting, wipe it off before it dries.

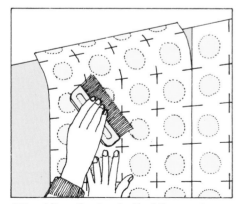

7 Align the top half of the next length of paper with the edge of the preceding length, butting up the edges closely. Brush and trim.

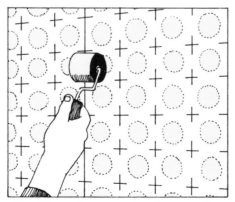

8 When the paper has been on the wall for a few minutes use a seam roller to press down the edges. Don't use on embossed paper.

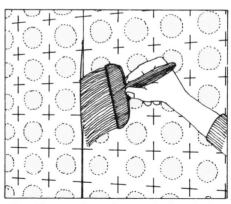

9 If any edges dry out before being brushed into place, or spring open later, carefully re-paste and brush back.

THE TRICKY BITS

CORNERS
Never try to take a large amount of paper around a corner: it will tend to crease up, especially when a corner is out of true, which most of them are.

WINDOW REVEALS
The trick here is to paper the wall leaving about 25mm (1 in) of paper to be turned into the reveal at both sides and at the top. Don't fix the edges into the reveal yet. First cut out strips of paper to fit the sides and top of the reveal, remembering, of course, to match the pattern with the paper already on the main wall. Hang the strips in the reveal, then brush the 25mm (1 in) margin of paper into the reveal.

FIREPLACE SURROUNDS
Fireplace surrounds come in a variety of designs and sizes, so just follow these general guidelines.

First, carefully measure and cut the length of paper so that most of the waste is removed. Leave yourself with about 75mm (3 in) of excess paper only. It is far easier to work this way rather than having to deal with a vast amount of soggy, pasted paper, much of which is not wanted.

Hang the paper on the top part of the wall in the usual way, smoothing it into the back edge of the mantel shelf. Make a crease line with the scissors, then cut off the excess. This will leave the lower half of the paper hanging beside the fireplace surround. If the side of the fireplace is straight, you simply brush the paper into it, make a crease line with the scissors and cut the paper to fit.

If the surround has a complicated outline, use a small sharp pair of scissors and gradually work downwards, pressing the paper into each shape before trimming it along the crease line. You then press the paper into the next shape and so on. If the paste starts to dry near the bottom, put on some more paste with a small brush and smooth the paper on to the wall.

If you are lucky, there will be a very small distance between the edge of the mantel shelf and the corner of the chimney-breast. Here, hang the top half of the paper, then make a neat, horizontal cut as shown. The lower half can then be hung separately and you won't be able to detect the join line later.

LIGHT SWITCHES & SOCKETS
There are two types of socket and switch: those that are on a block fixed to the wall and those that can be lifted away from the wall.

The first type is more difficult to work around. First hang the top half of the paper until the switch is covered.

Now press the paper on to the switch and, with the small scissors, make several cuts from the centre of the switch outwards to about 12mm (½ in) beyond the edge of the block. This will leave you with star-shaped flaps. Crease them against the edge of the block and trim them off. Then hang the lower half of the paper.

More modern, flush-fitting sockets and switches have two screws that hold the cover in place. **It is absolutely essential to turn off the electricity at the mains before loosening and removing the cover**.

Take out the screws and you can pull the cover forward a couple of inches without affecting the wiring.

Hang the top half of the paper as before. When you get to the switch, cut a hole from the paper about 6mm (¼ in) less in area all round than the cover. Now pull the cover through the hole, and you can brush the complete length of paper on to the wall. Refix the switch and you will have a perfect finish. There will be a 6mm (¼ in) margin of paper inside the cover.

Now, you can switch the electricity back on at the mains.

RADIATORS
If you have the know-how, you can remove a radiator so that the wall behind can be fully decorated. Otherwise you can simply tuck sufficient paper down the back and sides so that the wall has a fully papered appearance.

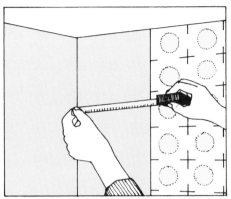

1 To take paper around an internal corner, measure the distance from edge of paper to the corner at the top, middle and bottom of the wall.

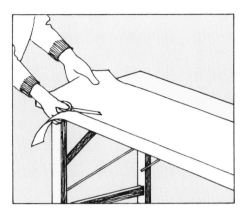

2 Add 12mm (½ in) to the longest measurements. Cut a strip of this width from the next length.

3 Hang it, turning the edge on to the next wall. Brush it tightly into the corner.

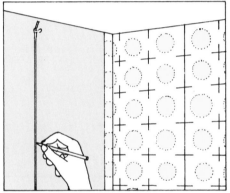

4 Measure the width of the matching strip, then draw a vertical line on the next wall that distance from the corner.

5 The inside edge of the matching strip goes into the corner to overlap the turned edge. Slight loss of pattern match is not noticeable.

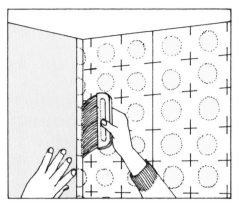

6 At external corners, again take measurements at the top, middle and bottom; add 25mm (1 in) to the longest. Cut and hang this strip.

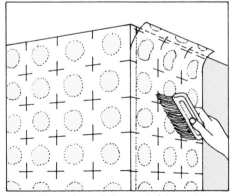

7 The edge of the matching strip aligns with the corner. A special overlap adhesive is used to stick down overlapping edge of vinyl.

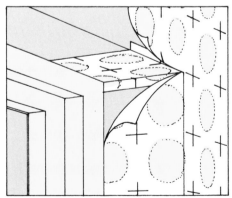

8 At window reveals, first paper the underside of the top, turning 25mm (1 in) on to the outside wall. The paper on the outside wall is cut as shown.

9 Provided that the reveal is not more than about 75mm (3 in) deep, the paper on the facing wall can be turned into it complete.

DOORWAYS

Hang full lengths of paper until a part length is needed to reach the frame. Remember that although only part of the length is needed alongside the frame, above it the paper must be hung to its full width to ensure the pattern continues.

You are probably going to need an L-shaped length of paper. With careful measuring and marking, you should be able to cut out an L-shape, leaving about 75mm (3 in) excess for final trimming. Be careful that the L-shaped piece can be hung to align with the pattern of the previous length. If you have a helper, it is easiest if one of you holds the full length against the wall, aligning the pattern with the previous length (remembering to allow 75mm (3 in) excess for final trimming into the angle of ceiling and wall) and the other to cut out the L-shape as required.

Having pasted the L-shape, hang the top part above the door until the top of the frame is

reached. Use the scissors to crease the paper along the top of the door frame. When you reach the corner, make a diagonal cut about 50mm (2 in) long away from the corner. This allows the paper to be smoothed into the door frame and creased and trimmed to fit.

ARCHES

If you try to paper an arch with one complete piece of paper, it is likely to stretch and bubble at the top. It would also be extremely difficult to ensure that the paper would follow the edge of the arch. In order to avoid these problems, proceed in the following way.

Cut two lengths of paper that will cover the inside surface of the arch – from skirting to apex on both sides plus 100mm (4 in) surplus. Trim each length to the exact width of the arch, at the same time matching the pattern at the edge with that on the adjacent wall. Turn the edge of the paper on the main wall into the arch by about 12mm (½ in);

you will have to cut notches in the edge to get it to lie flat on the curve of the arch. Then paper the arch, making a neat butt join at the top where the two pieces of paper meet: overlap the two lengths, cut through with a sharp knife, peel off the surplus and brush back the ends to butt closely together.

STAIRWELLS

Erect a safe working platform according to the particular situation. The one shown suits the needs here.

Hang the longest lengths first. A helper to organize positioning and brushing out the lower half is useful, but not essential. Rearrange the ladders and platform as needed while papering.

10 Where the mantel shelf of a fireplace surround is close to a corner, it's easiest to cut the paper carefully and hang two halves.

11 Other surrounds are papered by gradually working downwards, cutting the paper to fit the outline.

12 A fixed switch means having to cut V-shapes around the switch, then creasing and cutting around using small scissors.

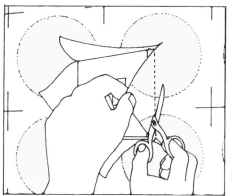

13 TURN OFF AT THE MAINS BEFORE PAPERING AROUND LIGHT SWITCHES. Loosen screws of cover plate, pull plate through paper and trim around.

14 Leave a margin of about 6mm (¼ in), which can be tucked behind the cover plate. Tighten screws and switch on again at the mains.

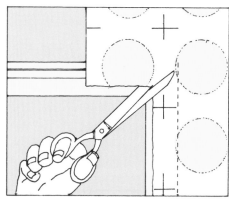

15 Before pasting, cut off most of the excess paper, leaving a margin of about 100–150mm (4–6 in) to tuck behind a radiator and fit against the bracket.

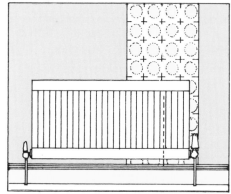

16 Hang the length, smoothing the paper behind the radiator by hand. Cut small pieces to cover any gap at the skirting.

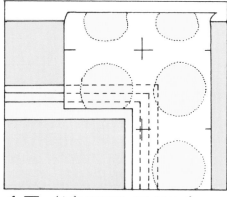

17 At doorways, cut a rough shape before pasting. Brush on paper, then cut a diagonal at the corner of the frame extending 50mm (2 in) on to the wall.

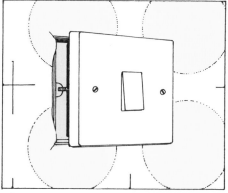

18 This cut will release the paper so that it can be brushed and creased into place before being trimmed neatly around the frame.

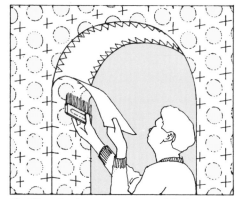

19 Arches are papered in two halves, making a join at the top. The paper on the facing wall has to be notched where it turns into the arch.

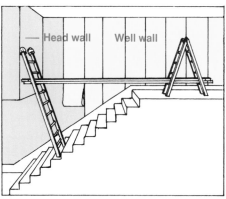

20 Papering stairwells. In this case, the facing wall is papered first. The ladder is then protected with rags while papering side walls. If you are going to paper the ceiling too, turn under the paper on the joining wall 25mm (1 in). Otherwise cut it flush with the wall/ceiling angle.

CERAMIC TILES

Preparation and planning are the most important aspects of ceramic tiling. It is absolutely essential that all surfaces are sound, dry and flat. Dry means that there must not be any dampness in the wall. If you have any reason to suspect that there might be dampness in a wall, first deal with whatever is causing the problem. If necessary, call in an expert. If you hang tiles on a damp wall, they will soon fall off.

A wall might appear to be flat, but often there will be sufficient bumps and hollows to make it difficult, if not impossible, to hang the tiles neatly. The quickest way to find out if a wall is flat is to use a 2m (6 ft) long piece of wood that you know has a perfectly flat edge. Place the wood in various places on the wall vertically, horizontally and diagonally, and see if there is any noticeable 'see-saw' movement or if large gaps appear between the edge of the wood and the wall.

If you find a hollow, you can make it flush by using filler or plaster. If a wall is really bad, it can be faced with plasterboard or you can call in a professional to replaster it (*see* 'Tools', 'Materials' and 'Techniques').

If you have a nice flat surface, remove any wallpaper or flaking paint. Old gloss paint (identifiable by its shine) has to be rubbed down with coarse glasspaper or an electric sander. The idea is to remove the shine and key the surface. Old ceramic tiles, provided that they are fixed firmly and are flat, make an ideal surface. You can refix the odd, loose one with ceramic tile adhesive after chipping the old adhesive off the wall with a chisel and hammer.

PLANNING

Have a look at tiled rooms in brochures and catalogues. Notice such things as equal-sized tiles either side of a window, no small strips of tiles cut to fit into a small space above a sink or bath and so on. This does not happen by luck; it is due to careful planning .

Notice, too, that the grout lines between the tiles run continuously around the room from wall to wall. They will even be aligned on items such as the side of a bath.

To plan a room, you need a gauging rod – a piece of wood about 2m (6 ft) long. Mark it off in tile increments according to the size of tiles you are using – normally 110 or 150mm ($4\frac{1}{4}$ or 6 in). Allow also for the joints between the tiles – a plastic tile-spacer can be used for measuring this.

If you hold the measuring stick on the wall all around the room, both horizontally and vertically, then you will soon build up a picture of how the tiles will best be placed. You will also, of course, establish the all-important starting point on each wall.

Few rooms work out perfectly. Inevitably, there will have to be a compromise or two. For example, in order to leave equal size tiles either side of a window – which is important to give the room a balanced look visually – you might have to accept a narrow row of tiles alongside a door frame. It's very much a case of taking each wall on its merits.

Do remember, however, that the horizontal join lines are continuous all around the room.

Having decided how the tiles are going to be best arranged, you need to establish the starting point for the first row of horizontal tiles and the first row of vertical tiles. You always start to tile *near* the bottom of a wall and *near* a corner. You never start to tile *at* the bottom of a wall, on a skirting board, alongside a door frame or window frame, in a corner or so on. None of these places can be relied upon to be perfectly horizontal or vertical. Use your spirit level to establish true horizontal and vertical lines, and fix a batten to the wall on your horizontal starting line, which is your guide to laying the first row of tiles. The batten will be removed after 24 hours, when the adhesive has set.

Fix the batten with masonry nails (wear eye protection) hammered partly in. The top edge of the battern should be

one tile width above the lowest point of the skirting or floor. That way you will not have to fit any thin slivers of tile into the gap when the batten is removed. The same principle applies to the distance of the vertical batten from the corner. For your vertical guide, you can fix a vertical batten to the wall or rely on a pencil line.

CHOOSING & BUYING TILES

You can pay as little or as much as you want for tiles, such is the extreme variety. They range from basic 110mm (4¼ in) square plain tiles to hand-painted tiles in odd shapes and sizes. Add to this the possibility of including random feature tiles, borders, friezes, or murals comprised of six or more tiles depicting anything from a countryside scene to a selection of vegetables and the choice becomes bewildering. A visit to a specialist tile centre and a browse through colour catalogues is well worthwhile. You will be amazed at the choice; it's far, far greater than the local d-i-y superstore could hope to offer.

The first thing to do is to decide which tile you want and how many border pattern tiles, feature tiles and so on are to be included. Expensive hand-painted tiles are not the best thing to practise on! Apart from anything else, they can be more difficult, so you will probably opt for more standard tiles, perhaps a straightforward square shape. Draw an outline of each wall in the room on graph paper. Don't forget to include doors, windows,

radiators and other features on the plan, as they all play an important role in the finished appearance – and, of course, in the number of tiles you buy. You can now chop and change your tiling plans until you have got exactly what you want.

From a scale plan you can quickly estimate how many tiles of each type to buy. If the same plain or patterned tiles are being used throughout, you can simply measure each area of wall to be tiled and divide it by the size of the individual tile. Add a little on for wastage through breakages and incorrect cutting, and you have the number needed.

You need also to buy sufficient adhesive and grout cement – the material that is used to fill the spaces between the tiles. The adhesive can be bought in ordinary and waterproof versions, and in powder or ready-mixed form. Powder form is cheapest, but you have to mix it with water according to the manufacturer's instructions. The same applies to grout.

Also available is a combined adhesive and grout, which is convenient but calls for cleanliness in use – if any gets on to the face of the tiles, it has to be wiped away quickly because it becomes very hard to remove once it has set.

Whereas standard grout and adhesive can be used anywhere, waterproof versions must be used on any area likely to be continually splashed by water – in shower areas, behind sinks and so on.

Normally, grout is white, but

there is a limited range of colours available. These are used in exactly the same way.

You may come across the expressions 'thin-bed' and 'thick-bed' adhesive. Thin-bed means that the adhesive can be used only in the normal thickness required – about 3mm (⅛ in). Thick-bed adhesive is for uneven surfaces, but not for use by the beginner. It requires tiling skill to leave a flat tiled layer over an uneven surface. The beginner must prepare an even surface on which to tile.

Heatproof adhesives are not needed in domestic kitchens or bathrooms, but might be required if you want to tile around a fireplace that is constantly in use. It is best to get on-the-spot advice from your tile supplier.

TOOLS NEEDED

Some of the tools needed for tiling are to be found in your basic kit – spirit level, hammer and pincers, for example. You will need to buy a tile cutter, and there are various types from which to choose. The simplest cutter has a hardened cutting tip. You draw the tip across the glazed face of the tile to leave a score line. Then you place the tile on a flat surface with a matchstick aligned below the score line, and press evenly on either side; the tile should break cleanly along the line.

However, for any sizeable job, it is worth paying a little more for a pincer-like tool, which will both score and cut the tile. You use the hardened cutting wheel

at the business-end of the tool to score the line where the tile is to be cut. Then you place the tile in the jaws of the tool so that the jaws are aligned with the scored line. A gentle squeeze on the handles and the tile will snap cleanly – efficient and quick.

A more expensive cutter that also scores and cuts is a guillotine-like device. Slightly easier and quicker in use, but the extra cost may not be justifiable for a one-off job unless using dual wall/floor tiles which are thicker.

Almost inevitably you will need to cut L-shaped tiles or a curved shape to fit around a basin, bath edge or similar feature. Here a tile saw is very useful. This comprises a tungsten-carbide coated blade in a simple metal frame. With a tile secured in a vice, any shape can be cut from it accurately and cleanly, albeit slowly.

Without a tile saw, you would have to nibble away with pincers to remove the waste and leave the desired shape. This is a slow exercise and tends to be frustrating, since the tile can easily be broken while chipping pieces away.

A tile file is a simple strip of abrasive coated metal. It is used to clean up cut edges, but is not an essential tool, as rough cut edges are normally concealed by the grouting.

An adhesive spreader – a plastic comb with notches in it – is usually supplied with the adhesive. It spreads the adhesive on the wall into a series of lines of the correct depth, which gives economical use of the adhesive.

An all-over coating of adhesive is unnecessary and wasteful.

Finally, it is worth buying a squeegee – a rubber blade in a plastic handle – in order to spread the grout into the joins. Some people prefer to use a small piece of sponge for this job; they feel you can work the grout more firmly into the joins. It's largely a matter of choice, although the squeegee is certainly quicker.

HALF-TILING

Where the walls are to be tiled only halfway up – often over previous half-tiling – a method has to be found to finish off at the top neatly. There are three choices. You can fill the gap between tiles and wall with a smooth layer of cellulose filler; fit wood beading or moulding (*see* 'Materials'); use a special tile quadrant to match the tiles.

You may want to tile a complete wall up to ceiling height where there was previous half-tiling. Since there is a difference in surface level between the lower and top halves of the wall, you either have to knock off the old tiles covering the lower half or build out the wall of the upper half. The first option is the least appealing since it means a lot of really hard work with a cold chisel and club hammer to remove the tiles before having to replaster the wall surface that is left. The easier option is to use plasterboard to bring out the upper half of the wall to the same surface level as the tiled lower half (*see* 'Plasterboard', pp. 49–51, for fixing details).

1 It is important to plan the room carefully to ensure that it has a balanced look. Note how the tiles are evenly spread around the window.

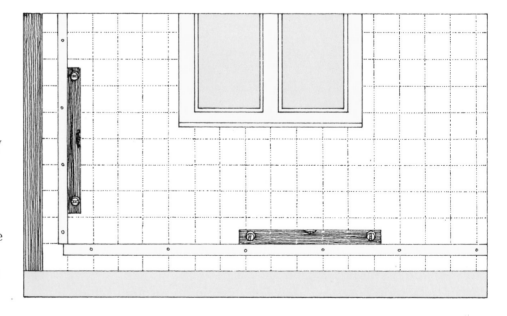

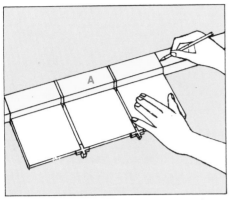

2 A gauging rod, made by marking tile increments and spaces on to a 2m (6 ft) long wood batten, will help you to plan the tiling.

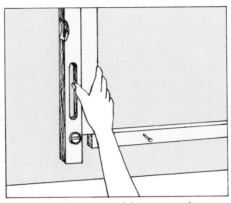

3 Fix a horizontal batten and a vertical batten to the wall as a guide to the starting point. These are removed later and the spaces filled.

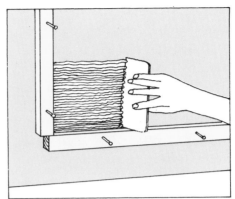

4 Spread a layer of tile adhesive over about 1 sq m (1 sq yd) of wall. Use a notched spreader (supplied with the adhesive) to do this.

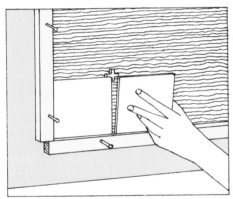

5 Place the first tile carefully into the intersection of the battens. Then build up the tiles in horizontal rows. Butt tiles carefully.

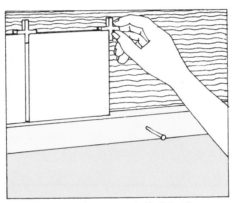

6 Unless there are 'nibs' in the sides of tiles to keep joins uniform, plastic spacers should be used at each intersection.

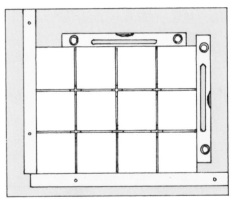

7 After each square metre (yard) or so of wall has been tiled, check that the edges are horizontal and vertical.

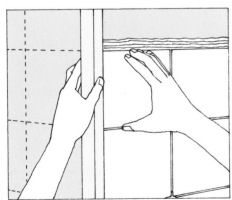

8 At external corners, fix a batten as shown. This makes it easier to cut and hang tiles accurately.

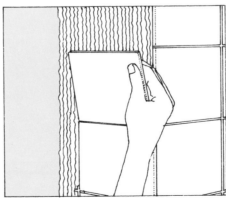

9 The tiles on the next wall are placed to butt up closely, with a glazed edge showing.

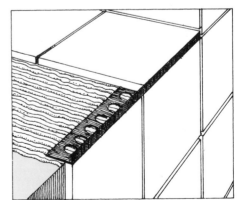

10 At windowsill edges you can align the vertical and horizontal tiles, or, simpler, use a plastic edge strip as shown.

ACCESSORIES

Items such as soap holders and toothbrush racks can usually be obtained to match your tiles, and occupy the space needed for one or two complete tiles. Some of these accessories are fixed with normal tile adhesive, others have to be fixed to the wall with screws.

When tiling, fit a tile (or two) into the required position with just a dab of tile adhesive – just enough to hold it in position. After 24 hours, the 'spacer' tile or tiles can be removed and the accessory fitted.

Screw-fixing into the wall is straightforward (*see* 'Techniques'). Adhesive fixing entails buttering adhesive on to the back of the accessory, pushing it into place and then using tape to keep it in position for 24 hours until the adhesive sets. The tape is then removed. You can tape the accessory to the surrounding tiles only when they are firmly fixed, that is when they have been in position for 24 hours. If you tried to do it before then, the weight of the accessory could pull the tiles off the wall.

Should you want to screw a fixture to the tiles later on then drill the screw holes with a masonry bit fitted in your drill. To prevent the drill skidding across the surface and scratching the tile, stick a piece of plaster on the tile and drill through this. Then peel off the plaster.

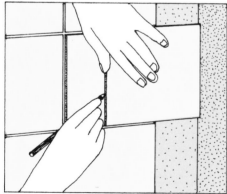

11 Place a complete tile over the last full tile and use another tile on top, edge pressed into corner, to mark off the cutting line.

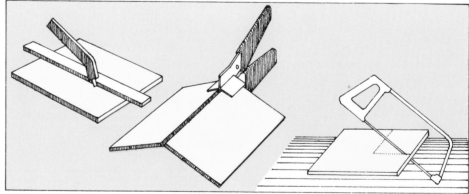

12 Straight cuts through tiles can be made with a scribing tool or pincer-like cutters.

13 L-shapes can be cut cleanly and accurately using a tile saw. When doing this, secure the tile in a vice.

14 Use pincers or special tile nibblers after first scribing the cutting line if you need to take just a fraction off a tile edge.

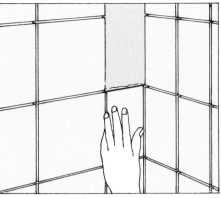

15 At corners, it is sometimes more convenient to butter tile adhesive on to the back of a cut piece before fixing it.

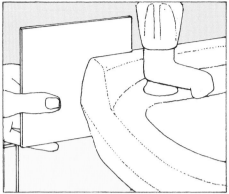

16 If you have to cut a tile to fit into an awkward shape, first make a cardboard template and transfer the outline on to the tile.

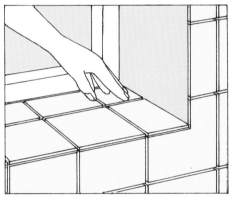

17 At window reveals, complete the outside wall, then fit tiles on the sill, keeping whole tiles to the front and overlapping those below.

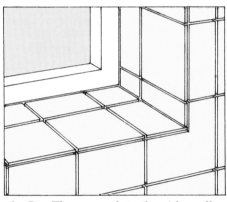

18 Then complete the side walls, again keeping whole tiles and glazed edges to the front. Join lines must always align.

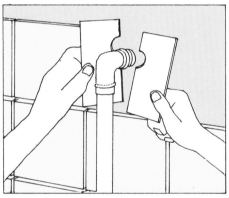

19 To tile around a projecting pipe, cut through the tile at the centre line of the pipe, then cut out two arcs; allow 2mm ($\frac{1}{8}$ in) clearance. Fit the halves neatly.

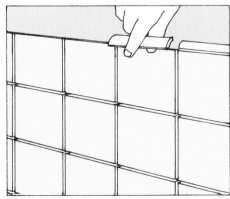

20 At the top of a half-tiled wall, you can finish with filler, a strip of wood beading or matching curved tile edge pieces as shown.

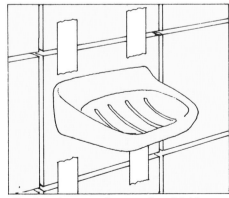

21 Accessories are fixed 24 hours after tiling is completed. A temporary tile (loose-fixed) is removed and the accessory taped until set.

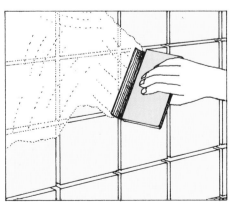

22 The final job is to smooth grouting cement into all the joins, using a squeegee. Wipe off the excess with damp cloth.

CORK TILES

Cork is an excellent material to use for insulation purposes. If you have a kitchen or bathroom wall that is especially prone to condensation, cork tiles provide a simple, effective and attractive answer to help cure the problem.

However, the use of 'warm' materials such as polystyrene and cork to reduce or prevent walls becoming steamed up is not the first line of defence. Initially you should think in terms of minimizing the cause of the steam, such as saucepans boiling away without a lid or laundry drying on radiators. You should also have a cooker hood and/or an efficient extractor fan, which will remove the steam quickly. When you buy an extractor, make sure it is the correct size for the room – too big and the room will be losing its heat quickly; too small and it won't clear the steam. Measure the room's cubic size – length x width x height – and ask your supplier for a suitable size fan.

Cork tiles that are to be used in kitchens and bathrooms must be steamproof – supplied pre-sealed with wax or varnish.

Lining a wall with cork is not a cure for dampness, which is entirely different to condensation. Dampness is caused by elements outside the house soaking through walls – for example, rainwater seeping through porous brickwork. If you line a damp wall with cork, the moisture will soon break down the adhesive used to fix the tiles and they will fall off. Cure the cause of the dampness in the wall and then you can hang cork tiles. Their use, of course, is not restricted to certain areas; they are ideal as feature areas in living rooms and bedrooms.

Most tiles are 300mm (11¾ in) square and about 3mm (⅛ in) thick. There is a good choice of shades, so look round before buying. Usually they are sold in packs of nine, which make nearly 1 sq m (1 sq yd).

There are various brands of special cork wall-tile adhesive, which you can buy at the same time as the tiles. On the side of the container it will tell you how many square metres of tiles the contents will stick. You must use a special adhesive.

When you get your tiles home, take them all out of their packs and mix them up. This allows the tiles to breathe and also ensures that any discrepancy in colour from pack to pack will be spread over the wall. You can get slight shade differences and it could be noticeable if a complete square metre of wall was covered with nine tiles from one pack. Mixed together there will be no problem.

It is essential to provide a flat, dry surface for the tiles. Old wallpaper has to be removed, along with flaking paint. Sound emulsion or gloss paint must be rubbed down with glasspaper to leave a key for the tile adhesive to grip to.

Plan the arrangement of tiles carefully. The wall should have a balanced look, with even-sized part tiles framing the edges. Avoid having tiles on either side of a window a different size and make sure you don't have thin strips to cut to finish off in corners. Whether you are only tiling halfway up a wall or going right to ceiling level, arrange to have a full tile in the top row. It is worth drawing the positions of the tiles on to the wall initially so that you can get an exact impression of how they will look.

While working, keep some soapy water and clean rags handy, so that you can immediately wipe off adhesive that gets on to the face of a tile. Also keep your fingers clean; otherwise they will transfer adhesive from tile to tile. If any adhesive dries on a tile, remove it by gently rubbing with a cloth moistened with white spirit. This might also remove some of the varnish coating. If so, you will have to touch in the mark with varnish later.

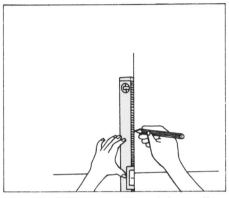

1 Find the centre line of the wall, vertically and horizontally, and work out how the tile arrangement will fall. Adjust to avoid narrow edge pieces.

2 Start tiling in the centre of the wall. Apply enough adhesive for one tile, with about 25mm (1 in) excess all round.

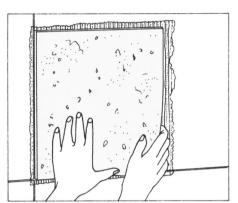

3 Position the first tile accurately in place with its edges aligned with the centre guidelines. Work from this tile outwards, butting tiles tightly together.

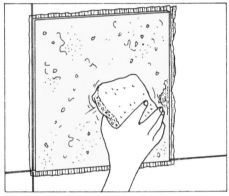

4 Should any adhesive be smeared on to the face of a tile, use water or white spirit (as directions) to remove it.

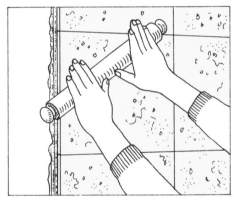

5 Having pressed each tile into place by hand, run a rolling pin firmly across the face to ensure it is well fixed.

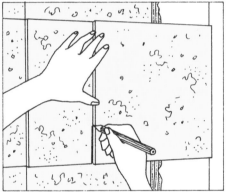

6 To mark a tile for cutting into a corner, place it over the last full tile. Place a spare tile over that, edge into corner, and mark cut line.

7 To cut the tile, place it on a flat surface, then use a sharp knife held against a straight-edge. Cut accurately along the guideline.

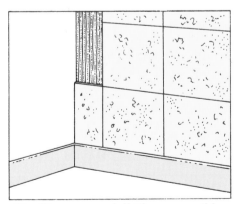

8 Fix as many full tiles as possible before marking, cutting and fitting edge tiles and awkward shapes requiring a template to be made.

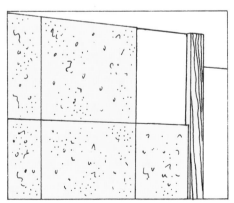

9 The edges of tiles at corners are susceptible to damage. Protect them by fixing an edge piece of wood beading.

WALL-BOARDS

Decorative wall-boards are ideal for permanently decorating walls, perhaps where the wall surface is less than satisfactory, and they can simulate a whole range of walling materials, such as a variety of timber woodgrains, ceramic tiles, brick and stone cladding. Often the effect is heightened by texturing the surface. Do not, however, be tempted to use wall-boards to cover a damp wall, as this could lead to rot and other structural problems. If there is dampness in the wall, get this put right before fixing the wall-boards.

Wall-boards are large – normally 2.4 x 1.2m (8 x 4 ft) – so they cover large areas quickly. Once fixed, are more or less maintenance-free, taking hard knocks and needing just an occasional wipe with a damp cloth to keep them looking fresh. They are also fairly cheap, quite light to handle and easy to fix.

If you have got really good, smooth, flat walls, you can use a contact panel-adhesive to stick the boards directly to the wall. However, in most cases you will first have to fix a framework of timber battens to the wall to give a flat surface on to which the wall-boards can be pinned.

FOR UNEVEN WALLS

The batten method is definitely the one to use if the wall surface is uneven.

Use a spirit level to get the battens perfectly vertical. If necessary, pack out any hollows with scraps of hardboard or plywood as the battens are fixed.

In most cases you can use 50 x 25mm (2 x 1 in) timber for the battens.

ON OUTSIDE WALLS

On outside walls use packing pieces under the battens to give a gap of about 6mm (¼ in) at top and bottom for ventilation. In an older house (pre-1930s) the wall is likely to be solid brick, and therefore cold. In this case use thicker timber (say, 50 x 50mm (2 x 2 in)) for the battens, and pack between them with insulation. Cover the battens and insulation with a layer of thick polythene before fixing the boards. The polythene will stop condensation from the room from soaking the insulation.

Fix the vertical battens at each end of the wall and, for 1.2m (4 ft) wide boards, at 1.2m (4 ft) intervals across the walls. This will ensure that the edges are supported. Horizontal battens are fixed at top and bottom, and at about 400mm (16 in) intervals in between.

The most secure way of fixing the battens is by screwing them into wall-plugs in the wall. But where the plaster is sound, for speed, you can fix them with masonry pins hammered into the wall. Wear safety spectacles in case one of the hardened pins shatters when it is struck with the hammer.

Because boards are usually 2.4m (8 ft) long, in most cases they can be fixed in one length between floor and ceiling. In a tall room you may have to add a small section above the main board.

If you have to cut a board, use a sharp knife to score the surface on the face side where the cut is to be made, then saw along the scored line with a fine-tooth saw, which will avoid splintering the surface.

SCRIBING TO FIT

Get the first panel ready for fixing by temporarily pinning it in place about 20mm (¾ in) from the side wall. With a pencil held against a 25mm (1 in) wide block of wood, and the block held against the wall, scribe a pencil line down the panel. The line will follow any undulations in the side wall.

Trim the panel to this line and fix it in place.

If the panels are to be glued to a flat wall surface, use bands of a gap-filling panel-type of contact adhesive. Secure the tops of the panels with panel pins until the adhesive sets.

Alternatively, fix the panels by pinning them to the battens with 25mm (1 in) long panel pins driven in about 150mm (6 in) apart. Use a hammer and nail punch to drive the heads of the pins just below the surface, then fill the small holes with coloured filler, called 'stopping'.

Finish off by pinning a skirting-board at the bottom.

1 Fix vertical battens to coincide with the edges of the wall-board. Secure them with masonry nails, or screws and wall-plugs.

2 Next, fit horizontal battens about 400mm (16 in) apart to support the boards in the middle. If wall is not flat, pack out battens with slips of hardboard.

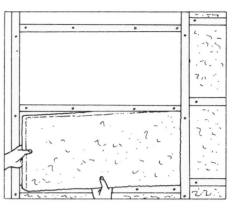

3 If you are fixing the wall-boards over a cold outside wall, it is sensible to add as much insulation as possible between the battens.

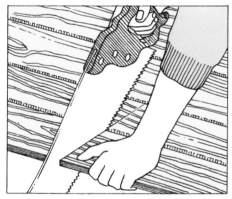

4 Try to fit wall-boards in one length between floor and ceiling. If cutting board, score line, then saw with face side up and firmly supported.

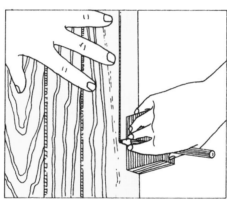

5 To fit the first board against side wall, temporarily pin board in place, then hold pencil against 25mm (1 in) wide block and scribe a line.

6 Lift the panel into place and hold it against the ceiling balanced on a wedge underfoot. It can be fixed to the battens with contact panel-adhesive.

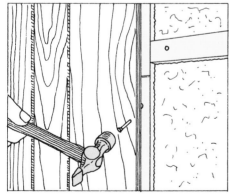

7 Alternatively, pin the board in place using 25mm (1 in) long panel pins. Drive these close to V-grooves in board so they are not seen.

8 If the positions of the horizontal battens are marked on the verticals, a string can be stretched across to guide fixing pins.

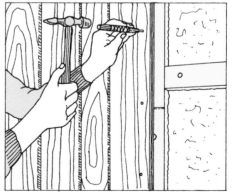

9 Use a hammer and a nail punch to drive the heads of the pins just below the surface. Fill holes with coloured filler.

CLADDING

Timber has a warm and welcoming look, and it is very attractive as a wall-covering. It is also very practical and hard-wearing, taking everyday knocks and scrapes in its stride, and only occasionally needs redecoration. It can cover up a poor or uneven wall surface, but if a wall is damp, get this put right before starting installation.

Because wood is a natural insulator, in most instances additional insulation under the cladding is not required.

However, wood is prone to movement according to the temperature and humidity of the room. If you were to use ordinary planks for cladding, gaps would soon open up between them. To overcome this, tongued-and-grooved boards or shiplap is used for cladding. The tongue of one piece pushes into the groove of the adjacent piece. With shiplap, adjacent strips overlap each other. Both methods permit a degree of movement in the wood without allowing cracks to appear.

STYLES OF FIXING

Cladding is fixed to timber battens that are themselves fixed to the wall. Although the basic technique of fixing will be the same, the way the battens are arranged on the wall will depend on the way you want the boards to look. If the boards are fixed vertically, they will make the room seem taller, and in this case the battens are fixed horizontally. If you want to make the room seem wider, fix the boards horizontally, in which case the battens will be vertical.

As a compromise between the two styles, it can look very striking to fix the boards diagonally, in which case the battens are fixed horizontally.

If you wish, you can arrange for the boards to run from floor to ceiling, or from wall to wall, in a single continuous strip. However, it is usual to butt-join boards that are not long enough to run in a single strip. As the diagrams show, joins must be arranged to fall midway at batten positions, and the joins on adjacent rows must be staggered.

There are four main types of cladding boards: tongued-and-grooved (known as T&G) wide V, narrow V, and moulded, which has a contoured surface; and shiplap, which looks somewhat like wide V when fixed. When estimating the amount of timber to buy, ignore the overall width and measure the covering width, which is the width of board, less the width of the tongue.

FIXING METHODS

The easiest way of fixing T&G boards is to pin them to the battens through the front. In this case you must use a nail punch to hammer the heads of the fixing pins below the surface of the boards and fill the indentations with wood-coloured filler, called 'stopping'.

For an invisible fixing, you can use the 'secret nailing' technique, driving panel pins at an angle through the shoulder of the tongue and into the batten. When the adjacent board is fitted, its grooved edge covers the nail head.

There is a tendency for the boards to split when secret nailing, so another method is to use metal fixing clips. The clips hold the grooves of the boards on to the battens.

To keep the timber in good condition it is important to encourage an airflow behind the boards. As long as you leave a small gap under the skirting and at the ceiling, there is natural ventilation with vertical battens. However, with horizontal battens it is important to fix pieces of thin plywood under the battens to allow natural airflow.

FINISHING OFF

At the planning stage think how you will finish off at the ceiling and floor. In most cases you can take the boards up to the ceiling and pin a timber scotia or quadrant moulding in place. However, if there is a plaster coving at ceiling height, it will probably be best to take the cladding boards to just below it and link the two together with a timber moulding.

At floor level the boards can stop just above the skirting, cover it, or partially cover it, giving a recessed effect. In all cases the boards should be

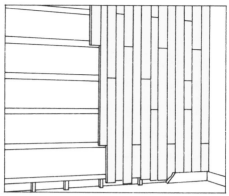

1 A common way to fit cladding is vertically, in which case the battens to which the boards are nailed are fixed horizontally.

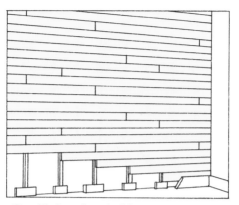

2 Fixing the cladding horizontally makes a room seem wider. In this case the battens are fitted vertically to the wall surface.

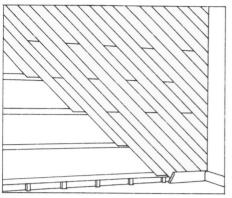

3 For something different it is possible to fit the cladding diagonally, in which case battens are fitted horizontally to the wall.

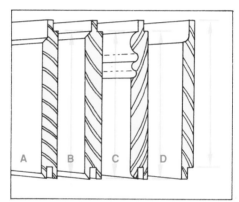

4 Cladding boards are available in many styles. These are the four basic types: tongued-and-grooved wide V (A), narrow V (B), moulded (C), and shiplap (D).

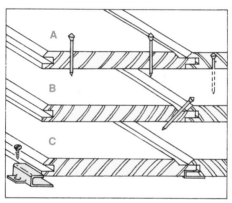

5 The three ways of fixing cladding: (A) nailing through the face, (B) secret nailing through tongue, (C) clip fixing

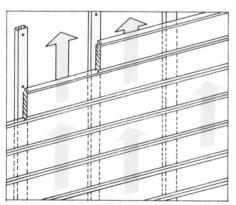

6 To keep the boards in good condition, it is important to get an airflow behind them. Vertical battens give natural ventilation.

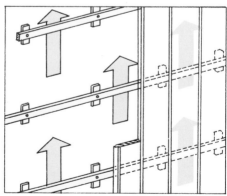

7 With horizontal battens, airflow can be achieved by putting packing pieces under the battens. Spacers can also level surface.

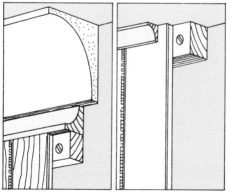

8 Think about getting a neat finish at the ceiling. Here are two methods using strips of curved timber, called scotia moulding.

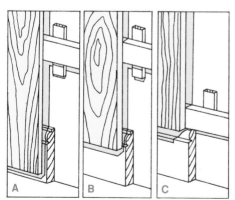

9 You must also decide how to finish at the bottom. Cladding can (A) cover, (B) partly cover or (C) come to the top of the skirting-board.

spaced slightly away from the skirting to give a clear airflow.

FIXING CLADDING

Start by putting up the battens, either vertically or horizontally, depending on how you have decided to fix the cladding. Use 50 x 25mm (2 x 1 in) softwood for the battens, unless you are fixing the boards over a cold, but dry, outside wall and want to add extra insulation. In this case use 50 x 50mm (2 x 2 in) timber for the battens and fit insulation bats between them. Cover the insulation and the battens with thick, clear polythene sheeting before fixing the cladding.

Whether the battens are horizontal or vertical, they should be fixed about 600mm (2 ft) apart using rust-proof (zinc-plated) screws 65mm (2½ in) long if fixing 25mm (1 in) thick battens, and 90mm (3½ in) long if fixing 50mm (2 in) thick battens.

If the battens are being fixed horizontally, remember to pack them out with pieces of plywood to keep an airflow behind the cladding. If the wall is uneven, adjust the thickness of the packing pieces to get the surface of the battens perfectly level.

GETTING A GOOD FIT

If the boards are to be fixed vertically, you need to be sure that the edge of the first board will butt tightly against the side wall. Therefore, the board will need to be 'scribed' to the wall. Do this by temporarily pinning the board vertically so it is about 20mm (¾ in) from the wall. Then, while holding a pencil against a small block of wood about 25mm (1 in) wide, draw the block from ceiling to floor to mark the contours of the wall on the edge of the board. Cut along this line. When the board is pushed against the wall it will be both a perfect fit and upright.

SECRET NAILING

Fit boards to be fixed by secret nailing with the tongue pointing outwards so the pins can be driven through the shoulders of the boards as shown in the diagram. After fixing the first board, use an offcut of cladding to protect the tongues of subsequent boards as they are driven home.

If using clips to hold the boards, fix the boards with the grooves facing outwards, as the clips slot into the grooves.

You will need to plane the tongue or groove off both boards where they meet at an external corner. At an internal corner you will need to plane only the board with the tongue edge. If there is a slight gap, you can hide it with a strip of moulding.

To finish off at the base, nail or screw a skirting-board over the boards, using spacers to keep the boards away from, and leave a small gap under, the skirting.

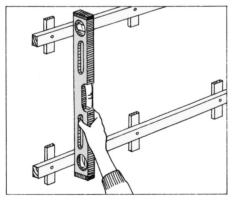

10 Whichever way the battens are fixed, make sure the surface is vertical using a spirit level and, if necessary, a straight length of wood.

11 If battens are horizontal, pack them out to give an airflow. Place insulation bats between battens on a cold outside wall.

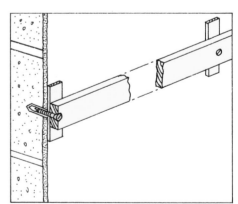

12 Battens should be spaced about 600mm (2 ft) apart and fixed using zinc-plated screws long enough to go right through the plaster into masonry.

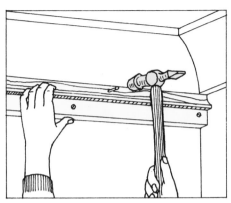

13 If you are keeping a plaster coving, fix the top batten just below it and fill gap by nailing a length of scotia moulding in place.

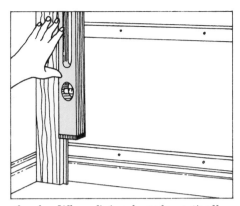

14 When fixing boards vertically, cut the first board to length and then lightly pin it in place vertically about 20mm (¾ in) from the wall.

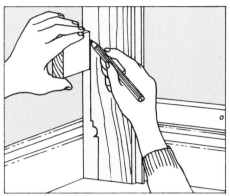

15 To get a close fit against the wall, the board edge must be shaped to the contour of the wall, called 'scribing'. Use a 25mm (1 in) block.

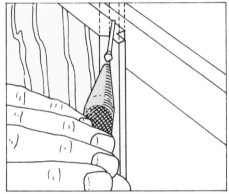

16 If fixing the boards by secret nailing, fit the boards tongue-side outwards and drive pins at an angle through the tongue near the shoulder.

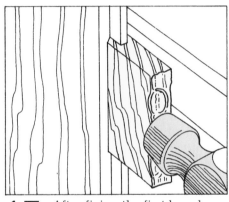

17 After fixing the first board, use a hammer and offcut of grooved board to drive the second board into place hard against the first.

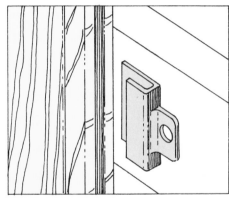

18 Purpose-made fixing clips are much easier to use because they cannot split boards. With clips, fix boards with groove side facing out.

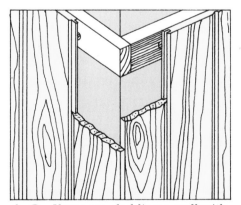

19 If you are cladding a wall with an external corner, plane the edges of the boards smooth and butt them together.

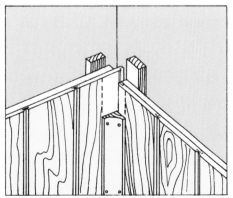

20 An easy way to finish an internal corner against another wood-clad wall is to use a strip of scotia moulding pinned in place.

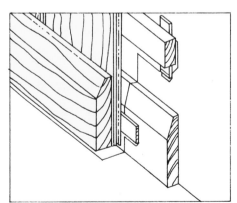

21 At the base you can add a strip of skirting-board or a timber batten for a neat finish. Keep it just off the floor to maintain airflow.

BRICK TILES

An exposed brick wall, chimney alcove or fire surround can be a very attractive decorative feature. You might think that the easiest way to achieve this effect is to chip the plaster off the wall to expose the bricks underneath. However, even if the plaster will come off, the bricks that may be exposed could be very poor quality, or there may be building blocks or even a hollow timber frame under the plaster.

TILE ADVANTAGES
To get an authentic brick-wall effect, it is better and easier to use brick tiles, which are available in a wide range of types. Some are authentic brick slips made from kiln-fired clay and produced by brick manufacturers in a range of facing brick (the best quality) colours. Because these brick tiles are heat-resistant, they can be used for fire surrounds (but not as firebacks).

Some brick tiles are made from plaster or cement-like materials. They may feel solid, but often the brick colour and texture are applied only to the surface, which is important to remember if the tiles are to be positioned in a passageway, around a corner or in any place where they may be rubbed as people pass.

Another type is made from thermo-plastic with sandy brick-like granules pressed into the surface. These tiles can be bent round corners after being heated with a hot-air gun, but they are unsuitable for fire surrounds.

It is important that brick tiles are positioned in exactly the same manner as genuine bricks. For example, be sure to stagger the vertical joins so that they are not directly above each other. Tiles can be butted together at internal corners. At external corners, avoid making a join line right at the edge by using special tiles that go around the corner. These are available in several sizes, as are the various odd-sized tiles you might need to complete a row. Be sure to stagger these so that they are not in the same position in every row.

USE A PHOTO-FIT
To help in planning it is a good idea to take a photograph of a section of wall with a corner or other feature you are trying to re-create. You can use this as a guide to positioning the tiles. Draw up an accurate plan on graph paper so you can be sure of buying all the specially shaped brick tiles you will need.

Lay out the bricks on the floor to get a good colour mix from the various packs. Use them to mark 'gauging rods', which will be helpful in setting out the work on the wall.

Gauging rods are simply straight timber battens that are marked across to represent the tile sizes, including the spacing joins. You will need one marked out in tile lengths, plus spaces, to centralize the bricks across the wall, and another in tile widths, plus spaces, to mark the brick course (row) heights on the wall.

Follow the diagrams and the manufacturer's instructions when it comes to fixing. Use only the recommended adhesive. In most cases the manufacturers recommend working upwards from a batten, but some manufacturers suggest working from the top down the wall to prevent fixing adhesive from getting on previously fixed tiles.

ADHESIVE TECHNIQUES
Some manufacturers recommend spreading adhesive on the backs of the tiles, which are then pressed on to the wall, while others suggest spreading adhesive on the wall and pressing the tiles into it while it is wet. In the latter case, the adhesive shows between the tiles to give a recessed grout line that does not need additional grouting or pointing (filling with cement).

When adhesive is spread on the backs of tiles, the spaces between the tiles need to be filled or grouted. An icing-bag type of applicator may be supplied for the grouting compound, which can then be squeezed into the spaces without getting cement on the surface of the tiles. Smooth off the grouting with a narrow pointing trowel.

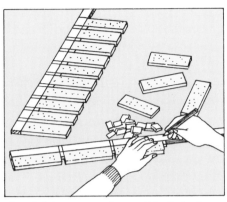

1 Make a gauging rod to help in setting out. Mark out straight battens in tile lengths and widths, including spaces.

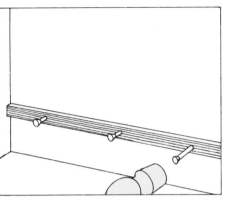

2 Fix a horizontal batten to wall to support bottom row of tiles but one. Remove batten 24 hours after tiling and add bottom row.

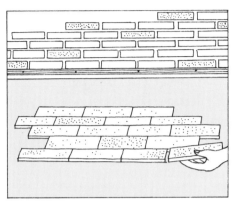

3 Open several packs and lay out the brick tiles to work out staggered vertical joins, and good colour mix.

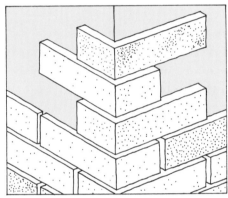

4 If the job includes a corner, fix the corner tiles first. If necessary temporarily support the specially shaped corner tiles on nails.

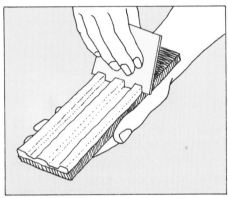

5 In some cases brick tiles are fixed using a special adhesive that is spread directly on the back of the tile with a notched spreader.

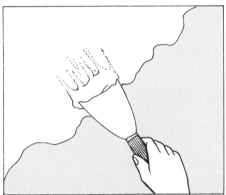

6 Another technique suggested by some manufacturers is to spread cement-like adhesive on the wall and press tiles in it, which saves grouting.

7 It is important to get each row of bricks level. Check frequently with a spirit-level and use a horizontal string line as a guide.

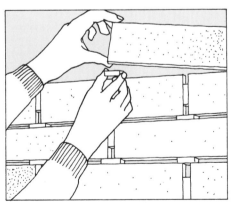

8 Use expanded polystyrene or wood-block spacers to ensure all vertical and horizontal join lines are kept to a uniform size.

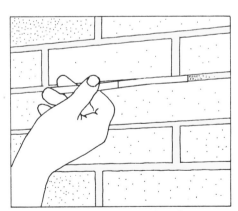

9 No grout is used if the tile adhesive is spread on the wall. If adhesive is on tile back, apply grout and smooth with pointing tool.

STONE TILES

A number of manufacturers make stone tiles that are fixed in a similar manner to the brick tiles shown on the previous pages.

The tiles may be made from a real stone, like slate, or from reconstituted stone. This is real stone that is ground, mixed with cement, sand, and perhaps pigments, and then compacted under hydraulic pressure to the shape and thickness required.

Reconstituted stone is usually available as natural, riven or ashlar. Natural resembles rough-hewn stone, riven has a ridged finish as though it has been split, and ashlar has a smooth finish like dressed stone.

You can also get tiles made from a plaster-like material, coloured, textured and moulded to look like real stone.

SHAPES AND SIZES
Stone tiles are available in more shapes and sizes than brick tiles. The basic choice is between random and coursed stones.

As the name suggests, random stones are available in various shapes and sizes and are used together to produce a 'crazy paving' effect on the wall.

Coursed stones are basically rectangular in shape, as though they are hewn from stone blocks. Although they are by no means as regular as brick tiles, they go together in a brick-like fashion. The edges are purposely not regular and the blocks can vary in height. There may be three different heights of blocks for working together, keeping blocks of roughly the same height together in a row. Alternatively, some blocks may be twice the height of the others and these can be introduced at random into two rows of the smaller blocks.

ALL-IMPORTANT STAGES
Like fixing brick tiles, planning the layout of the stones for a realistic effect is all-important. Study stone garden walls, cottage and barn walls to get ideas for the layout of the stones, and, if possible, take photographs of good walls that you can copy. With both coursed and random stone walls, the main thing is to break up the vertical joins as much as possible. A vertical join between two stones should be broken by the stone placed in the row above. You should never be able to trace a vertical joint virtually unbroken from the bottom to the top of the wall.

For fixing, follow our diagrams and the manufacturer's instructions. Use only the adhesive recommended for the tiles you have selected.

Some manufacturers recommend fixing the tiles from the bottom working upwards, while others state that fixing should be from the top downwards.

Whether you are fixing random or coursed tiles, walls should be structurally sound, dry, free from dirt, grease and any loose material, like wallpaper or flaking paint.

With stone tiles, you cannot get corner tiles as you can with brick tiles, so at external corners you must butt-join adjacent tiles.

CUTTING EDGES
Particularly with coursed stones, you may need to cut tiles to fit. The plaster-based imitation-stone tiles can be cut with almost any saw, but real and reconstituted stone tiles are much harder. You can saw them with a tungsten-carbide coated saw file blade (as used to cut ceramic tiles) fitted in a hacksaw frame. A quicker method is to fit a masonry cutting disc in an electric circular saw or small angle grinder tool, and to deeply score the back of the tile with this before snapping it over the edge of a bench.

Stone tiles tend to be heavier than brick tiles, so they may need the support of a couple of nails hammered into the wall beneath them while the adhesive sets.

After fixing, use an icing-bag type of applicator full of grouting compound to fill the mortar gaps, and take care not to get the grout on the surface of the stones. A small stiff-bristled brush gives a good, natural-looking finish to the grout.

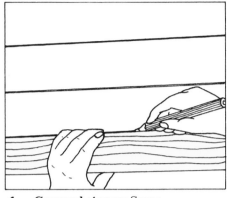

1 **Coursed stones:** Some manufacturers recommend working from the top downwards to avoid soiling stones with cement. Draw level guidelines on the wall.

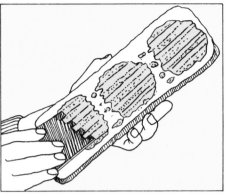

2 Apply adhesive cement with a notched spreader.

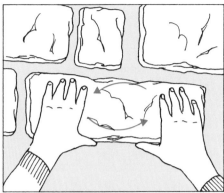

3 Press the stone hard against the wall with a twisting motion for good adhesion. Until adhesive sets, nails may be needed under heavier stones.

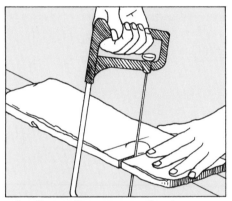

4 Some tiles may need to be trimmed. For real stones you may need to use a saw file in a hacksaw. For softer types, any saw will do.

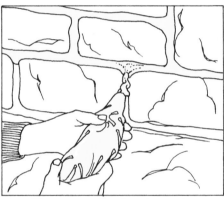

5 Use a grouting bag to apply grouting compound easily between the stones. Wait for the adhesive to set before you begin.

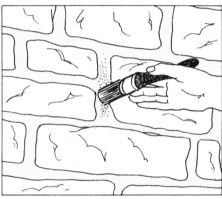

6 Take great care not to get grouting compound on the face of stones. Use a small, stiff-bristled brush to finish off grout.

7 **Random stones:** Stones are laid out on the floor in random fashion so that join lines are irregular.

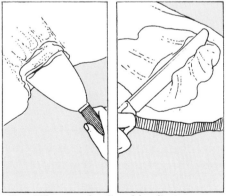

8 Tiles can be fixed by first spreading a smooth coat of adhesive to wall or by buttering the backs of stones.

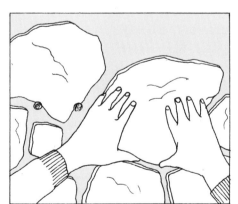

9 Press the stones firmly into position with a twisting motion. Support large stones on nails until adhesive sets.

FRIEZES & BORDERS

Although most friezes and borders are made to complement a wall-covering design – and it's usually safest, in terms of design and general appearance, to use the combination suggested by the manufacturer – you can follow your own ideas. If you feel a different border will set off the wall-covering design far better, then use it. Even using a border with plain emulsion-painted walls can enhance the appearance of a room.

Friezes and borders can be purely decorative or can serve a definite function, such as altering the proportions of a room visually or hiding a crack at the ceiling-to-wall join.

For decorative purposes, apart from being used at the top of the paper, they can be used to create the effect of a dado rail and to frame doorways, windows, light switches and so on. They can be used effectively in loft rooms to follow the sloping ceiling line. If you feel really creative, you can form squares, rectangles or even a stepped effect to bring plain walls alive.

You can reduce the height of a high ceiling visually by creating a 'picture rail' border around the room, and a short room will seem longer from one end as the eye picks up and follows a border. The same tactic can be used to make a short hallway seem longer from the front door.

Traditionally, a cove or cornice is used to mask the crack that occurs in many rooms at the ceiling-to-wall angle (*see* 'Coving'). You can rarely fill such a crack successfully, as it is caused by normal movement of the house during the different seasons of the year. An alternative is a frieze or border – just choose a design that can be turned on to the ceiling, if necessary, to cover the crack.

There are two types of friezes and borders: ordinary and ready-pasted. The pros and cons applying to them are the same as for wall-coverings – some people like to use ready-pasted, other people find them a bit messy.

You must always use them over a smooth, dry, clean surface, so flaking paint needs to be removed. If you have just painted a surface, wait a week before hanging a frieze or border. If you have just put up a wall-covering, let 48 hours elapse before adding one.

It is sometimes difficult to get a frieze to stick properly on a heavily embossed wall-covering. All you can do is try it out first on a small area. Rather than buying the frieze, cut a strip of any left-over paper for your trial run.

A paper frieze is hung with ordinary wallpaper adhesive. A vinyl frieze or any frieze being used on top of a vinyl wall-covering normally requires a heavy-duty paste, but do check the frieze manufacturer's instructions first.

Where the frieze is being hung to follow the ceiling line, it is advisable to prepare first for the ceiling being uneven. Although a ceiling may look fine, most are slightly undulating along their length. If you hang a frieze perfectly horizontally, you may well see the neat appearance marred by small bits of the wall-covering or painted wall appearing between the top edge of the frieze and the ceiling. To avoid this, take the ceiling paint about 12mm ($\frac{1}{2}$ in) on to the wall. When the frieze is up, any undulations will not be detectable because the eye will not easily distinguish the ceiling and wall line.

You don't need to worry about doing anything like this at skirting level if you are applying a frieze there. Apart from it being unlikely that the top edge of the skirting will be undulating, the edge of the frieze can always be squeezed down between the skirting and the wall if necessary. Besides, the eye will not pick up any slight fault when looking downwards.

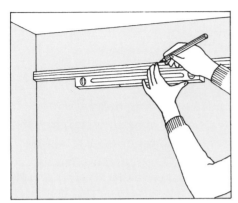

1 Since you can never rely on ceilings being horizontal use a straight wooden batten with a spirit level to draw a guideline on the wall for the bottom edge of the frieze.

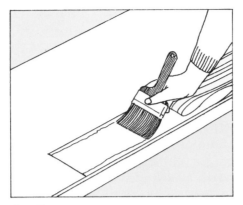

2 Paste the frieze carefully. Align the edges with the table edge to prevent paste being transferrred from the table to the decorative face.

3 Align the edge of the frieze with the guideline, then carefully brush it out. If you start to wander off the guideline, start again.

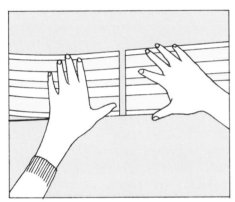

4 If possible, avoid having to make joins in the middle of a wall. If you have to, then butt-join the ends very carefully.

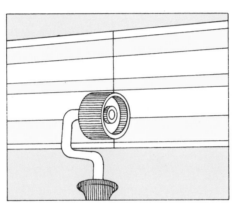

5 Use a seam roller to press the join down tightly. Don't use on an embossed design in case it flattens the texture.

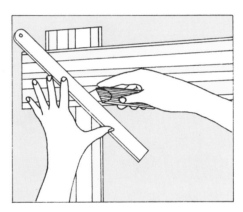

6 At corners, overlap the two pieces, then use a sharp knife and a straight-edge to cut through both layers.

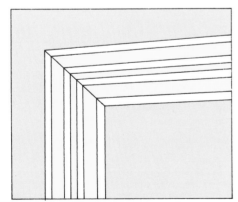

7 Trim off the waste, ease the edges together to make a neat mitre, and use the seam roller.

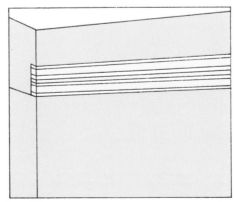

8 When turning a corner, external or internal, take about 12mm (1/2 in) at the end on to the next wall.

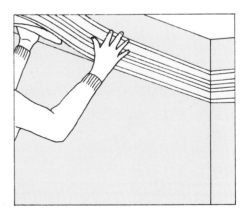

9 Draw a guideline on the next wall and hang the offcut of frieze to overlap the 12mm (1/2 in) margin.

REPAIRS & DECORATION

FOAM WALLPAPER

Sheet expanded polystyrene will minimize or eliminate condensation problems, which usually occur on a cold outside wall in a kitchen or bathroom –

the two rooms where most steam is generated – but can also crop up in any room in the house.

Expanded polystyrene is a 'warm' material. It is too thin to have any great insulation value and it is certainly not a cure for dampness in a wall, which must be treated separately before using any wall-covering.

You can buy the polystyrene in rolls at any decorating shop. It is very light in weight and must be handed gently since it can tear fairly easily. When you get it

home, lay it on its side, not on its edge. You will also need to buy the adhesive recommended by the manufacturer of the polystyrene.

You can hang ordinary wallpaper over polystyrene but use lining paper over it before hanging a vinyl wall-covering.

It is possible to butt-join lengths of polystyrene, as when hanging wallpaper (see p. 23), but you may prefer to use the overlap method shown here.

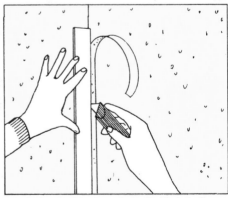

1 Polystyrene must be cut to length before hanging. Get as neat a fit as possible. Do not take it around corners.

2 Brush paste over the area of wall to be occupied by one length of foam. Take the paste about 25mm (1 in) beyond the area on both edges.

3 Offer the sheet into position, aligning its edge with a vertical pencil line made on the wall. Use a roller to smooth it into place.

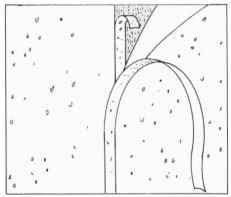

4 Hang the next length to overlap the first by 25mm (1 in). Then, using a sharp knife held against a straight-edge, cut through the overlap.

5 Remove the two strips of waste, then press the two edges back into place for a neat join. If preferred you can use butt-joins.

6 Run a wooden seam roller down the edges to make sure they are in firm contact with the wall.

PLASTER-BOARD

Although it is unlikely that you will want to partition a room by building a new plasterboard wall, there are many occasions when plasterboard can be used in more minor jobs to make life much easier for yourself.

As its name implies, the object of plasterboard is to provide a solid plaster surface on a wall or ceiling that is to be decorated. Plasterboard consists of a plaster core sandwiched between sheets of paper. If you live in a modern house, many of the internal walls separating rooms and hallways will be made of plasterboard fixed to a timber framework – they are sometimes called hollow walls. The ceilings will certainly be made from plasterboard. In older houses, old lath and plaster ceilings may have been replaced or covered with plasterboard.

It may sound like a daunting material to use but it's no more difficult to handle and fix than plywood or chipboard.

You are most likely to use it if you have a small wall or walls that need to be made perfectly smooth for decorating – usually with tiles of some kind, mostly ceramic. It is the modern equivalent of employing a plasterer. It's also useful for patching small areas of damage in a ceiling, caused, perhaps, by a plumbing leak, and it can also be of great benefit if you want to insulate a particularly cold exterior wall.

You buy plasterboard at a builder's merchant. The most popular thicknesses are 9.5 and 12.7mm ($\frac{3}{8}$ and $\frac{1}{2}$ in). The thinner version is perfectly adequate for fixing direct to a wall to create a flat surface. The strength of the thicker type is useful where it is being nailed to a framework of battens, as may be the case when completing a whole wall or when building a new partition wall.

The board is sold in a standard size of 2.4 x 1.2m (8 x 4 ft). This is very heavy and cumbersome and requires two people to carry it. A board should always be carried on edge, not like a stretcher, which could cause it to bow and crack in the middle. Without suitable transport, you will have difficulty getting a sheet home so, unless you are going to need a full-size board, cut it into two or more smaller, manageable pieces at the builder's merchant, or pay to have it delivered to your home, where you can slice it up to the exact size required.

Although it can be sawn, the easiest way to cut plasterboard is by using a sharp handyman-type knife. If possible, lay the board flat and slice through one paper face. Next, stand the board on edge and bend it backwards (away from the cut) to a 90° angle so that it breaks through

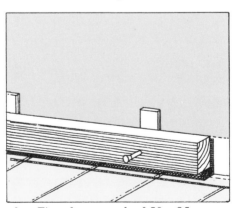

1 Fix a framework of 50 x 25mm (2 x 1 in) sawn softwood battens to the wall. They can be fixed with screws or nails placed at 1m (3 ft) intervals.

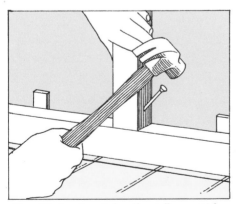

2 Fix horizontal rails at floor, mid-wall and ceiling level. Then add vertical pieces at 600mm (2 ft) intervals, skew nailed as shown

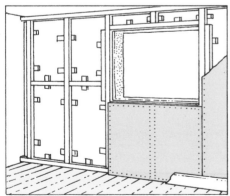

3 Add battens around doors and windows. Use hardboard packing to make surface of battens level with each other. Plasterboard joins over centre of battens.

the plaster core. Finally, use the knife to cut down through the paper backing. The only time you need to saw it is when you have to cut a curve for it to fit around an awkward shape, such as a wash basin; in this case a padsaw is used.

You will notice that the plasterboard has one ivory-coloured paper side and one grey paper side. For decorating purposes, have the ivory-coloured side showing. The grey side is for applying a skin coat of plaster, as required in some professional building work.

SMALLER AREAS

If you just want to use small pieces of board – for example, to level the 400 or 500mm (16 or 20 in) of wall space between the top of the work-surface and the wall cupboards in order to tile it, or perhaps to bring the upper half of a wall to the same surface level as a half-tiled wall below – then you can fix them in place with adhesive. In this case the wall cannot be severely

undulating – just sufficiently awkward to make hanging tiles too difficult. You must use the correct type of adhesive, which is called panel adhesive. It is supplied in a cartridge, which has to be fitted in a 'skeleton' applicator gun (*see* 'Tools').

If you are going to line a complete 'outside' wall, it makes sense to insulate it at the same time. This means first fixing up a framework of 50 x 25mm (2 x 1 in) softwood battens at 400mm (16 in) intervals and horizontal pieces at the ceiling and floor.

Where you are dealing with a straightforward flat, plain wall, you just need to remove the skirting-board before fixing the battens. Skirtings are normally fixed by nailing them to the wall. You can prise them away by tapping a bolster chisel down behind them and levering them clear. If you work carefully you can remove them without damage. They can be replaced later outside the new plasterboard; the quickest way to

refix them is with panel adhesive.

Life becomes more complicated if a wall has a radiator, switches and sockets, windows or doors on it. There's a lot of work to be done here, such as altering door frames and repositioning the radiator on the new wall surface. You would need a very good reason not to have all this done for you by a professional.

Filling the joins between the boards is done using special wallboard filler and tape. These are supplied with full instructions for use. The special applicator and sponge (*see opposite*) can be obtained at the same time. You do not need to fill the joins if you are going to tile over the top using ceramic, cork or mirror, only for papering or painting.

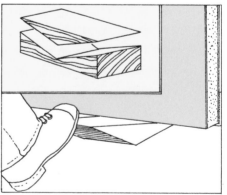

4 Start fitting the plasterboard in a corner, ensuring it is vertical. If necessary, scribe it into the corner, then use a padsaw to cut it.

5 Each board should be cut 12mm ($\frac{1}{2}$ in) shorter than floor-to-ceiling height. Make a footlifter from wood so you can raise a board.

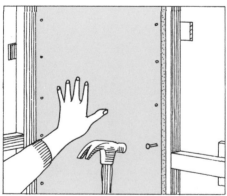

6 Align each sheet in centre of batten. Fix with galvanized plasterboard nails at 150mm (6 in) intervals. Don't nail within 12mm ($\frac{1}{2}$ in) of edge.

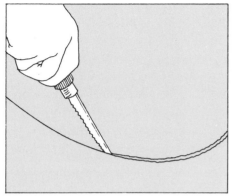

7 Cut curves with a padsaw. Use sandpaper to clean up any rough edges. Use a panel saw for straight cuts.

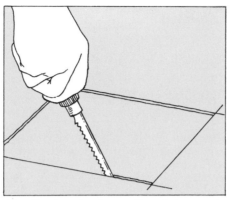

8 Rectangles for wall switches and sockets should be marked off accurately and cut out with a padsaw.

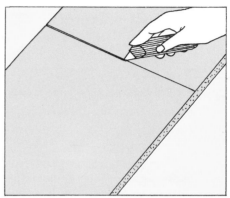

9 An easier way to cut plasterboard is with a sharp knife. First, cut through to the plaster core of the board.

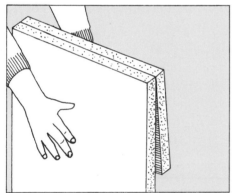

10 Turn the board back along the cut line until it snaps cleanly. Then cut through the paper backing.

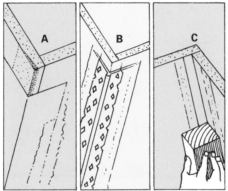

11 Internal (C) and external (A & B) corners have to be reinforced where the edges of the boards butt up. Using paper tape (A & C), or metal angle bead (B).

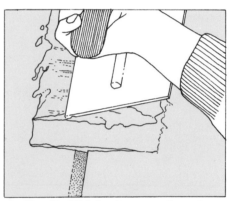

12 To fill joins between boards, apply a 100mm (4 in) band of joint filler using a steel float.

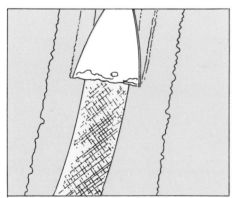

13 Then cut a length of jointing tape and use a filling knife to press it firmly into the filler. Leave for five minutes.

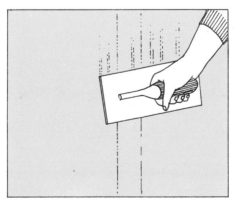

14 Use the steel float to apply a 200mm (8 in) wide band of joint filler over the tape.

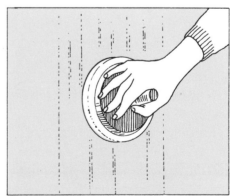

15 Use a special sponge, moistened, to *feather* out the joint filler. Allow to dry. Apply a 300mm (1 ft) band of joint filler, *feathered* with the sponge.

REPAIRS & DECORATION

MIRRORS

Mirrors serve a dual purpose: they are both functional and decorative. In bedrooms and bathrooms they are essentially practical. In other parts of the house they can be used to reflect light and create an illusion of space. A small hallway with a mirror extending down a complete wall will be dramatically altered; a mirror in an alcove in a small lounge will suggest another room. The permutations and possibilities are enormous. The one place not to site a mirror is on a chimney-breast with a fire below; people using the mirror risk standing too close to the fire and getting burned.

There are framed and unframed mirrors. The best types will be made from 6mm ($\frac{1}{4}$ in) thick good quality *float glass*. This will be perfectly flat and have no imperfections, giving a perfect reflection.

Where a mirror is to be used in steamy conditions, such as a bathroom or shower room, or some kitchens, check that it has a well-silvered steam-resistant backing. If it doesn't, then the silvering might well come away in places and you will not be able to anything about repairing it, since silvering is a factory process.

AIR SPACE

In every situation, you should ensure that there is a little space between the mirror and the wall so that air can circulate and prevent the silvering from being damaged. This can be done by using plastic spacers or washers, which are usually provided with the clips and screws fixing kit. If you need to provide your own washers, when rehanging an old mirror, for example, use tap washers. Avoid rubber washers, which can deteriorate in time and attack the silvering.

The wall to which a mirror is fixed must be perfectly flat. Test it by holding a straight-edged piece of wood against it horizontally, vertically and diagonally in various places and see if there is a noticeable 'see-saw' movement. If there is, then you will need to line the wall with a piece of plywood, chipboard or plasterboard 10 or 12mm ($\frac{3}{8}$ in or $\frac{1}{2}$ in) thick. If you try to screw a mirror to a badly uneven wall, you will risk cracking it as the screws are driven home.

There are three ways of fixing mirrors: with clips, screws or plates. A small or medium-sized framed mirror can be regarded as a picture and hung in the same way, but a really large mirror needs to be screwed through the frame into the wall and supported on a length of 50 x 25mm (2 x 1 in) wood below.

If a mirror is supplied with holes pre-drilled for screw fixing, it is just a matter of *offering* it into place, marking off the four holes and fixing it using the wall-plugs and screws provided. If there are no holes and you want to fix it with screws, ask a glass merchant to drill the holes for you. It is possible to drill holes in a mirror yourself, but it requires a special drill bit and some skill.

Brass mirror screws are available, but there is no reason why you shouldn't use ordinary steel mirror screws, which will be provided with decorative dome covers. Screw these on to the head of the screws holding the mirror.

Fixing clips are probably the most popular way of fixing a mirror. They are normally provided with wall-plugs, screws and *spacer* washers. There are two fixed clips, which support the mirror from below the bottom edge, and four sliding clips, which go at the sides and, possibly, top of the mirror to hold it in place.

Fixing plates and corner plates are also available, but are used only with smaller mirrors. The mirror plates are screwed to the back of a mirror frame and the wall; the corner plates (for unframed mirrors) are screwed to the wall only.

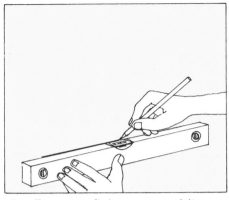

1 For screw fixing, use a spirit level to mark a horizontal line on the wall to serve as a positioning guide.

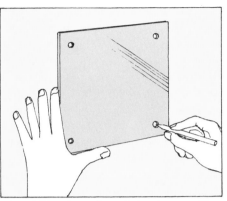

2 Offer the mirror into place, with its base on the pencil line, then mark the positions of the holes on the wall.

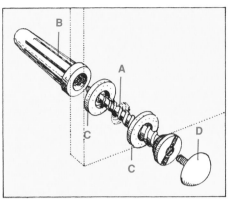

3 Drill holes (A) in the wall, and insert a wall-plug (B). Drive in each screw with washers (C) behind and in front of mirror. Screw home covers (D).

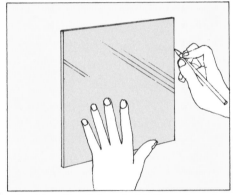

4 For clip fixing, hold the mirror in position and lightly pencil its outline on the wall.

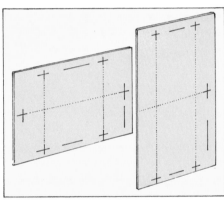

5 Mark clip-fixing positions 19mm ($^3/_4$ in) in from top and sides, and 13mm ($^1/_2$ in) from bottom.

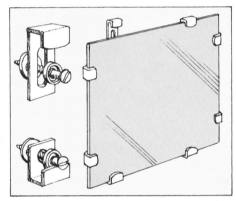

6 Use fixed clips at the bottom of the mirror to support it. Use sliding clips at the top and sides.

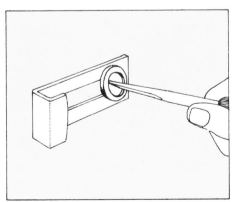

7 Secure the fixed clips first, then screw sliding clips into position tight enough to just allow movement.

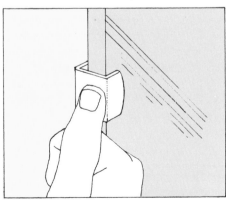

8 Put the mirror in place on the fixed clips, then push in the adjustable clips to hold it in position.

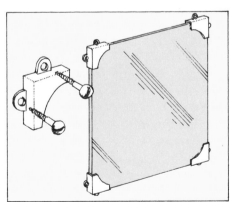

9 Hold mirror and corner plates in place. Mark off and drill all holes. Fix bottom plates, insert mirror with top plates and fix these.

MIRROR TILES

The advantage of mirror tiles is that they can be used to cover any shape or area that you have in mind. They come in a range of sizes, patterns and scenic designs. As with all wall-tiling jobs, the secret of success lies in the preparation of the surface to which the tiles are fixed. This must be perfectly flat. If it isn't, some of the tiles may not adhere properly and, even if they do, the reflected image could well be distorted.

If there is any dampness in the wall – be suspicious of loose wall-coverings and flaking paint – cure this first. Next, test the wall. Place a long straight-edged piece of wood against it – horizontally, vertically and diagonally – in various places. If you detect any 'see-saw' movement, you will need to create a level base for the tiles. Do this by screwing a sheet of 12mm (½ in) thick plywood or chipboard to the wall.

Where a wall is very uneven, you should fix to it a framework of 50 x 25mm (2 x 1 in) softwood battens. Set them at a maximum of about 750mm (30 in) apart and fix them to the wall with 75mm (3 in) long No 8 screws (*see* 'Repairs and Preparation').

If a wall is flat enough to receive tiles directly, remove any wallpaper or scrape off flaking paint. Seal a porous surface – plaster, emulsion paint, chipboard or plywood – and seal it by applying a coat of gloss paint. You must not use vinyl gloss. Allow 72 hours for gloss paint to dry before you tile, otherwise the weight of the tile might pull the paint film from the wall.

If the wall has been freshly plastered, allow four weeks for it to dry before tiling.

The adhesive tabs used to fix the tiles in place do not react favourably to a cold surface. In an unheated room, it is likely that the adhesive will reject a cold plaster surface, so warm the room thoroughly before attempting to fix the tiles.

Although tiles come in a variety of sizes, you might not be able to find exact sizes to fill the area you have in mind without having to cut some tiles. The simplest solution is to tailor the area to a number of full-size tiles. If you have to line a wall with chipboard, lay the tiles on the board, and pencil around the outline. Cut the board to this size and you have a tailor-made base.

You can cut mirror tiles with a special glass cutter, or you can ask a glazier to do it for you.

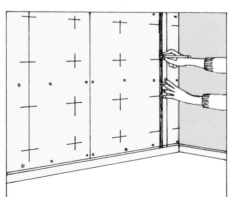

1 Line an uneven wall with a board or a board fixed to 50 x 25mm (2 x 1 in) wall battens.

2 Use a gauging rod (*see* 'Ceramic Tiles', p. 28) to work out the best positions for the tiles.

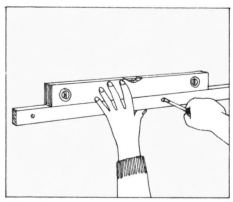

3 As a temporary guide, for the bottom row of tiles, fit a 25 x 25mm (1 x 1 in) batten to the wall.

4 Mirror tiles are sometimes supplied with self-adhesive fixing tabs on the back. If separate tabs are needed, fix one at each corner.

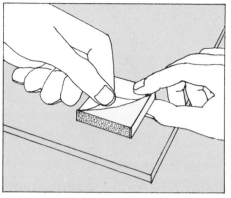

5 Peel off the top protective paper after fixing each tab in place. Do this just before fixing tile to wall.

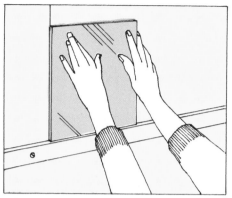

6 Draw a vertical pencil guideline on the wall. Then press the first tile neatly into the place. Only apply pressure over the tabs.

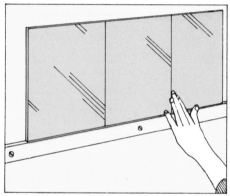

7 Add further tiles in horizontal rows. Make sure each one neatly butts up to its neighbour.

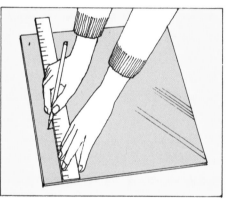

8 When you need to cut a border tile, first calculate carefully the exact tile size required.

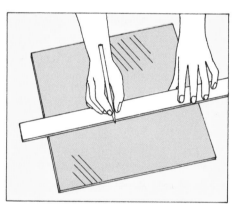

9 Use a *chinagraph* pencil and a straight-edge to mark an accurate cutting guideline.

10 Carefully score the cutting line with a glass cutter held against a straight-edge.

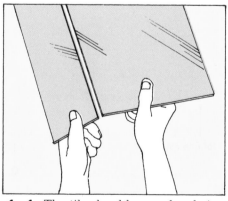

11 The tile should snap cleanly in two with even pressure exerted on both edges.

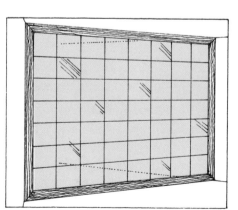

12 Where an area is an awkward size that will require leaving narrow border tiles, an edging of hardwood can frame the area instead.

PAINT

Whatever surface you are painting – walls, windows, radiators or ceiling – it must be prepared properly beforehand. A clean, smooth, dry surface is essential for good, long-lasting results (*see* 'Repairs and Preparation'). It is also important to use the correct equipment and paint (*see* 'Tools' and 'Materials').

WALLS AND CEILINGS

It is usual to use emulsion for the walls and ceilings. Remember that a flat matt paint will help disguise any surface imperfections in a wall, whereas a shiny emulsion, for example silk finish, will highlight them.

How many coats of paint you will need on any wall is never certain. If you are using the same colour as before, one coat might be enough. However, if you are changing the colour, you might need two or more coats in order to get a perfectly flat, even finish. Ceilings, especially where white paint is used, can require three or more coats. If you are painting a bare plaster surface, the first coat of emulsion should be diluted with water, following the instructions on the can.

So it can be difficult to estimate the amount of emulsion paint to buy. Given the circumstances above, work out the area of wall to be painted, then refer to the spreading rate given on the side of the can. The spreading rate indicates how many square metres (yards) of surface will be covered by 1 litre (about 1¾ pt) of paint. So if the total wall area of a room is 50 sq m (60 sq yd) and 1l (1¾ pt) paint will cover 15 sq m (18 sq yd), then you are going to need about 3½l (about 6 pt) of paint for each coat.

Before you start to paint, take as much of the furniture as possible out of the room, gather whatever is left in the centre of the room and cover it to protect it.

Vacuum clean the room after preparation and before starting to paint to prevent dust from settling on the wet paint.

Open the window to impede the rate at which the paint will dry out. This is worth doing because, when applying paint, you do not want the edge of a painted area to dry. If it does, that edge line will be evident when the wall is completed. For this reason, you must never take a break in the middle of painting a wall or ceiling. If you do, the paint will dry and the edge will show through. So always plan to finish a complete wall in one work session. If you then need a break, you can have one since a dried edge is not seen in corners.

It's unlikely that you will be able to reach to the ceiling without a stepladder, but if you have to paint only up to the picture rail, you may be able to reach comfortably, depending on your height. A sturdy plank placed between strong supports, such as stepladders, trestles or packing cases, will save having to continually reposition a stepladder, although not everyone feels comfortable on a plank.

Anything not being removed from a wall, such as light switches, can be protected from splashes by covering them with masking tape. If you don't intend repainting door frames, window frames, dado rails and so on, cover them with masking tape too and sheets of newspaper for larger areas such as radiators.

Always work away from the main window in the room. Working this way allows you to see which areas of the wall have been painted, so it prevents you from going back over a painted area, that has started to dry. Not only is this wasteful but it can leave obvious patches of paint on the finished wall.

If you are using a roller or pad brush, first go around the perimeter of the wall with a 25mm (1 in) wide brush. A roller or pad won't get into tight corners without smudging adjacent surfaces, so paint them first. Also paint around light switches, radiator pipes and so on in the same way.

Whatever type of applicator you use – brush, roller or pad brush – always work in a random direction on walls. Just load the applicator generously with paint and aim to work in an organized way, such as 600mm (2 ft) wide vertical bands. Don't overspread the paint, and work quickly to avoid that dry edge.

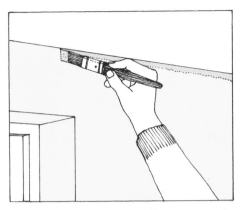

1 Before painting walls, go around the room with a 25mm (1 in) brush. Paint a narrow margin around all corners where the roller won't reach.

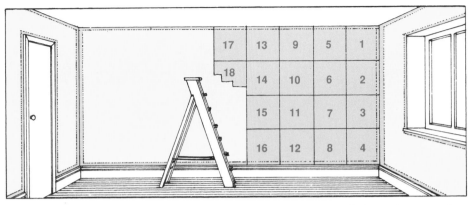

2 Paint one wall at a time completely, working in squares, following the sequence shown. If you are left-handed you will find it more convenient to work from the opposite corner. Work quickly to join up the squares before the paint edges dry.

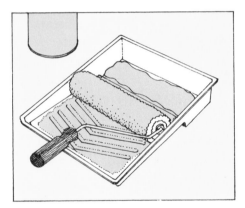

3 Load a roller correctly. Pour some paint into the well, dip the roller in it, then work it up and down the tray to cover it completely.

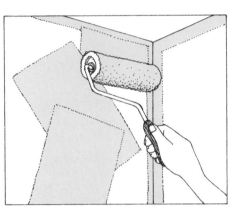

4 Start painting in a corner, allowing the edge of the roller to overlap on to the 25mm (1 in) margin of paint. Use the roller in random fashion.

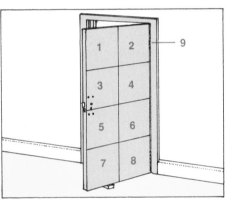

5 Paint a flush door in the order shown. Again, if you are left-handed, you will probably prefer to work from the opposite side.

6 A panelled door should be painted in this sequence. This will enable you to work towards wet edges, joining them up before any dry. Use two brushes – a 25mm (1 in) size for the mouldings and a 50 or 75mm (2 or 3 in) size for the main panels and sections.

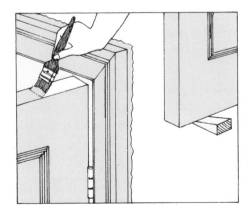

7 Where walls are to be papered, take a 12mm (½ in) margin on to the wall. Paint top edge of door if overlooked; remove wedge when paint has dried.

Normally, you can apply a second coat within hours – the instructions on the can will be specific. However, you really need to see the room in good, natural daylight in order to judge how the first coat has dried. If you are lucky, the walls will have an even, flat finish. There won't be a patchy effect or brush or roller marks apparent. Have a look at the walls from different points in the room before deciding on a further coat. Should only one or two walls need a further coat, then do just those. However, it's likely that if one wall needs to be done again, they all will.

DOORS

When both the ceiling and walls have been painted, you can concentrate on doors, windows and radiators. There is no specific order for dealing with them.

Remove all the door furniture, then, tap a wedge underneath the door to keep it absolutely firm. If you keep it sufficiently open for someone to enter the room if necessary, that will prevent work being interrupted.

There is a strict order for painting doors, as shown in the diagrams; it is a logical process that will ensure an excellent all-over finish.

Using gloss paint is much more difficult than using emulsion. You must work carefully and neatly in order to prevent the paint running or going on too thickly.

How you start painting is determined by whether you are facing a new, bare surface or old gloss. Assuming, again, that all preparation work has been carried out carefully (*see* 'Repairs and Preparation'), you are ready to start.

The conditions for painting are important. First, the room must not be dusty, so vacuum it well, otherwise a draught from a window or someone deciding to sweep up while new gloss is drying can result in a dust-speckled effect on skirting boards and door bottoms. Next, make sure the room is not freezing cold – this can cause the paint to lose some of its gloss on drying. Finally, the light must be good, so paint gloss only when natural light in the room is at its best. Shadows and artificial lighting can lead you to paint over previously painted areas resulting in a patchy finish.

Clean any dust from the lid of the can before removing it – you don't want that falling into the paint. You can paint straight from the can if you like, though many people find it is well worth transferring small amounts to a smaller can called a paint kettle and working from this.

A paint kettle is light and convenient to carry. Since only a small amount of paint is in it, it won't tend to thicken up and have to be restirred, which can happen, especially if you are working in direct sunshine.

One of the secrets of gloss painting is never to overload the brush. At the most only 25mm (1 in) or so of the bristles need be immersed in the paint. The bristles are then wiped on the inside of the can or kettle to remove any excess and you are ready to work.

Whether you are applying a coat of primer, undercoat or gloss, always put the paint on in the same fashion. First apply the paint in the direction of the grain of the wood. Assuming this is vertical, brush three or four vertical strokes with a gap of about 12mm ($\frac{1}{2}$ in) between them. Next, without reloading the brush, join the vertical bands by spreading the paint across in horizontal strokes. Finally, make more vertical strokes to finish off using the tips of the bristles only. Work quickly, reload the brush and move on to the adjacent area immediately. By working in this systematic way, you will avoid dried edges and eliminate brush marks.

The technique of 'working with the grain', that is starting and finishing in the same direction as the grain, should be followed on all wood surfaces. With panelled doors, some sections – the horizontal rails – will normally have the grain going across.

Allow 24 hours for each coat of paint – primer, undercoat and gloss – to dry before applying the next coat.

When painting door frames, assuming the walls are to be papered later, take a 12mm ($\frac{1}{2}$ in) margin of the gloss on to the wall. The same applies to window frames and above skirting boards and below picture rails. This is good insurance against any slight errors in cutting the paper to fit into the angles.

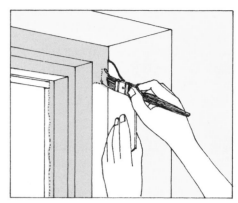

8 **Sash windows:** Push the top sash down close to the sill, and the bottom one up over it so that they overlap by 250mm (10 in). Paint the meeting rail and vertical sections of the top sash, then push it up and complete it. Paint the lower sash next. Finally, paint the frame and runners.

9 Although a margin of gloss is needed on the glass, you don't want smudges. If your hand is unsteady, use masking tape or a shield. A shield keeps gloss off the reveal too.

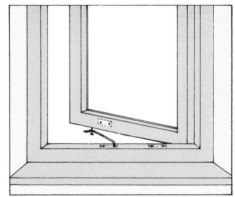

10 **Casement windows:** Work from the inside towards the outer surfaces. First complete the rebates, crossbars and crossrails. Then do the sides and edges and, finally, the frame. Don't forget to take a 2mm ($\frac{1}{8}$ in) margin of gloss on to the glass.

11 Remove fittings from frame before painting. Use an improvised stay made from a coat-hanger to hold window open until it dries.

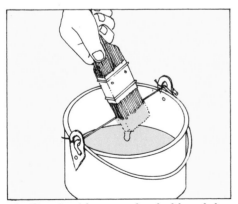

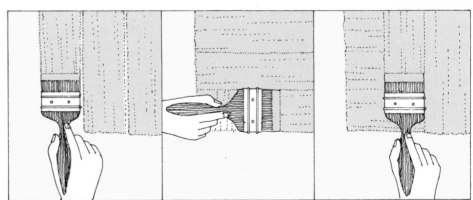

12 Avoid an overloaded brush by wiping the bristles on the edge of the can or on a string tied across.

13 The correct way to apply gloss. Brush on with the grain, leaving a 12mm ($\frac{1}{2}$ in) between strokes. Then, without reloading the brush, work across. Finally finish with the grain, using the tips of bristles.

Also, especially where a door is overlooked from a staircase, paint the top edge. Apart from the visual aspect, this is also a dust trap if unpainted.

WINDOWS

The first rule about windows is to paint any openable ones that are accessible to intruders as early as possible in the day so that they are dry and closable at night.

The order of painting casements and sashes is shown in the illustrations and should be followed closely. Do use at least two brushes – 25 and 50mm (1 and 2 in) wide – on window frames; you will find you are able to work much more quickly and accurately by matching the narrow and slightly wider brushes to relevant surface widths.

Cutting-in around glass is the slowest part of the job. However, the idea is not to keep the paint off the glass altogether, but to take a margin of the gloss coat about 2mm ($\frac{1}{8}$ in) on to it. By doing so, you will prevent any condensation running down the glass from getting into the framework and causing it to rot.

If you have a steady hand, then you will be able to do this without smudging the glass. If you have an angled brush, it will be even easier. If you can't keep a steady line, use masking tape or a paint shield. Should you choose tape, remove it before the gloss coat dries. If you leave it too long, as you pull away the tape it might bring some of the paint film with it.

SKIRTING BOARDS

However much you try to keep dust off the floor, some is bound to settle. When painting skirtings it is easy to pick up dirt on the bristles and brush it on to the work. To avoid this, use a piece of cardboard, which you can slip below the skirting and move along as you work.

PICTURE RAILS

Together with dado rails, these usually require a fairly narrow brush. Do ensure that the top of a picture rail has been cleaned out before painting, otherwise dust will adhere to the brush.

RADIATORS

Paint them when they are cold and don't turn them on again for at least 48 hours. Don't paint the valves on either side: you will need to be able to operate them in the future and having them jammed by paint won't be convenient.

Paint a radiator slowly, *laying off* the paint in each of the recessed areas carefully to avoid paint runs. Check back every 600mm (2 ft) to make sure you haven't missed any runs.

FAULTS

The commonest problem with painting technique is overloading a brush, which results in runs. This can be avoided by using the technique described earlier. Should you still be overloading, then tie a piece of string across the can or paint kettle and get into the habit of wiping the bristles on it.

Continually overloading causes the bristles to be clogged with paint, making the brush drag across the surface. If this happens stop painting and switch to a new brush if you have one. If not, quickly clean and dry the brush before restarting. Also stir the paint frequently so that it doesn't start to thicken.

As with emulsion painting, don't take a break in the middle of painting, say, a flush door or you will see the dried edge when you have finished.

There is no need to clean the brush when you stop for short breaks; just wrap the bristles in foil. The paint will stay wet and the brush will be ready for re-use immediately.

Overnight, suspend the brush in white spirit or a proprietary brush cleaner. Work off the excess spirit on a clean piece of wood or brick so that the bristles are dry before you use the brush again. If you don't dry off the brush, the white spirit will make the paint too runny.

VARNISH

Apply varnish and lay it off in the same way as paint except that you can use a more flowing coat, but do watch for runs.

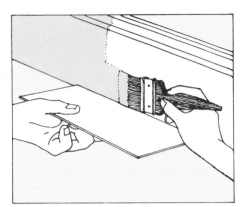

14 Small sections such as a cornice or dado rail can be tackled more quickly and neatly with a small brush.

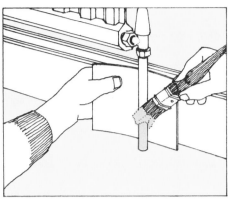

15 A piece of cardboard held below the skirting will prevent the brush contacting the floor and picking up dust.

16 You can avoid getting paint on to a freshly painted skirting while painting radiator pipes by using a piece of card as a shield.

17 Paint radiators with a small brush to avoid runs. Work in a good light and brush away from the grooves. Don't paint the bleed nipple.

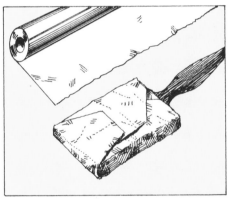

18 Taking a short break? Wrap the brush in foil. The paint will stay wet and the brush will be ready for immediate re-use.

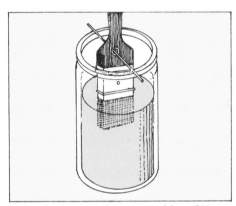

19 Overnight suspend brush in cleaner. Keep the tips of the bristles about 25mm (1 in) above the bottom so that they are clear of the sediment.

PAINT EFFECTS

Painted walls and woodwork do not have to be dull and boring. There are lots of special paint effects that will let you get away from the plain painted look.

SPLATTERING

Also called spattering, this is one of the easiest techniques. You can achieve a speckled effect by splattering one or more colours on to a previously painted surface.

The base coat can be emulsion, satin finish, eggshell or gloss paint, which should be allowed to dry. This background will be the dominant colour, so it should be a fairly neutral one.

The technique is fairly messy, so cover the floor with dust sheets and mask features such as doors, windows and light switches with newspapers.

For the splatter colours, use an oil paint thinned down with white spirit, so that it will splatter, but not run. Pour the paint in a tray, dip a stiff bristled brush in it, hold the brush upside down, then draw a ruler towards you across the bristles to flick paint droplets forwards. Practise on an old board before embarking on the area you want to decorate.

SPONGING

This gives an attractive speckled appearance to a surface and involves using a small sponge to dab irregular patches of colour over a base coat that will show through.

Start by applying the base coat evenly and allow it to dry. You can use emulsion paint on walls, while an oil-based eggshell or satin finish is best on wood.

The best effect is achieved by using a small natural sponge, which should be soaked in water so it expands to full size. Squeeze out the water and dip the sponge into a little thinned top coat. Dab the sponge on a board to get rid of excess paint and then work as evenly as possible over the surface to be painted.

RAGGING

This is a very similar technique to sponging, except that a bunched-up rag is used to apply the top coat of paint. Allow the base coat to dry, then dip the rag into the thinned top coat, work it on a board and then dab it on to the surface. Change the rag for a clean one as soon as it gets clogged up. Experiment with different types of cloth and vary the bunching of the rag for different effects.

RAG-ROLLING

As the name suggests, a rag about 400mm (16 in) square is folded into quarters and twisted into a roll before being rolled across the wet paint surface to create a pattern.

The top coat will be the dominant colour, so it should be darker than the lighter satin-finish base coat. Let the base coat dry, then apply the top coat, which can be an oil-based eggshell or satin paint thinned with an equal amount of white spirit, or a decorator's oil-glaze also thinned with white spirit. Apply the top coat thinly, and smooth out with a wide brush used lightly. A good supply of rags will be needed, because as they get soaked in paint they become less effective and must be changed. Soak each rag in white spirit and wring it out before use. Roll each rag across the surface of the wet paint, trying to avoid 'skids'. Change the direction to avoid a repetitive pattern.

DRAGGING

This is a simple form of wood-graining used on wood and panelling. It involves dragging the bristles of a dry brush over wet paint to produce regular parallel lines. It takes a bit of practice!

Allow an off-white base-coat of satin-finish oil-base paint to dry first. Apply a transparent oil glaze that has been thinned with an equal amount of white spirit and tinted with artist's oil paint in the wood shade required. Brush this on to the surface. Now draw a dry, long-bristled brush over the surface to create the grain effect. To get the effect of sharp wood joints at corners, mask previously treated areas with glasspaper sheets held upside down. These will not smudge the wet paint.

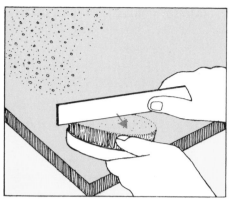

1 **Splattering:** One of the easiest techniques. Apply any base coat and allow it to dry. Scrape ruler over stiff bristled brush to make flecks.

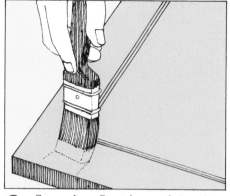

2 **Sponging:** Start by applying the base coat. This can be emulsion paint on walls, or eggshell or satin-finish oil-based paint on wood.

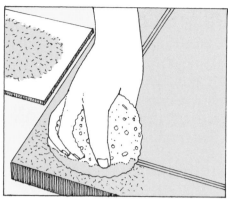

3 Use a real marine sponge soaked in water and wrung out so it is full size. Dip the sponge into a little thinned top coat and dab on to base coat.

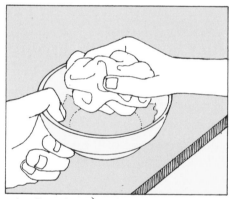

4 **Ragging:** Apply base coat and allow to dry, as for sponging. Pour a little top coat into a bowl and dip a bunched-up rag into paint.

5 Lightly dab the rag on to the dry base coat and gradually build up the required pattern – several light coats are better than heavy ones.

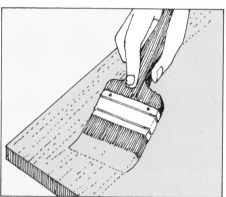

6 **Rag rolling:** Use an eggshell paint or an oil glaze of darker colour over a pale base coat. Thin it with white spirit and apply by brush.

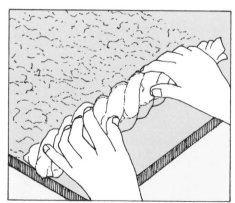

7 Form rag into rolled-up sausage shape and roll across the wet paint surface to produce a pattern. Change direction, but do not 'skid'.

8 **Dragging:** A finish for wood and panelling to represent wood grain. Apply a base coat and allow it to dry. Then apply a tinted glaze.

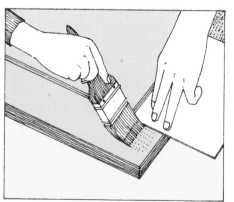

9 With a light touch and a steady hand, drag the bristles of a dry brush over the wet paint. Mask with glasspaper at corners for wood look.

STIPPLING

Stippling is a very easy effect to achieve, requiring only a large stippling brush with a flat, square head measuring about 100 x 75mm (4 x 3 in) to produce a delicate, flecked effect. The bristles are flat on the underside so you can hit the wet paint surface of the top coat to produce the stippled effect. Purpose-made stippling brushes are available from good decorators' outlets. However, it is worth experimenting with other types of brush you may find around the house. For example, the old-fashioned type of gentleman's hairbrush could be ideal, or an old clothes brush.

The effect looks best if a pale oil glaze (from good decorating shops) is applied over a base coat of a slightly lighter colour to keep the effect 'open'.

The oil-based satin – or eggshell – finish base coat should be smoothly applied and allowed to dry. For the top coat use 4 parts of a transparent oil glaze thinned with 1 part white spirit. Tint it to the colour required with some universal stainer (also from decorating shops).

Brush the diluted top coat sparingly over the dry base coat, then brush more of the top coat on to the bristles of the stippling brush. Hold the brush absolutely parallel to the wall and bang it firmly into the wet top coat so the base colour just shows through. You will have to hit the surface squarely or the effect will be smudged. Practise on a piece of board to perfect the technique before tackling a large area.

BAG-GRAINING

This technique is similar to ragging, but it gives a finer textured finish, looking a little like crushed velvet. Allow the base coat to dry, then paint on a top coat of oil glaze thinned with white spirit. Wrap a damp sponge or crumpled rags in a thin plastic bag and dab it on to wet oil glaze.

GRAINING

Graining is a very old technique that is used to give painted woodwork the appearance of a high-quality wood, such as mahogany. It has the advantage that you do not have to strip off the existing finish, but it is definitely a difficult technique – one to leave until you have gained some experience of the other finishes. You will need to use a special glaze called 'scumble', which is available from specialist paint and decorators' suppliers.

Apply a coat of a wood-colour eggshell oil-base paint to match the lightest colour of the wood effect you wish to achieve.

Next, apply a coat of wood-colour scumble glaze thinned with an equal amount of white spirit and rub this on to the surface. Use a brush on the wet glaze to form a light basic grain pattern. Leave this for 24 hours to dry thoroughly.

Next the swirling heart-grain can be applied. Use black gloss paint in oil glaze thinned with white spirit. Apply this very lightly to the panel in semi-elliptical brushstrokes and then, with a long, soft-bristled brush, soften these grain lines, working out from the centre.

When you are satisfied with the result, let the panel dry before giving it a protecting coat of clear varnish.

STENCILLING

Stencilling is a very quick and easy technique for applying motifs and designs.

Careful setting out is required to get the patterns level and at even spacing.

Probably the best way to start is with a stencil kit from a decorating shop. You can buy ready-cut stencils, fast-drying stencil paints (although ordinary emulsion paint can also be used) and special stencil brushes, which are used with a stippling action so that the paint does not get under the edges of the stencil.

Traditionally, stencils are made from oiled stencil card, but clear acetate is becoming popular because it is transparent and therefore easier to align.

If you cut your own stencil, work from a tracing of a very simple design. Children's books are good sources of designs. It is helpful to have a separate stencil for each colour.

Working to guidelines, tape the stencil in place with strips of masking tape. Apply the paint to the brush sparingly, dab excess paint on to scrap paper, then work from the edges of the stencil towards the middle using a circular stippling motion of the brush. Allow each colour to dry before proceeding to the next.

10 **Stippling:** Before stippling apply a coat of thinned oil glaze over the dry base coat. Use brush; apply sparingly.

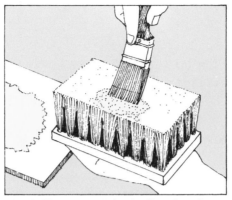

11 Use a special stippling brush or old hairbrush. Brush more of the top coat on to the stippling brush.

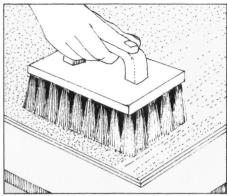

12 Next, stipple the brush into the wet top coat to make the base colour show through. Strong, firm brush pressure will be needed.

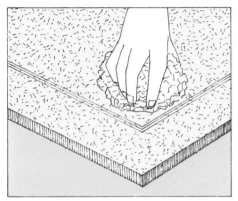

13 **Bag graining:** A delicate effect is achieved by wrapping a damp sponge in a well-crinkled thin plastic bag, which is dabbed on wet glaze.

14 **Graining:** Give painted woodwork the appearance of wood grain. Apply wood colour eggshell paint. When dry, paint with scumble glaze.

15 Leave scumble glaze in basic grain pattern and allow to dry. Apply thinned black gloss in semi-elliptical strokes; soften with brush.

16 **Stencilling:** Buy stencils from decorating shops, or trace simple design and cut your own. Cut separate stencil for each colour.

17 Use emulsion paint or special stencil paint. Work paint into stencil brush and dab on to paper.

18 Tape stencil in place and stipple paint into cut-out, working from edge to middle with a light circular movement of brush.

TEXTURED COMPOUNDS

Most people see textured compounds as being a quick way of redecorating a wall that is sound and stable but perhaps suffers from excessive minor cracks or crazing. This situation is discovered after stripping off an existing wall-covering, possibly in the hope of finding nice, flat plastered walls that can simply be painted with emulsion. In older houses, which have endured many years of wear and tear from the occupants, and natural movement, you will rarely find walls suitable for emulsion painting – unless you are prepared to put up with obvious defects showing through.

Before the arrival of textured compounds – which are simply thick, buttery paints – you would have had three choices if you wanted to emulsion walls: to spend hours filling and smoothing the walls with cellulose filler or plaster; to hang lining paper before repainting; or simply repaper using a thick, textured paper, such as woodchip or Anaglypta, which is specially made to be painted.

Textured compounds offer a fourth alternative, giving a patterned surface that you can paint as normal using emulsion or, more rarely, gloss paint.

Textured compounds are sometimes referred to as Artex. This, however, is just one of many brands.

The material remains flexible for its lifetime, which means that it will continue to conceal cracks that might open through normal house movement. However, it will not conceal serious cracking that may result from a bad structural fault, a plumbing disaster or the like, nor can it be applied to hide cracks that are more than 1.5mm ($\frac{1}{16}$ in) wide. If you come across these, fill them first, as described in 'Repairs and Preparation'.

The compounds come in two forms. The ready-mixed form comes in a plastic tub, from which it can be applied straight to a wall or ceiling. Cheaper, but less convenient, is the type that come as a powder for you to mix with water to the right consistency as described in the manufacturer's instructions. Provided you do the mixing correctly – which simply means adding the right amount of water – this type is as easy to use as the other.

SURFACE PREPARATION

Any wallpaper or ceiling paper has to be completely stripped off. Should you find bare plaster below the old paper, you should apply a coat of stabilizing primer as directed by the manufacturer.

Surfaces that were previously painted are suitable provided the paint is sound – just rub down with glasspaper or a power finishing sander to slightly abrade the surface. To test paint that is suspect, wipe it vigorously with a wet rag and press some sticky tape on it, then pull it away. If either test brings paint away, you need to wash away as much loose material as possible before applying a stabilizing primer – again as recommended by the manufacturer. Happily, this situation is not common, since poor quality paints and old distemper have largely disappeared over the years.

Some of the compounds provide a texture simply by applying them using the required tool – usually a foam roller. This will give a stipple texture. With others, you do your own texturing using either a proprietary tool or an implement of your own making – this gives you a chance to be totally individualistic, provided you are reasonably artistic of course.

Don't forget, you can always practise first on an old piece of hardboard or plaster until you get proficient.

Because the compound sets rock hard and is very difficult to remove later, there are several things to remember. First, be certain you can live with the finish for a long time before using a textured compound.

Second, you usually get an hour or so to complete making a pattern after applying the texture, so don't work on too great an area at a time.

Third, always mask off windows, doors, sills and any other surface that could be splashed by the compound, which sets rock hard and is very difficult to remove later.

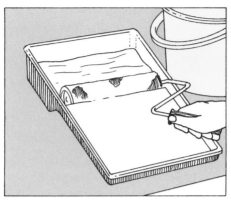

1 Pour the compound into a roller tray and load the roller thickly by working it up and down the tray.

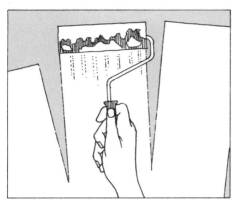

2 Working in random directions, apply a thick coat of compound to the surface. Don't wave the roller about or specks will fly everywhere.

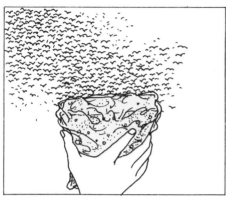

3 To achieve a stipple finish, wrap a sponge in polythene so that the surface is flat, then 'bounce' the sponge on the compound.

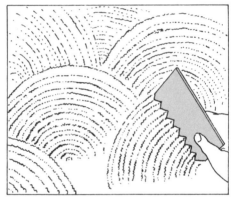

4 A combed effect is created using a serrated scraper which you can buy or make. Aim to overlap each arc.

5 Popularly called the Roman swirl, this design is created with a sponge. Just place the sponge on the surface and take it through a circle.

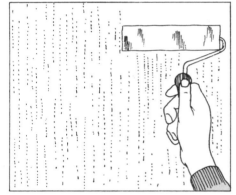

6 A pleasing, very light pattern consisting of vertical lines, like the bark of a tree, is achieved with a foam roller.

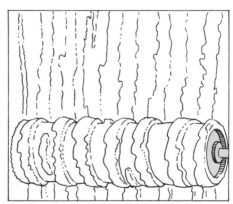

7 A more pronounced bark-like pattern can be created using a special roller bought at decorating shops. Just run it up and down vertically.

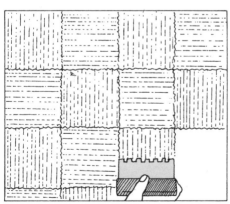

8 A basket-weave, criss-cross design is very easy to do. Use a notched plastic comb – shop bought or home-made.

9 Around ceiling roses, light switches and so on, use a 12 or 25mm ($^1/_2$ or 1 in) brush to cut in. Draw a straight band or try to match the texture.

FLOORS: CARPETS

There are not too many jobs that d-i-yers should be wary of attempting, but measuring for and laying fully fitted carpet is definitely one of them even if you are very experienced at other d-i-y jobs.

It is worth remembering that many carpet suppliers offer a measuring and estimating service, which is often free, and, from time to time, a genuine free fitting service. Considerable skill is needed to lay a fully fitted carpet, such as a good quality hessian-backed Axminster or Wilton. (These names are not brands; they describe the method used to make the carpet.) In a large awkward-shaped room, perhaps an L-shaped lounge or one having more than its fair share of alcoves and recesses, the carpet may have to be fitted as a number of pieces, joined together while it is being laid. In some cases the job of joining the carpet is done in a workshop so that the roll is delivered to the house ready for the fitter to install.

The key to professional installation lies in the way the carpet is stretched. Gripper rods – lengths of timber strips with angled nails protruding from them – are nailed around the skirtings. The carpet is fixed to one side of the room and then is stretched across the floor by using a device called a knee kicker. The carpet is then engaged on the gripper rods on the opposite wall, where it is held under tension. The process is repeated at the top and bottom walls of the room too, taking the carpet into any bays or alcoves and around corners. Only by correct stretching will you be ensured that your carpet will wear well.

However, the job of laying a foam-backed carpet is one that can be tackled with confidence. It's a job that can be done when a carpet is new or is replaced after decorating or, perhaps, after having moved house.

CARPET SIZES

Carpet squares come in an enormous range of sizes and have bound edges. A gap will be left between the edge of the carpet and the skirting, so the floor has to be in good condition or be *sanded* and *sealed* to improve its appearance. As it is not fixed down, a square can be turned from time to time so that it wears evenly. It is also easier to protect when the room is being decorated. Obviously there is no problem in fitting a carpet square and there are unlikely to be any problems when moving house.

Fitted carpets cover the complete floor and make a room more spacious. They give excellent insulation against heat loss and reduce noise. It is not practical to turn a fitted carpet in order to spread wear, and there is the problem of removing and refitting it at decorating time. When moving to a new house, the carpet will have to be laid in a smaller room so that it can be cut and fitted again, or it can be used as a carpet square if you bind the edges.

Fitted carpet is obtainable in a range of widths, the most common being 2.7m (9 ft), 3.6m (12ft) and 4.5m (15 ft). You buy a piece slightly bigger than your room and then trim it to fit.

SEAMS

At the planning stage joins in the carpet have to be considered, bearing in mind traffic lanes, carpet pile, economy in cutting and appearance. *Seams* are best avoided, where possible, in heavy traffic areas such as doorways.

PILE

The direction of the pile – that is, whether it leans towards a window or away from it – affects the shade of the carpet.

Carpet always appears to be darker when you look into the pile; lighter when you look in the direction it is flowing. For a dark, rich colour from the doorway, lean the pile towards the door. If you want the rich effect from inside the room, lean the pile towards the light.

It is important that wherever pieces of carpet are joined the pile is running in the same direction. If it isn't, light and dark shading will be seen side by side. Find the direction of the pile by brushing your hand along the carpet. If it lies smooth, you are brushing with the pile; if it brushes up, you are going against the pile.

PATTERNS

The top of the pattern should lie away from the door so that you are looking at the design the right way up as you enter.
If the pattern is random, then the direction of pile is the deciding factor. Often you have to compromise between seams, pile and pattern.

UNDERLAY

However good the quality of a carpet, its performance depends completely on durable, well-laid underlay. Never skimp on the cost of underlay – an old piece of carpet or sheets of newspaper are worthless. A proper underlay provides a buffer between the carpet and the floor, ensuring even wear. It protects the carpet backing from rubbing against the floor or rotting, and prevents dust coming up through the floorboards from working its way

through to damage the pile. It will also overcome any slight unevenness in the floor.

Foam-backed carpets do not require a separate underlay but they do need to be prevented from sticking to the floor. If this happens, it can be impossible to lift the carpet with the backing intact. It can also cause the carpet to wear prematurely.

Paper felt – thick, grey paper sold in 900mm (3 ft) or 1.8m (6 ft) widths – is normally used as an underlay.

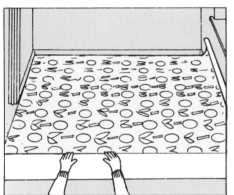

1 Take the carpet into the room and position it roughly, with the pattern aligned to best advantage.

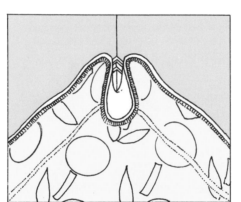

2 Initially, have about 150mm (6 in) of surplus carpet lapping up the skirtings.

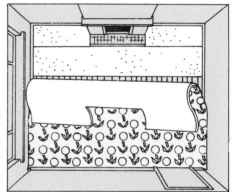

3 Roll back the carpet halfway across the room to leave part of the floor accessible for fixing felt paper.

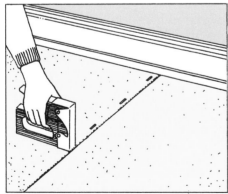

4 Staple felt paper to floor, with adjoining sheets overlapping by 25mm (1 in). Complete both halves of floor.

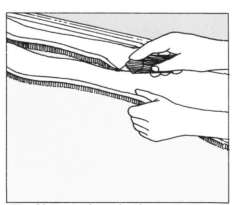

5 Using a sharp knife, cut away most of the surplus material, leaving about 50mm (2 in) for final trimming.

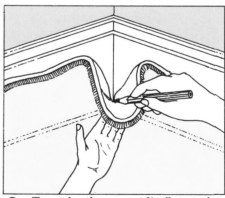

6 To make the carpet lie flat, make release cuts in corners. First, feel the floor through the carpet.

Felt underlay is 1.3m (about 4½ft) wide. There are many different grades, made from jute, animal hair, wool waste or a combination of materials. Sometimes rubber is incorporated.

Polyurethane foam or rubber is much more springy and resilient than felt and gives the carpet a softer feel. Rubber underlays should never be used where there is underfloor heating, because the rubber will start to smell and can eventually disintegrate.

To prevent them moving, strips of underlay should be joined at the edges either with self-adhesive tape or by tacking or stapling. Use adhesive on concrete floors.

Underlay is never stretched like carpets, but must be pulled taut to eliminate any wrinkles.

LAYING THE CARPET

Take off the door to the room if it opens inwards. It will be easy to replace later. Bear in mind that if a carpet has not been laid in the room before you might have to trim some wood from the door to allow it to clear the carpet. While the door is in position, measure it against a piece of the carpet and mark off how much is to be removed. Draw a line on the door and saw off along it after you have removed the door from its hinges.

The carpet should be laid using double-sided carpet tape, which is bought in rolls. It is either 25 or 50mm (1 or 2 in) wide, and the smaller size is sufficient where the carpet is to be fixed only around the skirtings. The wider version is needed if two pieces of carpet have to be joined, although two pieces of 25mm (1 in)-wide tape, laid side by side will suffice.

To save having to handle a large amount of excess carpet, if possible take the carpet into a larger room, even into the garden, and cut it to leave only about 150mm (6 in) of excess all round for final trimming.

Fix the carpet tape to the floor all around the edge of the room. Don't peel off the upper layer of protective paper yet.

Take the carpet into the room and unroll it so that the excess laps up against the skirting boards. Adjust the carpet so that the pattern is lying correctly. Now roll back half of the carpet to expose the floor below. Fit the paper felt underlay to this half of the room.

The felt can be fixed using large head tacks or, much quicker, a staple gun. Unroll about 60mm (2 ft) and fix the edge just inside the tape. Now gradually unroll the felt right across the room, fixing it at the edges every 1m (3 ft) or so. Once it is cut and anchored at the other side of the room, the neighbouring strip can be laid, overlapping the first by 25mm (1 in) and again fixing at 1m (3 ft) intervals.

When half of the floor has been covered, roll that half of the carpet into place, then roll back the other half and fix the remainder of the felt paper. By using this method, the paper felt is not disturbed on the floor.

It is best to start cutting the carpet to fit along two reasonably plain walls – ones that don't contain radiators, doors, a chimney-breast or other such features. This is not always possible of course.

When final trimming is complete, pull back the edges of the carpet and peel off the protective cover paper from the double-sided tape. Push the carpet edge on to the tape all round the room with foot-pressure.

Make cuts at corners to allow the carpet to lie flat and then start the final trimming, as shown in the diagram.

If you have to join two pieces, make sure the pile of both is going in the same direction. Fix carpet tape to the floor along the join. Press the larger piece of carpet into place on the tape. Now, using a small artist's brush, apply some carpet adhesive to the edge of the pile to prevent it from fraying. Lay the adjoining length, making a tight *butt-join*. Keep a wet sponge handy to wipe away surplus adhesive immediately.

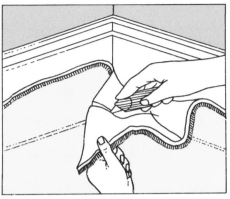

7 Turn the carpet back and make two cuts (one from each side of the corner) through the foam backing down to the floor line.

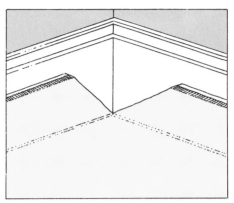

8 Press the carpet back into position; it will lie flat on the floor ready to be trimmed along skirtings.

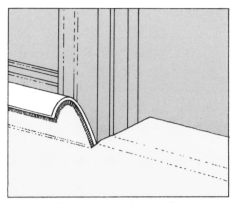

9 At doorways make a release cut as shown, allowing the surplus to pass through the door frame.

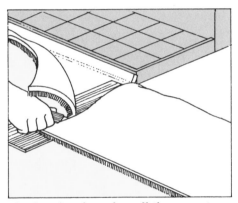

10 At a hearth, pull the carpet forward, place hardboard on the floor and initially cut a loose fit; trim later.

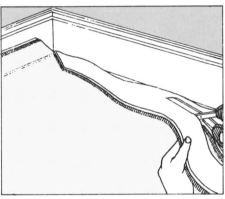

11 Carefully make final trimming cuts along the skirting with knife or scissors.

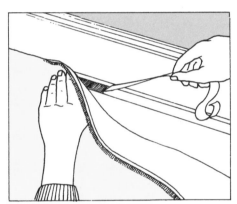

12 Pull protective tape from carpet tape, then press down carpet edge firmly.

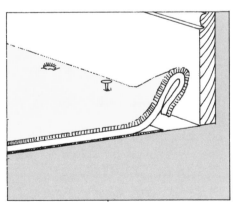

13 If you prefer to use 37mm (1½ in) carpet tacks, cut the edge oversize, turn under and tack through double thickness.

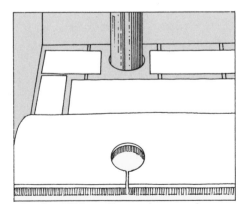

14 With radiator pipes, make a cut from the edge of the carpet inwards, then cut out small circle for pipe.

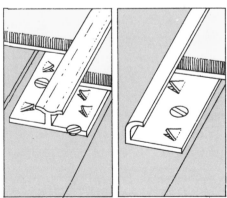

15 Fix a binder bar centrally at doorways. Cut carpet edge to slot it completely under the bar. Where two coverings meet, fit a double-sided binder bar to cover both edges.

CORK, CARPET & VINYL FLOOR TILES

For the beginner, the advantage of floor tiles over complete sheets of material – a roll of vinyl or carpet – is that they are far easier to lay. The problem areas – around obstacles such as fitments, basin pedestals and so on – are easily navigated. With a complete sheet, a cutting error can be disastrous, whereas with tiles you are doing the work in easy stages so that, at worst, you will spoil only one tile. Even that may be of use somewhere else in the room.

All tiles, whether being laid on floorboards or a solid concrete floor, must be put down on a perfectly flat, dry and clean surface. If they are not, they will work loose and any imperfections in the *sub-floor* will soon become evident on the surface.

Essentially, each type of tile is laid in the same way. Tiling must always start from the centre of the room, with tiles being laid outwards to the skirtings, where any cutting has to be done.

The reason for starting in the middle of the room is that very few walls can be relied upon to be *square* to each other. If they were, then you could happily use a skirting-board as the guide to laying the first row of tiles. Unfortunately, this is not the case.

Take some tiles and try it for yourself. Just lay them 'dry' – without glue – against the skirting-board. The first row will be all right, but the second or third row will not lie square to the preceding row and by the time you reach the end of the room an odd-shaped space will be left to fill at the skirting-board.

By working outwards from the middle of the room you will have to cut only the border tiles to an exact fit.

CORK

You can lay cork tiles over well-fixed pvc tiles, but not over any other floor-covering. Do not lay them where there is underfloor heating. When you get your cork tiles home, unpack them and leave them in the room where they are to be used for 24 hours. Shuffle them around so that they can 'breathe' and become conditioned to the room's atmosphere. It is possible that not all the packs of tiles will be exactly the same shade, so, by mixing them up, any shade differences will be spread over the complete floor and will not be noticeable.

Plan to lay the tiles in a warm room. This will make them more pliable and easier to handle.

Most cork tiles are supplied with a sealed finish already applied. If not, then refer to the manufacturer's instructions on what sealer to apply over them once they have been laid.

Special cork floor tile adhesive is required to lay them and this will be available where you buy the tiles. The instructions on the can will tell you how many square metres (yards) the contents will fix.

Keep some soapy water and rags available while laying the tiles so that you can immediately wipe off any adhesive that gets on to the decorative face of the tiles or your fingers. Dried adhesive can be removed by wiping with white spirit, but this might also remove some of the varnish on the tile surface. If so, you will have to touch up the marks later with clear varnish.

CARPET

Carpet tiles are usually *loose-laid,* so if any get stained they can be taken up and cleaned. If you are laying more than 10 sq m (10 sq yd) of tiles, fix every third row with double-sided adhesive tape; also use tape to fix tiles at doorways.

VINYL

Do not lay self-adhesive vinyl tiles over linoleum or cork. As with all tiles, it is best to finish off at doorways by using a binder bar to protect the edge of the tiles from being loosened by foot traffic (*see* 'Sheet Vinyl', page 80).

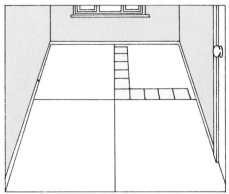

1 Find centre line of room. 'Dry' lay tiles. If necessary, adjust starting point by half a tile width to avoid narrow edge pieces.

2 Start laying the tiles in the order shown. Complete the room in four quarters.

3 Carpet tiles sometimes have arrow lines on the back to indicate direction of laying. See manufacturer's instructions.

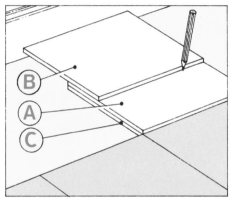

4 To cut an edge tile: place tile to be cut (A) over last full tile in row (C). Press tile (B) against skirting and mark cut line on (A).

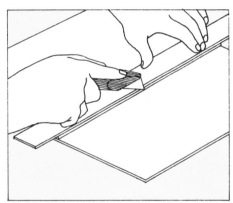

5 Tiles of all types can be cut with a sharp knife held against a straight-edge. Make a firm, clean cut.

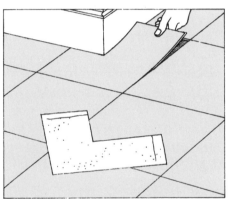

6 Always leave the backing paper on self-adhesive vinyl tiles until the tile is to be laid.

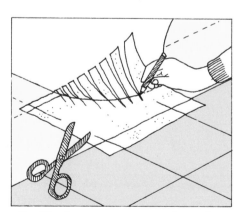

7 The best way to cut awkward shapes is to first make a pattern to transfer to the tile.

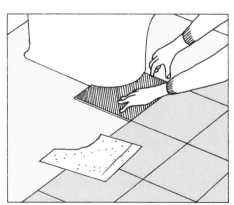

8 A template made from cardboard or stiff paper is needed at awkward shapes. Use a profile gauge for door architraves.

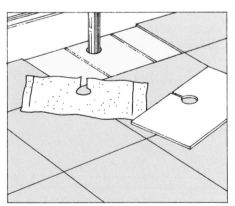

9 At radiator pipes, make a paper template. Mark on the full tile width and allow 2mm ($1/8$ in) clearance.The cut behind the pipe won't be seen.

CERAMIC & QUARRY FLOOR TILES

Preparation, planning and setting out for ceramic and quarry floor tiles is as for other floor tiles, except that you need to strengthen a timber floor by covering it with plywood.

CERAMIC TILES

Work out where the last rows of full tiles will fall at the corner of the longest side and adjacent wall of the room and nail straight timber battens to the floor to get these edges straight and at right angles to each other.

If you *loose lay* a block of 16 or more tiles in the corner, these will help to confirm the battens are at right angles.

With a notched spreader, apply ceramic floor tile adhesive direct to the floor, and push the tiles into this with a slight twisting action to ensure firm bedding.

Floor tiles rarely have built-in spacers, so they must be accurately spaced using plastic spacers. Spacers for floor tiles tend to be thicker than those for wall tiles. They can be left between the tiles and are *grouted* over.

Floor tiles are cut by *scoring* and snapping in the same way as ceramic wall tiles, but as floor tiles are thicker, it is best to use a professional type of cutter, as shown in the diagram.

Special grout for ceramic floor tiles is available in various colours and this is *worked* into the gaps between tiles using a rubber-blade squeegee.

QUARRY TILES

Quarry tiles are bedded on a one part cement to three parts sharp sand mortar mix, which is laid to approximately the same thickness as the tiles.

To get this bedding layer even, the mortar is smoothed out with a levelling board, notched at the ends, and drawn between two battens that are laid level and spaced exactly four tiles, plus spaces, apart – see the diagrams.

Dusting the mortar with dry cement helps to ensure the tiles stick firmly. The action of tapping them down level with the battens (the levelling board lays mortar to leave them 3mm ($\frac{1}{8}$ in) above the battens) brings some mortar into the spaces between tiles.

When the mortar has set, the edge tiles can be cut and fitted. The easiest method of cutting is to deeply score both sides of the tile using a masonry cutting disc fitted in an electric circular saw or in an angle grinder tool. Then the tile will snap if tapped with a hammer and cold chisel.

Use a small piece of board notched to the tile depth less 3mm ($\frac{1}{8}$ in), to ensure an even depth for the bedding mortar for the border tiles.

Grout tiles with a cement-based waterproof grouting compound. Finally, apply quarry-tile sealant or a non-slip liquid wax polish as recommended by the supplier.

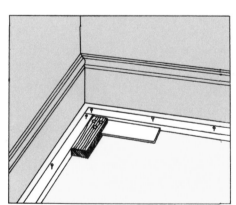

1 Ceramic tiles: Set out the floor to get the border tiles even. Fit guide battens to the floor to align the full-size perimeter tiles.

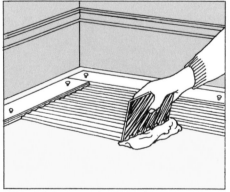

2 Make sure battens form an exact right angle in corner (check using a try-square). Use a notched applicator to spread tile adhesive on the floor.

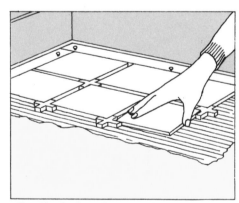

3 Push the tiles into the adhesive with a slight twisting motion. Keep them square with plastic spacers.

4 Lay the tiles in small blocks, then press a straight-edge along their edges to ensure they are square.

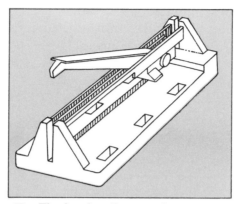

5 The border tiles are almost certainly going to need to be cut. A tile cutter like this makes cutting floor tiles accurate and easy.

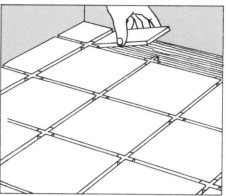

6 Maintain the spacing for the grouting when laying the border tiles. Either spread the adhesive on the floor or on back of the tiles.

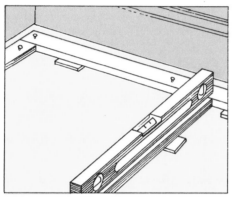

7 **Quarry tiles:** Use battens twice the thickness of tiles. Fix them at perimeters and four tiles plus spacers apart. The tops must be perfectly level. *Pack out* as needed.

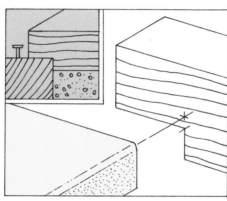

8 A levelling board is notched at ends to tile thickness less 3mm (1/8 in). This levels mortar to correct depth.

9 Pour the mortar at one end of the row. Pull the levelling board along the two battens to spread the mortar evenly.

10 Sprinkle surface of mortar with dry cement, then lay tiles, ensuring correct spacing. Tap down to level of battens with back of the levelling board

11 Adjust spacing with point of trowel and leave for at least 24 hours to set. For border tiles, use notched hardboard as leveller.

12 Apply cement-based waterproof grout between the tiles with a rubber-blade squeegee. Sponge off surplus cement.

WOOD PARQUET FLOORS

A very economical way of laying an attractive hardwood floor is to use parquet panels. You can lay this type of floor over timber floorboards, chipboard flooring panels or any solid floor – it just needs to be smooth and dry.

Traditional parquet flooring is made up of individual hardwood blocks, which are quite thick. This type is not only expensive, but it is difficult to lay, so you are much better off with wood mosaic panels. Each panel is made of five to seven hardwood fingers in four separate parts arranged at right angles to one another and held together on a *bitumen felt* backing. When the panels are laid side by side they make a basket-weave pattern. Wood mosaic panels are available in a number of attractive timbers.

A FITTING TIP

About the only hard part in laying wood mosaic panels is cutting the panels to fit around intricate parts, such as the moulding around doors, called the *architrave*. To get around this problem, trim the bottom of the architrave before you do anything else. Place a panel on the floor as a guide to where to cut, then, holding a panel saw on its surface (with the panel upside down so you don't scratch it), cut through the bottom of the architrave as shown in the diagram. Now, when you get round to fixing the border tiles, you will get a very neat result by simply tucking the panel under the architrave without having to trim to match the intricate moulding.

SETTING OUT

Setting out to find the centre of the room for an even border is as for other floor tiles. You can start laying from the last full panel at the corner of the room farthest from the door or at the centre of the room.

The tiles are stuck down with flooring adhesive, which is like black *mastic*. Apply it in sections of about a square metre (yd) at a time with a serrated spreader.

Lay the panels into the adhesive. Take care to follow the guidelines, and to *butt* adjacent panels closely together. As each panel is laid, tap it down into the adhesive, using a scrap of wood to protect the surface from the hammer blows.

DEALING WITH THE BORDERS

Once the main part of the floor has been laid, there is a special technique for ensuring that the border tiles fit neatly against the skirting with the requisite 10mm (³⁄₈ in) gap to allow the wood to expand and contract, which it will do depending on temperature and humidity.

First, place the panel to be cut precisely over the adjacent full tile. Then, put a 10mm (³⁄₈ in) thick board against the skirting-board as a spacer. Place another parquet panel on the loose panel, with one side butting against the spacer; the opposite side acts as a guide for marking a cutting line on the panel beneath.

With the panel face upwards, cut along this line with a fine-tooth saw. This panel will be an exact fit in the space between the last full panel and the wall. Glue it in place.

When you get to obstructions, such as central-heating pipes, the best way to deal with them is to separate the fingers by cutting through the felt at the back. Glue down all the whole fingers. You can then cut cardboard *templates* of the cut outs required on the remaining fingers. Cut out these shapes using a fine-tooth saw, such as a coping saw, fretsaw or electric jigsaw. Press the fingers into place.

There are two ways to finish off the *expansion gap* that has been left around the perimeter of the floor. You can cover it with a shaped timber batten, called a moulding, which is pinned to the bottom of the skirting-board, or you can glue a cork strip into it.

The panels are usually supplied *unfinished*, so the final task is to sand the floor smooth, vacuum it clean, wipe up the last traces of dust with a rag soaked in white spirit and finish the floor with two or three coats of polyurethane varnish or proprietary floor sealer.

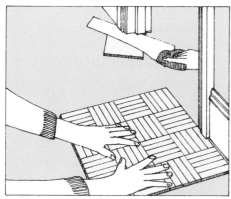

1 To save fiddly cutting around door surrounds, undercut the base of the architrave using a parquet panel as saw guide.

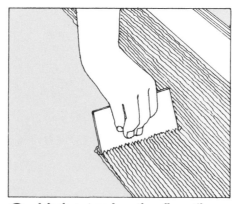

2 Mark out as for other floor tiles. Spread mastic-type floor adhesive with a serrated spreader over an area of 1 sq m (1 sq yd).

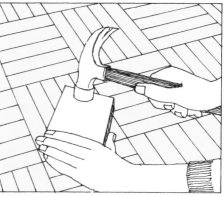

3 Press the panels into position butting up to guidelines and to each other. Bang them down firmly, using old timber to protect surface.

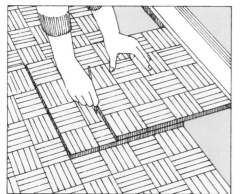

4 For edge tiles, place panel to cut on the adjacent full tile, and another panel against 10mm (³⁄₈ in) spacer batten on skirting. Mark line on middle panel.

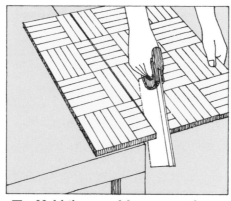

5 Hold the panel face-upwards overlapping the edge of a workbench and saw along the cutting line with a sharp fine-tooth saw.

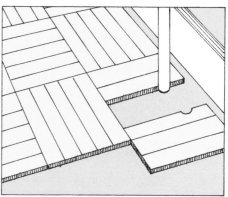

6 To get round obstructions like heating pipes, separate fingers of parquet by cutting through backing. Cut out shapes with fret saw.

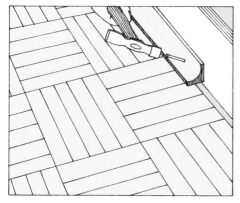

7 Leave 10mm (³⁄₈ in) gap around perimeter of floor to allow for natural expansion and contraction. Hide the gap by pinning on a wood moulding.

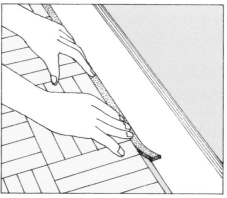

8 Alternatively, buy special cork *expansion strip* and glue it into place in the expansion gap. After fitting, this can be sanded.

9 Sand the floor smooth after laying, vacuum clean, then wipe over with rag moistened with white spirit. Finish with varnish or seal.

WOOD-STRIP FLOORS

You can make a luxury floor with solid hardwood strip flooring. For the most part solid tongued-and-grooved boards, about 75mm (3 in) wide and 20mm (¾ in) thick, are used for this type of flooring. Wood-strip flooring is available in various types of hardwoods from good timber merchants and from flooring specialists.

There are also proprietary wood-strip flooring systems, where the hardwood strips are bonded to a tongued-and-grooved plywood backing that has grooves cut in its underside, allowing adjacent boards to be held together by metal clips. Such floors are not fixed down at all, but 'float' on the surface of the sub-floor.

The traditional wood-strip floor is supplied in random lengths that slot together to look like a high-quality dance floor. The boards are fixed by nailing them to the *sub-floor*, which is usually floorboards, although they can be fixed directly to the floor joists, perhaps where the old floorboards have been removed because they were uneven or woodworm eaten. The wood strips are laid at right angles to the joists or the existing floor-boards.

If you want to lay a wood-strip floor over a solid floor, it is easiest to use a proprietary 'floating' floor, which will be suitable for any sound, dry surface.

GETTING INTO CONDITION

To minimize the chances of a wood-strip floor shrinking, swelling or twisting after laying, it is best to 'condition' the boards before laying them. You can do this very simply by opening up the packs of wood in the room where you are going to lay them and leaving them loosely piled for at least 48 hours. This gives the timber time to acclimatize to the temperature and humidity of the room. It also lets you look at the boards to check the colours and grain formations of the timber. With natural timber, some variation between the boards is desirable, but by checking them through before laying, you will be able to ensure that any colour differences are spread over all the floor.

Even when the wood strips have been conditioned, there will still be some movement of the boards, so make sure there is an *expansion gap* of about 10mm (⅜ in) all around the perimeter of the floor. As with a wood parquet floor, this gap can be filled with a cork expansion strip or it can be covered with a decorative timber moulding.

Before laying the floor, cover the existing floor with *waterproof building paper,* which will help to separate the two floors and will stop the transfer of dirt and draughts.

FIXING THE BOARDS

The first board must be fixed by driving the nails through the surface of the board, but subsequent boards are fixed by *'secret' nailing* through the *shoulder* of the tongue. Drive the nails home using a nail punch to leave the nail heads beneath the surface of the wood.

Boards not long enough to span the floor in a single length can be *butt-joined*, but ensure that butt-joins between adjacent boards are well staggered.

This type of traditional wood-strip floor needs sanding and sealing in the same way as mosaic wood panels (see pp. 76–7).

PROPRIETARY STRIP FLOORS

Follow the manufacturer's fitting instructions. Basically, for the type that is held together with metal clips, the first stage is to cover the sub-floor with heavy-gauge polythene on which a sound-deadening rubber underlay is laid. Next, the tongued-and-grooved flooring is laid, with the first strip wedged away from the skirting to give a 10mm (⅜ in) expansion gap. Strips are held in place by metal clips, which lock on to grooves in the underside of the boards as they are driven into place. An *offcut* of board protects the tongue of the board being positioned in this case. When the flooring is laid, it remains only to fill or cover the expansion gap.

1 Nail tongued-and-grooved boards at 90° to the sub-floor through shoulder of tongue.

2 Lay first board 10mm ($\frac{3}{8}$ in) away from skirting. Use offcut of wood strip to protect edge as you fit subsequent strips.

3 Boards are unlikely to span room in single strip, so butt-join shorter strips. When marking out, allow for 10mm ($\frac{3}{8}$ in) gap against side wall.

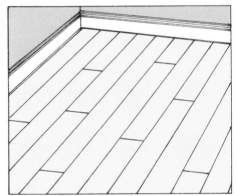

4 Butt-joining means joining strips end-to-end. Stagger these joints so they appear at random and do not align across adjacent strips.

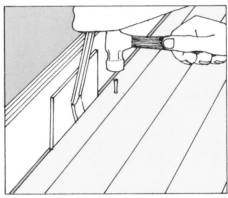

5 Lever last strip in place with a bar held against the skirting. Note the scrap board to protect the paintwork. Fix by *face nailing*.

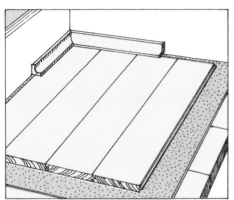

6 Expansion gap can be covered by nailing timber moulding to skirting. Note paper underlay.

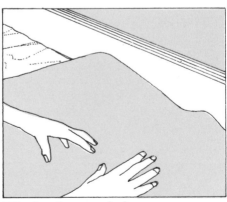

7 Lay foam underlay over polythene for strips that clip together. Lay first strip leaving an expansion gap.

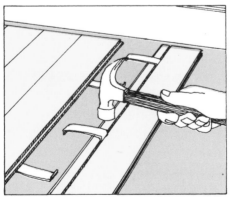

8 Each board is held with fixing clips that hook in a groove on underside of the next board. Fit clips at 600mm (2 ft) intervals.

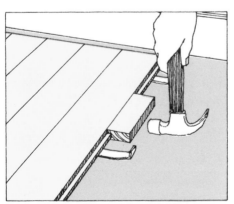

9 Clips are fitted so they are slightly apart; the next board is turned right way up and the boards are hammered together so the clips lock into groove.

REPAIRS & DECORATION

SHEET VINYL

Vinyl is extremely popular where a floorcovering has to be durable, easy to clean and attractive, qualities that make it a leading choice in kitchens and bathrooms especially. Provided that the floor below has been properly prepared, vinyl can be expected to last for some years with only normal washing and polishing needed to maintain its appearance.

There are many qualities of vinyl, from fairly thin types through to those having a cushioned backing to make them both warm and comfortable underfoot. There are plenty of textures, colours and patterns, so you will certainly find something to suit your needs and taste.

Lay-flat vinyl is the easiest to lay. It is manufactured with a strong backing to make it lie flat on the floor. It has to be stuck down only in doorways and where two pieces have to be joined with a seam.

Rolls of vinyl are manufactured in 2, 3 or 4m (about 6½ ft, 9¾ ft and 13 ft) widths. Obviously it is preferable if you can cover the floor with a single piece of vinyl without a seam. However, not all types of vinyl are made in a choice of widths and there will be occasions when it is uneconomical or will cause tricky installation problems to use a single piece.

Its always a good idea, especially for a room with alcoves and window bays, to make a scale plan on graph paper and take it with you when you buy your vinyl. Include windows and doors on the plan. An experienced salesman will be able to advise you on choice of pattern and roll width. He should also be able to tell you where it will be easier to cut the vinyl and join another piece to it by making a seam. The direction in which a pattern is laid can be determined not only by the size of the room but also by the way it is viewed from a doorway.

Clear as much of the furniture and appliances from a room as possible before starting. In the kitchen, take out the washing machine and dishwasher even though it means dismantling plumbing. In the long term it will be quicker to do this rather than try to work around items.

Also take off any door that opens into the room – it can make life so much easier. Just unscrew the side of the hinge set into the door frame and you will have no trouble putting it back later. Be careful, though: some doors are really heavy, so have a helper on hand or open the door and stand it on wedges tapped underneath.

The hardest part of the job is trimming the vinyl to fit around obstacles such as the basin pedestal. The easiest way to overcome this – especially in a small bathroom or kitchen – is to make a template of the complete floor first. Use pieces of paper felt taped together. Then lay out the roll of vinyl in another room and put the template on it. If you mark out the position of the door on the template, you will be able to centralize the pattern of the new vinyl. Cut out the vinyl allowing 50mm (2 in) all round for final trimming in the room.

When you first get the roll of vinyl home, store it in the room where it is to be laid for 24 hours so that it becomes conditioned to the atmosphere. This makes it more manageable to lay. The roll should be loosened with the pattern facing outwards.

Never leave the vinyl in a very cold room; make sure the room is warmed to a comfortable working temperature. If you don't do this, the vinyl could become brittle and crack slightly.

Finally, if you make a trimming error at the skirting-board edge and there is a gap between it and the vinyl, then a strip of timber quadrant moulding pinned to the skirting is a good face-saver.

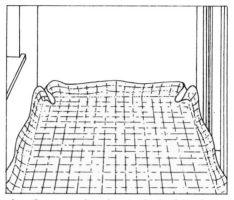

1 Lay out the sheet of vinyl in the room and position the pattern properly.

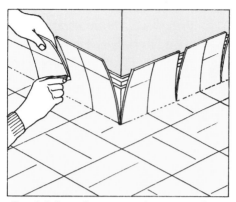

2 Make release cuts in external corners and at intervals along the skirting.

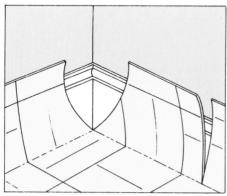

3 Also cut down to the floor in internal corners. At this stage the vinyl should be flat on the floor.

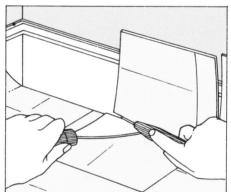

4 Using a sharp knife cut along skirting line. A *scraper* can help to push vinyl in tight.

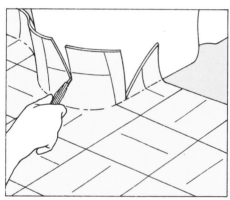

5 At obstacles such as a basin or toilet base, make several downward cuts before final trimming.

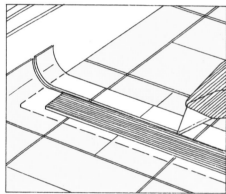

6 To join vinyl, align the pattern and overlap the two pieces. Cut through both layers.

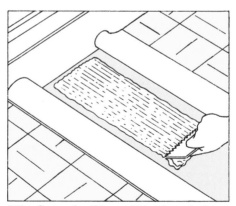

7 Spread a 75mm (3 in) band of adhesive on the floor using a notched spreader. Then press down vinyl.

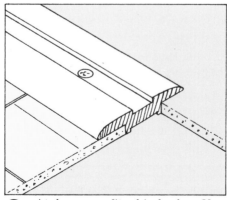

8 At doorways fit a binder bar. You can get types to join vinyl to vinyl, or vinyl to carpet.

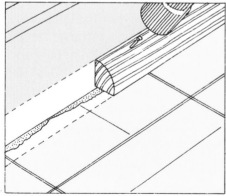

9 If the edge is not trimmed accurately into the skirting, pin quadrant moulding to skirting to cover the error.

REPAIRS & DECORATION

POLISHED BOARDS

An inexpensive yet very appealing floor can be achieved by sanding clean old floorboards before coating them with a *decorative seal*. The finished effect will be determined by the condition of the boards and the amount of preparation work done.

Quite often, even in very old houses, the floorboards can be in excellent condition – usually where they have been kept covered with carpeting over the years. Here, all that may be needed is a light sanding to *skim off* the surface to reveal fresh wood below.

On the other hand, you may be unlucky and be faced with a floor that has warped in places, has extensive gaps between the boards and maybe has been stained or painted around the edges. Before the arrival of wall-to-wall fitted carpets and vacuum cleaners, it was normal to have a carpet square that stopped some distance short of the walls. This allowed the carpet to be taken outside for cleaning, but it meant that the floorboard border had to be painted or stained.

No floor will be so bad that it can't be rejuvenated, but there will be a lot of work involved.

Whether you are prepared to take it on will depend on how badly you want to achieve the polished look. Getting the floor ready is described in 'Repairs and Preparation'.

A floor sander can be obtained from a local hire shop. As with all equipment being hired, it is advisable, in order to minimize hire charges, to have the room ready so that sanding can be started immediately. You will need an industrial drum floor sander for all of the floor except the corners, where it won't reach. Here you you will need a power-operated edging sander.

The industrial sander has a large revolving drum and is used in the same way as a vacuum cleaner. There is a knack to using it, which you should be able to master quickly. First, tilt it back so that the drum is clear of the boards. Next, switch it on. Lower the revolving drum carefully on to the boards and move it slowly forward. The machine will tend to pull forward under its own steam so, on one hand, you will have to restrain it and, on the other, you must make sure it moves sufficiently fast not to oversand one small area. If this happens, it is likely to gouge out too much wood.

When you hire the sander, get a supply of abrasive sheets. You will be given instructions on how to fit a sheet in place on the drum. In most cases you will need a medium-grade abrasive paper to start and a fine grade to finish off and leave a smooth surface. Only where the boards are very uneven would you need

a coarse grade abrasive to start. You would also require an extra coarse grade if you were clearing a thick film of old wax from the floor.

The edging sander is used with similar abrasive grades, and you might need to finish off with hand sanding to get into really tight spaces.

Although sanders are fitted with dust-collecting bags, they are generally far from being totally efficient. This means that you will be working in an extremely dusty environment for several hours, so a dust mask is essential – and perhaps even safety spectacles.

It is quite surprising how much dust can escape into the house from under and around doors, so seal these up before you start sanding.

After sanding is finished, vacuum the floor thoroughly, wash it and allow it to dry. You can now apply a polyurethane-based or a oleo-resinous seal. The former type lies on the surface and can have a clear, gloss or matt finish. The latter soaks into the wood and is a scratch-resistant, lustre finish.

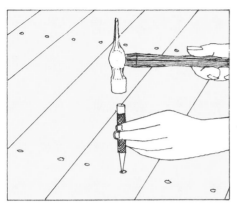

1 Use a nail punch and hammer to drive any protruding nailheads below the surface of the boards.

2 First fit a medium-grade abrasive sheet to the sander. Tilt it back, then switch on.

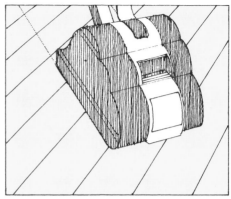

3 Lower the sander to the floor and move it slowly forward. Don't allow it to stop or it will gouge the floor.

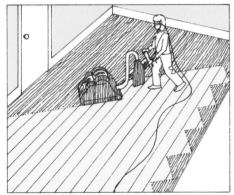

4 Work away from the socket outlet to avoid the flex. The first pass should be made diagonally across the floor, with minimal overlaps.

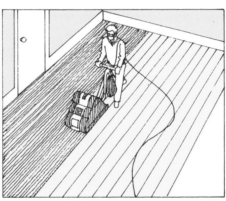

5 Then work in the direction of the boards. Two or three passes may be needed.

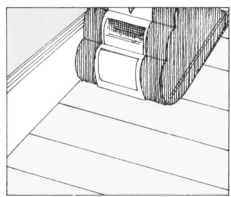

6 If there are any high spots on the boards, sanding at right angles will level them off.

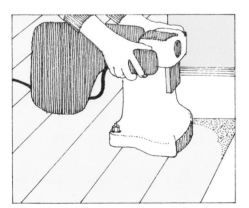

7 To get into corners and skirtings where the main machine can't reach, use an edging sander.

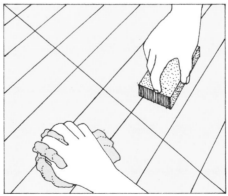

8 If necessary, finish with a hand sander. Vacuum to remove all traces of dust. Wipe floor with a rag moistened with white spirit.

9 The first finishing coat of sealer should be applied with a cloth. A roller can be used for subsequent coats.

PAPERING A CEILING

Exactly the same techniques used for hanging wallpaper are used when papering a ceiling. The one great difference is that you have to contend with the laws of gravity, which can cause great difficulties. Because the paper will be inclined to drop away from the ceiling, you must follow the correct technique for supporting it until each length is completely fixed in place.

Normally, you start to hang the paper parallel with the main window in the room and then work backwards into the room. In this way if the edges of adjoining lengths overlap slightly, they will not cast a shadow and draw attention to the error. However, this rule can be broken if the ceiling is much shorter in the opposite direction; this will mean you can handle much shorter lengths of paper, which is a great advantage.

You can't hang ceiling paper with just a stepladder to work from, because when you get down to move the ladder along, the paper, being unsupported, will peel off the ceiling.

Therefore you must arrange a continuous working platform to allow you to walk completely across the room within easy reach of the ceiling. A strong scaffold board supported by stepladders, trestles or even stout boxes is needed. You have to walk backwards along the board when hanging the paper, so feel behind you with one foot to ensure you are standing safely in the middle of the board at all times.

The technique, when working alone, is to support the folded paper with one hand, while you brush the paper on to the ceiling with the other. If you fold the paper into sections no more than 1m (1 yd) long, and keep as close to the ceiling as possible, you can release each fold as soon as the previous section is brushed in place. Not everyone can master this technique, and if that is true in your case, have a helper stand just behind you to support the paper while you concentrate on the brushing out only.

Any ceiling that is sound, clean and dry can be papered. Flaking paint or old paper must be removed. If the ceiling is a new one made from plasterboard, it must be coated with a primer-sealer first.

For the best appearance, the ceiling has to be painted afterwards. It is best to allow at least 48 hours for the paper to dry out thoroughly before painting. Use one or two coats of emulsion paint, as needed.

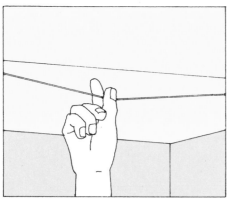

1 Pluck a chalked string, fixed to opposite walls 12mm ($\frac{1}{2}$ in) less than the width of paper away from window. Snap it against ceiling to make guideline.

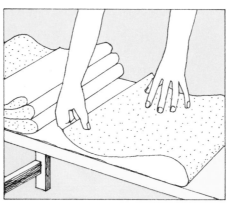

2 Cut paper to length plus 100mm (4 in). Paste and fold into a series of 600–900mm (2–3 ft) sections, paste side to paste side.

3 Align edge of paper with chalk line. Turn 50mm (2 in) on to end walls, 12mm ($\frac{1}{2}$ in) on to window wall. Brush out each section. If working alone, support the folded length with a spare roll of paper.

4 If two people are working together, one can support the folded length while the other concentrates on brushing out.

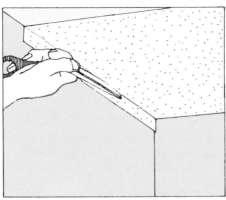

5 After hanging each length, press into wall-to-ceiling angle and crease with scissors

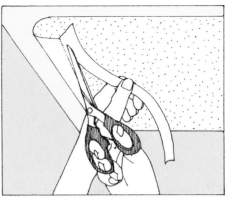

6 Peel back paper and trim carefully along crease line; brush back into place.

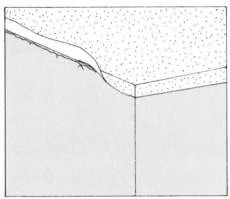

7 As an alternative to coving, if there is a crack between wall and ceiling, leave 12mm ($\frac{1}{2}$ in) margin on wall.

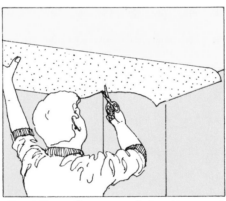

8 Where there are obstructions, cut paper roughly to size before pasting; allow for trimming. Make release cut at external corner.

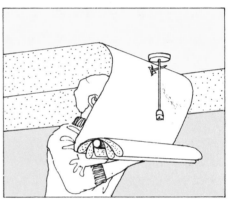

9 Paper up to a ceiling rose. **TURN OFF ELECTRICITY**. Take the paper over the rose and mark the position of rose.

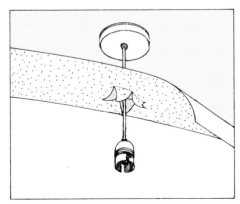

10 Make a hole in the paper and pull the fitting and flex through.

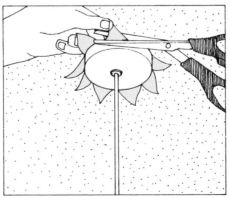

11 Hang remainder of length. Then make star-shaped cuts around rose before trimming neatly.

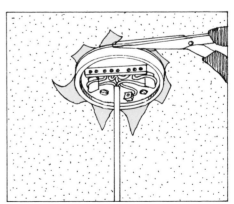

12 Or, remove rose cover, slacken fixing screws, trim near base. Paste must not enter rose. Refix screws and cover. Restore power after 12 hours.

PAINTING A CEILING

Always plan to paint a ceiling in one continuous work session and in natural daylight. If you take a break, the paint at the edge of the area where you stopped will dry and harden. When you complete the ceiling, the hardened paint line will show.

Start to paint parallel with the main window and work backwards across the room. This way you will be able to see where you have painted. If you paint over an area several times, it will show up as an uneven patch on drying.

Make sure you can reach the ceiling easily; your head should be only a few inches from it.

If you are using a roller, use a 25mm (1 in) wide brush to 'cut in' around the edges and any light fitting. *Cut-in* the edges as you work to remove any risk of dried edge showing.

Paint in strips about 1m (1 yd) wide. Work quickly so the edge of the painted area is wet when you overlap it painting the next strip.

Allow the paint to dry before deciding on whether a further coat is needed.

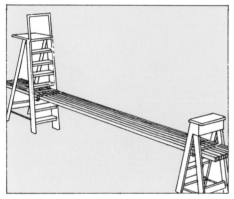

1 Provide a continuous support using a strong scaffold board lashed to stepladders or trestles.

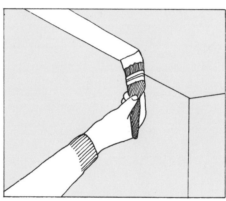

2 If using a roller, first cut into edges using a small brush.

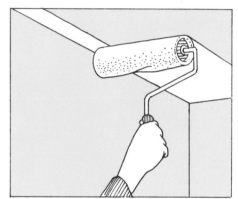

3 Follow up with the roller used in random directions. Work quickly to join wet edges.

4 Alternatively, use a roller with a broomstick handle or telescopic extension fitted so that you can paint in comfort from the floor.

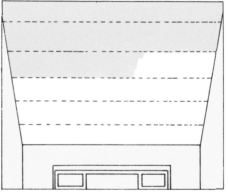

5 Work away from the main window applying the paint in bands. Merge in the joins between them.

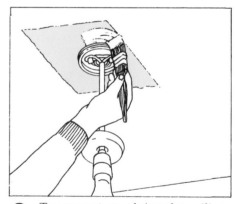

6 To prevent smudging the ceiling rose, **TURN OFF THE ELECTRICITY**, unscrew the cover and paint around the base.

REPAIRS & DECORATION

TILES

Expanded polystyrene tiles can be used in any room in the house, although they are most often used in kitchens and bathrooms. Their insulation quality prevents condensation problems and helps to reduce heat loss in a small way.

The tiles can be fixed to any clean, dry surface; old ceiling paper and flaking paint must be removed. Although they provide a good, quick cover-up over minor cracks, do not use tiles on a structurally unsound ceiling.

As with floor tiles, you start fixing in the middle of the room, then work outwards to the edge. If starting at the centre leaves a narrow border strip, adjust the starting point accordingly. When determining the starting point, also bear in mind how the tiles are likely to finish around a fluorescent light.

The tiles can be cut to *butt-up* closely to the walls or polystyrene cove can be added later. This can provide a useful cover-up where the edge tiles have not been cut accurately (see p. 92).

You don't have to paint the tiles, but if you are planning to, it's worth considering doing so a couple of days before fixing them. **NEVER USE GLOSS OR OTHER OIL-BASED PAINTS.**

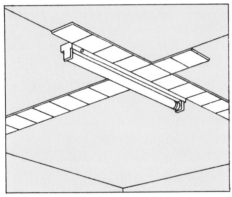

1 Find mid-point of ceiling. Adjust as necessary to avoid narrow strips at lights and edges.

2 Coat the back of each tile completely with tile adhesive.

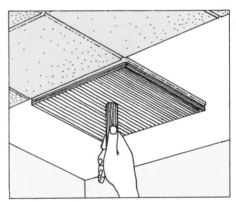

3 Finger pressure can indent tiles, so use a piece of hardboard or plywood to press each one in place.

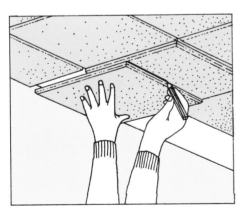

4 At edges, place tile to be cut over last full tile; press marker tile into wall and draw cutting line.

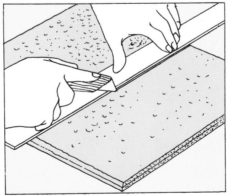

5 Place tile on flat surface. Use a sharp knife and straight-edge to cut it.

6 Mark the position of a ceiling rose on a tile. Measure the diameter of the rose and cut out correct size circle.

TIMBER CLADDING

Fitting a *tongued-and-grooved* timber ceiling is a job requiring only basic carpentry skills. The important thing is to condition the wood before it is used (*see* 'Materials'), and, especially where it is to be used in a kitchen or bathroom, to *seal* it on both sides to prevent condensation affecting it. You can seal the back of the boards before they are fixed; you can treat the fronts before or after fixing.

You cannot fix the boards to the ceiling with adhesive because the ceiling won't be sufficiently flat. First fix 50 x 25mm (2 x 1 in) battens to the ceiling joists at 600mm (2 ft) intervals at right angles to the joists. Determine the joist positions by knocking until you hear a dull noise, then probe with a *bradawl*. Mark the centre lines of the joists on the ceiling. The battens can be *rough sawn* timber (*see* 'Materials') and must provide a perfectly flush surface. Insert pieces of hardboard to pack out any hollows. Use 75mm (3 in) No 8 screws for fixing – one at each end and in between every 1m (3 ft). The ceiling light rose will have to be lowered to the new ceiling surface.

If you want to lower a ceiling in order to improve insulation or to install concealed downlights, you have to fix a framework of 50 x 50mm (2 x 2 in) sawn softwood battens. Fix a horizontal supporting batten around the perimeter of the walls at the new ceiling height. Add cross-battens, with 50 x 50mm (2 x 2 in) supporting pieces in the centre of each one to prevent them sagging when the tongued-and-grooved boards are nailed on.

It is difficult to cut the ends of the boards to be an exact fit into the walls, since the wall surface is likely to be undulating. The simple solution is to cut the ends as accurately as possible and fix moulding to conceal the edges.

The boards can be fixed in place using 25mm (1 in) panel pins. They can be inserted through the face of the board or through the tongues. If *face-fixing*, you can leave the pinheads on show as a feature. In this case you should make sure that the nails are arranged systematically at regular intervals.

Alternatively, you can drive the pinheads below the surface with a nail punch and fill the holes with woodfiller before decorating. In either case do not insert the pins closer than 13mm (½ in) to an edge, or you risk splitting a board.

Concealed fixing is neater. The pins are inserted through the tongue and are covered by the next board.

1 **Lowered ceiling:** Hold 50 x 50mm (2 x 2 in) batten in place and tap screws through pre-drilled holes to mark positions on wall.

2 Drill the hole to accept 90mm (3½ in) No 8 screws.

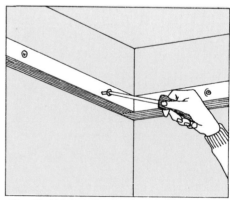

3 Butt joint the horizontal battens where they meet at a corner.

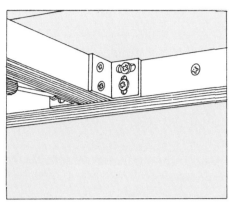

4 Use L-shaped adjustable fixing plates to fix cross-battens. Secure with 25mm (1 in) No 8 screws.

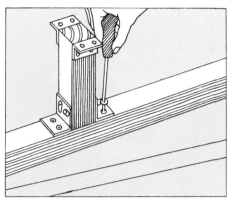

5 Use L-shaped plates to fix supports 50 x 50mm (2 x 2 in) to middle of cross-battens.

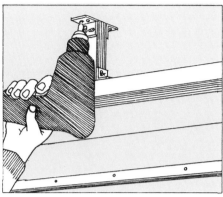

6 Screw to ceiling joists with 37mm (1¹⁄₂ in) screws.

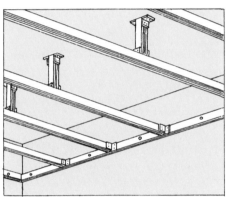

7 Space cross-battens across the room at 600mm (2 ft) intervals.

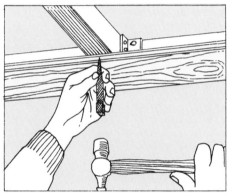

8 Fix first board to each batten with 25mm (1 in) panel-pins through the tongue, and tap home with hammer and pin punch.

9 Continue to slide home further boards, pinning each one in position.

10 Fix downlights as work progresses, as you need access above ceiling. Drill hole inside pencil guideline to allow padsaw to be used.

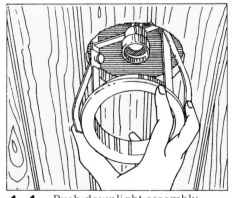

11 Push downlight assembly into place.

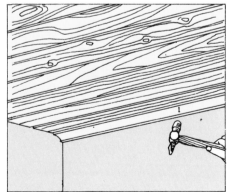

12 When the ceiling is completed, pin moulding around the perimeter to conceal gaps.

REPAIRS & DECORATION

PLASTER COVE

In many houses cracks may appear along the wall-to-ceiling join line. If you fill them with an ordinary plaster filler, they will probably reappear within a year or so. The cause is normal seasonal movement that happens to all houses.

You can often hide the cracks behind ceiling paper or a decorative frieze, but the most popular and effective measure is to fix a cove of plaster, timber or expanded polystyrene.

Plaster cove comes as a plain curve or in ornate form. It is fixed with a special adhesive and can be painted or papered later.

The advantage of plaster cove is that it will overcome the problem of an uneven ceiling or wall. The adhesive that squelches on to the surface as the cove is pressed into place can be used as a filler to conceal the gaps caused by the uneven surfaces.

Cove is sold in 2m (6½ft) lengths by d-i-y stores – usually in packs of six lengths – or in much longer lengths by builders' merchants. Longer lengths can be more economical and reduce the number of *butt-joints* that have to be made, but they are more cumbersome to handle. Most people would welcome a helper to lift a length in to place. However, if working alone, you can bang a couple of nails into the wall as supports for the lower edge of the cove.

The adhesive is supplied as a powder to be mixed with water to a creamy consistency as directed by the manufacturer.

The cove has to be joined neatly at internal and external corners. This can be done by *scribing* the end of the length to make a *mitre* joint – templates for both internal and external mitres are supplied with a pack of lengths.

The alternative is to use separate preformed mitre pieces, usually sold in pairs for internal and external corners. These are fixed in place using the cove adhesive.

The job will be completed more quickly if you first prepare all the lengths required. Dry fix cove in place using nails banged into the wall and ceiling to support the edges. Make sure all edges butt up tightly. Cut lengths and mitre corners. When you have completed all preparatory work, begin fixing cove to surfaces with adhesive.

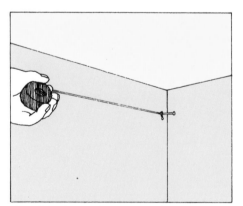

1 Mark out the area to be covered by the cove using a string line.

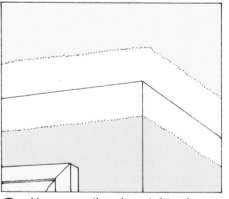

2 Use a pencil and straight-edge to transfer the string guideline on to both wall and ceiling.

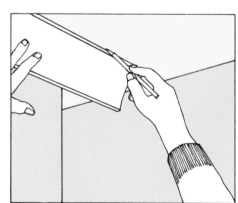

3 First set out all the full lengths and cut pieces. Where possible measure small lengths *in situ*. Allow extra cove for external mitres.

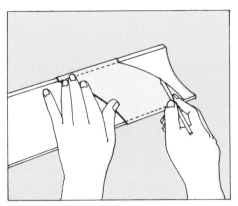

4 A paper template is provided with a cove kit to mark out corner mitres.

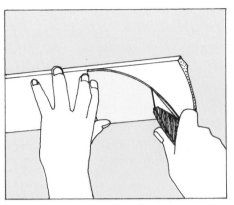

5 If you have a lot of mitring to do, it is worth making a durable template from thin metal. Cut around this with a sharp knife.

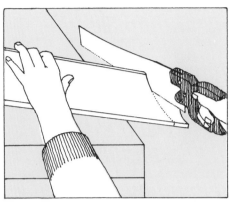

6 Cut the cove using a fine-tooth handsaw. Work slowly to make a clean cut.

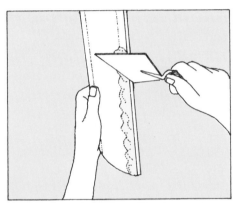

7 Butter the cove adhesive on to the top and bottom edges of the cove.

8 Press the cove firmly into place. It should stick well in seconds.

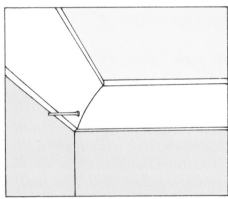

9 If the surface is uneven and the cove is not in tight contact, bang two masonry nails below the edge to take the weight.

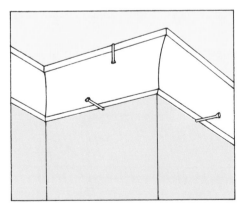

10 Position nails above and below the cove to hold it in place for a few hours while adhesive sets.

11 Scrape away excess adhesive while it is still soft. Wipe off any from the face of the cove.

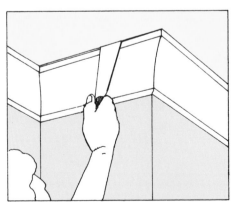

12 Use a filling knife to press remaining adhesive into gaps and joins between lengths. Smooth with wet cloth.

POLY & TIMBER COVE

Both these types of cove will cover up ceiling-to-wall cracks effectively. Expanded polystyrene cove, which has a simple curved profile, is often used to complete a ceiling to which similar tiles have been fixed (see p. 87). It can also be used with a painted ceiling.

It is very light in weight and is fixed using a special adhesive. It is used only where both the ceiling and wall are more or less flat. The cove cannot be forced on to an undulating surface – it will spring back once pressure on it is released. Check the surfaces first by holding a long straight-edged piece of timber along them to see if there are noticeable gaps.

If you do have problems fixing a cove, then switch to a ceramic tile adhesive, which is thick and buttery and will fill any gaps caused by minor surface unevenness. Immediately wipe off any adhesive that gets on to the surface of the cove; if it is allowed to set, it will be difficult to remove without damaging the cove.

Preformed mitre pieces are used at corners so you don't have the problem of making tricky mitre cuts. Where a straight length of cove has to be cut, use a sharp handyman's knife.

Paper or flaking paint must be removed from the wall or ceiling. You can use a length of cove and a pencil to mark off the area to be covered by the cove and prepare only this area. The cove can be painted, if you choose, 24 hours after it has been fixed. **NEVER USE GLOSS OR OTHER OIL-BASED PAINTS.**

TIMBER COVE
Ornate timber cove is supplied in 24m (8 ft) lengths and is fixed to the wall using special plastic clips. One half of the clip is fixed to the wall and the other to the back of the cove; when the two are brought together the cove is locked in place.

Special mitre pieces are supplied for external and internal corners. These are also fixed with clips, but if the corners of the room are not *square*, you might need to pin the top and bottom edge of the mitre piece to the wall and ceiling to align it correctly.

If slight gaps remain after fixing the cove, use a proprietary filler. Larger gaps can be concealed by pinning a thin decorative moulding on to the cove. A thin moulding will have enough flexibility to conceal any gaps. The cove can be painted or stained.

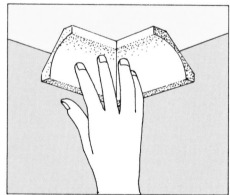

1 Poly cove: First fix a preformed expanded polystyrene corner piece in position.

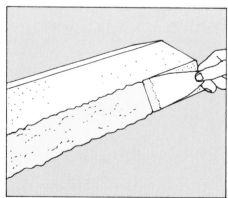

2 Butter a liberal amount of cove adhesive on to the back edges of the cove.

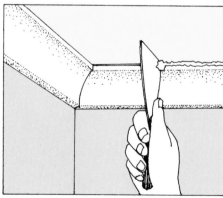

3 Press the cove in place. Use a filling knife to remove excess adhesive and to fill gaps at edges.

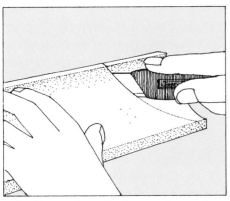

4 Use a sharp knife to cut cove to length. Cut firmly and cleanly.

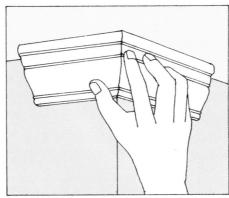

5 **Timber cover:** Start by fixing preformed external corner pieces to form a mitre.

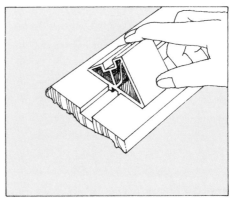

6 Slide the plastic triangular blocks into rear groove of cove so it can be correctly positioned on wall.

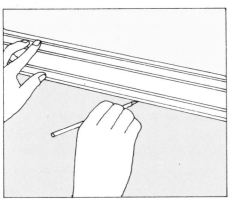

7 Hold cove on wall and draw a line to indicate its correct position.

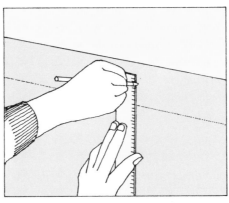

8 Mark 27mm ($1\frac{1}{16}$ in approx) above the guideline and draw another line parallel with it.

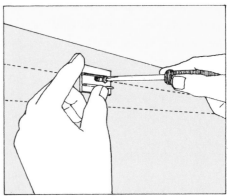

9 Upper line indicates position at which the plastic clips are to be screwed to the wall at 400mm (16 in) intervals.

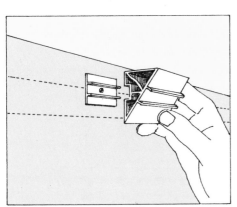

10 Fix the triangular mounting blocks on to the plastic clips.

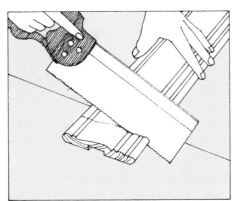

11 Cut cove to required lengths with a tenon saw. Sandpaper smooth cut edges.

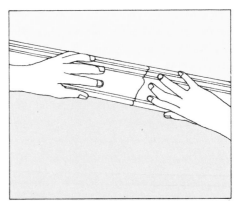

12 Press the cove on to the mounting blocks. A little sideways movement is possible to butt up lengths tightly.

SUSPENDED CEILINGS

An effective way to hide a sound but poor ceiling, or to lower one that is too high, is to install a suspended ceiling. Proprietary systems are simple to install and provide very good sound and thermal insulation. The ceiling consists of an aluminium framework into which the panels are dropped from above. The only part of the ceiling that is permanently fixed is the edge trim, which is nailed or screwed to the walls. It supports the long main tees, which, in turn, support the cross-tees.

An illuminated suspended ceiling consists of translucent panels with fluorescent lighting above. Alternatively, you can have downlights set into mineral fibre panels or fluorescent lighting fixed below the panels.

To prevent the main tees sagging – especially in larger rooms where there is a considerable weight to support – intermediate fixings are needed. Drill a hole in the central main tee, thread a length of galvanized wire through it and tie the wire to a screw eye fixed in the ceiling joist above. Supports fixed at 2m (6 ft) intervals will normally be sufficient.

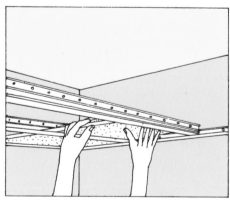

1 Use a spirit level and pencil to mark a horizontal guideline for edge support trim around the room.

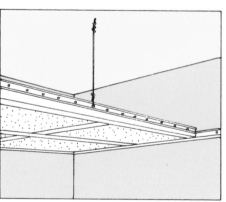

2 Nail or screw the edge trim to the wall.

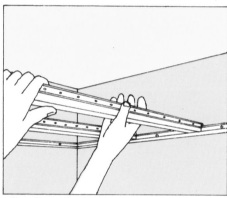

3 Rest the main bearers on the edge trim.

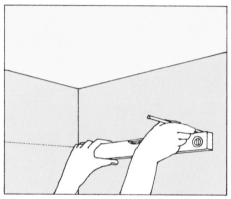

4 Add cross-tees and drop panels into place from above as work proceeds.

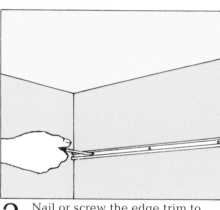

5 To prevent main bearers sagging, tie wire to both bearer and a screw eye in ceiling.

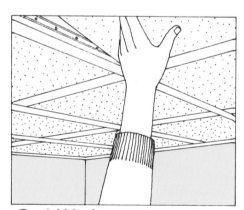

6 Add further cross-tees and panels to build up the framework and ceiling.

HOME MAINTENANCE

Routine repair and maintenance
to electricity, plumbing and the central-
heating system are basic to ensure
the smooth running of a house. When the
lights go out, an overflow starts to run
or a pipe freezes, you need to know how to
rectify the fault. Simple repairs can be
carried out by anyone using a basic
tool kit, as this section shows.
Knowing how to deal with faults and
emergencies, apart from being convenient,
will also save you the cost of calling in a
professional. Don't wait for trouble to strike;
get to understand the jobs in this section
first and you will be well prepared.

MAINTAINING · THE HOME

HELP!

PLUMBING

If a pipe bursts or a water tank starts to overflow, put a bucket below the leak, then turn off the house water supply at the main stopcock, which is usually found underneath the kitchen sink. Next, turn on all the taps in the house and flush the toilets to drain the storage tank. The leak will soon stop.

Everyone in the house should know where the stopcock is located. A stopcock can jam if it is not used regularly, so two or three times a year turn it on and off a few times. If the stopcock does jam, raise the ball-valve in the water cistern in the loft by tying it to a piece of wood. This stops water coming into the tank from the mains.

ELECTRICITY

If all the electricity in the house goes off, see if there is power coming to neighbouring houses. If not, then there is a general mains supply failure. Notify the electricity company. If other houses have power, your main fuse has blown and, again, your electricity company should be notified. You cannot repair this.

If only the downstairs or upstairs lights fail, or if more than one appliance fails, replace the fuse in the consumer unit – the fuse-box – or switch on the miniature circuit breaker. If this doesn't solve the problem, call in a professional.

If an appliance starts to overheat, turn off the socket and remove the plug. Have the appliance checked professionally. If a socket, switch or plug overheats and starts to smell, turn it off at the consumer unit, remove the relevant fuse and call an electrician.

GAS
IF YOU SMELL GAS, PUT OUT ALL CIGARETTES AND FLAMES. DO NOT OPERATE ELECTRIC SWITCHES. Turn off the gas supply at the meter and open all windows. Check that an appliance has not been left on unlit and, if not, call the gas board.

DAMP
If a damp patch appears on a ceiling in wet weather and starts to leak, it is likely to be caused by rainwater penetrating through the roof. Go into the loft and look and listen for a dripping sound. A torch is handy for tracing the water back to its point of entry, which may be some way from where it falls to the floor. Put a bucket under the drip; stand it on a board across the joists. You can then decide how to deal with the fault. Most roof repair work has to be tackled from outside, which requires the correct access equipment.

Damp patches on walls do not necessarily constitute an emergency, but the cause should be rectified as soon as possible since dampness can lead to the serious problem of wood rot. Damp patches starting from skirting level and spreading upwards could indicate rising damp, which means that the house damp-proof course has been bypassed. Check whether earth is bridging the damp-proof course. If not you may need a professional diagnosis.

Dry rot, usually found under floors or other badly ventilated, damp places, is evident by a musty smell. A cotton-wool like growth may be seen on the wood and there could even be fungus. Speedy professional attention is required.

GUTTERS AND DRAINS
Fix an overflowing gutter as soon as possible, since it can eventually cause dampness to start. Overflowing or blocked drains are extremely unhygienic, so sort out any problems as a priority.

FIRE
When a fire is discovered, immediately raise the alarm and get everyone to safety. A small fire can spread at a terrifying rate, so don't attempt to tackle it before everyone is safe. If the fire is still small and you can deal with it quickly, then do so. However, take no chances; if necessary, leave the room, closing the door behind you, and call the fire brigade.

Install one or more smoke alarms in your house and keep a small extinguisher and a fire blanket in the kitchen. Learn how to use them – don't wait until confronted with flames to read the instructions.

CHECKING WIRING

NEVER take chances with electricity. Check the system visually to satisfy yourself that it is modern, with up-to-date built-in safety factors. If you are in any doubt about the safety or suitability of your electrical wiring, contact your electricity supplier to carry out the work, or ask the supplier for a list of approved, qualified electrical contractors.

IMPORTANT SAFETY NOTE: When working on the electrical system, always switch off the mains first. Always unplug an appliance before working on it.

CHECKING OUT THE SYSTEM
Start at the fuse-box, where the meter is situated. Signs of old wiring will be evident here, such as rubber-covered cables, untidy wiring, separate switch fuse-boxes and cracked covers. Replace such wiring as soon as possible.

Ideally, your check will reveal a neat, modern consumer unit (fuse-box) with tidy plastic-covered wiring, miniature circuit breakers (MCBs) and, perhaps, residual current device (RCD) protection. MCBs are alternatives to fuses, and in case of overload, they trip (switch off). When the fault has been repaired, the MCB that has tripped is simply switched on again. An RCD trips if there is a fault current and gives valuable protection against electric shocks.

If the fuse-box has cartridge fuses, the *blown* fuse is replaced with a new cartridge. With rewirable fuse-holders, the blown fuse is repaired as shown on p. 98.

With the main switch OFF, pull out the individual fuse-holders. Inspect them for cracks and check that fuse wire of the correct rating is fitted by comparing its thickness with new fuse wire.

Check that green-and-yellow, or green, electricity board earthing cables are connected to clearly marked earthing terminals attached to a clamp on the incoming supply cable, or to a metal earthing rod driven into the ground.

Check the hidden wiring with the mains OFF. Ease the sockets forwards and check that the cables connecting them are the sound plastic-covered type, that the terminal fixing screws are tight and the earth wires are properly covered in green-and-yellow earth sleeving.

Complete the checks by examining lighting flex, lampholders, and appliance plugs for perished flex, insecure flex sheathing, cracked casings and loose terminals. Replacement is explained on pp. 98 and 99.

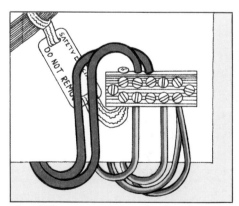

1 When examining the fuseboard look for green-and-yellow, or green (on earlier installations), electricity board earthing cables connected to earthing terminals.

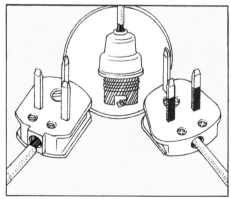

2 At least once a year check light flex, lampholders and plugs for loose flex sheathing, perished flex, cracked casings and loose terminals.

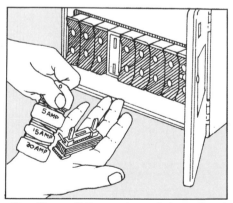

3 Turn off the main switch, pull out individual fuse holders and inspect for cracks. Ensure fuse wire is correct rating by comparing with new.

PLUGS & FUSES

Most plugs have post-and-screw terminals: each core of the flex is pushed into a hole at the top of the pin and secured by a small screw that drives into the hole. In some plugs the core is wrapped around a stud (clockwise) and secured by a screw. In others, the core wire is placed in a slot and held by a clip that snaps over it.

Take care not to cut the insulation of the inner cores when removing the outer sheath. Cut the inner cores to length to suit the spacing of the terminals. Bare only sufficient wire on the inner cores to fit into or around the terminals so that the insulation goes right up to the terminals.

When fitting a plug to a new appliance, cut off the soldered flex ends first.

Some appliances are double insulated (marked with a square-within-a-square symbol); they do not have an earth core in the flex, and the E terminal in the plug is left unconnected.

If a fuse in the consumer unit blows, turn off at the main switch, unplug appliances on the affected circuit and, depending on the type of consumer unit, reset MCBs, replace cartridge fuses or fit new fuse wire.

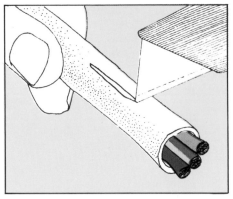

1 To wire a plug, start by removing the outer sheathing of the flex so that the cores are long enough to reach the plug terminals.

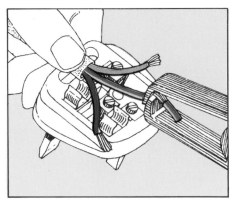

2 Carefully strip a few millimetres of sheathing from each of the cores. Flex should be 3-core unless appliance is double insulated.

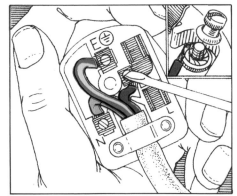

3 Connect the three cores to plug terminals. Green/yellow core to terminal marked E or ⏚ (earth); blue core to N (neutral); brown to L (live)

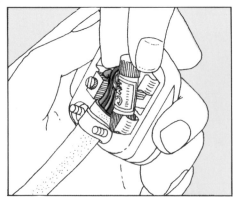

4 Check that the terminal screws are tight and that the outer sheathing is held under the cord grip. Fit fuse of correct rating. Replace cover.

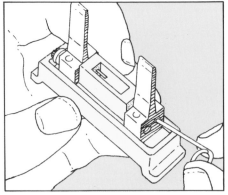

5 To replace a rewirable fuse, turn **OFF** power and pull out fuse-holder. Look for melted fuse wire. Slacken terminals and remove old wire.

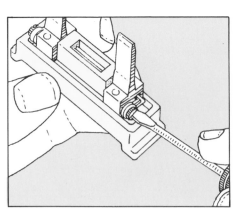

6 Pass fuse wire of correct rating through fuse-holder and wrap clockwise round terminals. Tighten screws and twist to snap off surplus.

REPLACE LIGHTING FLEX

You should replace brittle, discoloured and old twisted flex. The same technique can be used to fit new flex if a longer length is required.

Before starting work, **SWITCH OFF THE ELECTRICITY AT THE MAINS**. It is not good enough merely to switch off the light switch, as wires at the ceiling rose may still be live.

Various methods are used to wire ceiling roses, so before disturbing any wires, make a clear drawing of how the cores are connected. Also note whether 2-core or 3-core flex is used to connect the lamp-holder.

Generally, 2-core flex is used for a plastic light fitting, while 3-core flex, with an earthing core, is used with metal lamp-holders and metal light fittings.

If there is an earth terminal connected in the ceiling rose, it is easy to wire in 3-core flex, but if you have a metal light fitting and no earth terminal, call in a qualified electrician to provide an earthing point.

Fit the lamp-holder to the flex before connecting the flex to the ceiling rose, and make sure the outer sheath of the flex is within the cover of the lamp-holder and ceiling rose.

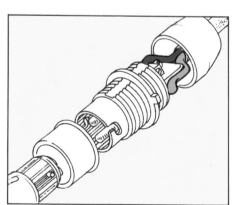

1 To renew old ceiling light flex, first **SWITCH OFF THE ELECTRICITY AT THE MAINS**. Now unscrew and remove the cover of the ceiling rose.

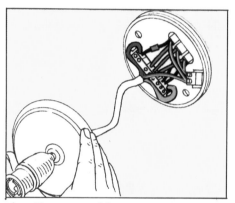

2 Before disturbing any of the electrical connections at the rose, draw a diagram showing clearly where wires are connected.

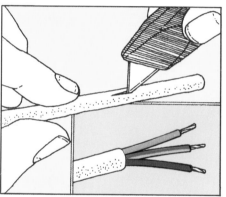

3 Prepare the ends of new flex. For plastic lamp-holders and light fittings 2-core flex is used; metal fittings use 3-core with earth.

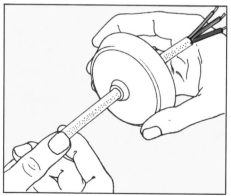

4 With a plastic lamp-holder, the ends of the flex are connected to two terminals. Metal fittings have a terminal for earth also.

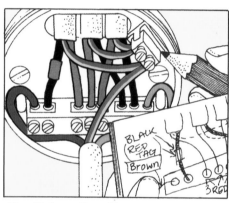

5 Cut the flex to length, prepare the ends for reconnection and thread the flex through the ceiling rose cover.

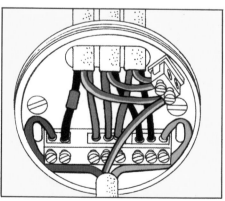

6 Finally, re-make the flex connections at the ceiling rose as original. Make sure the flex wires are located over the support lugs.

REPLACE DAMAGED SOCKET

NEVER be tempted to try to repair a damaged socket; it MUST be replaced. However, this is an easy job and it gives the chance to change a single socket to a double, and a surface-mounted type (the most prone to damage) to a neater, flush type.

Before starting work it is most important to **SWITCH OFF AT THE MAINS**. Release the socket securing screws and ease the plate forward to permit the terminal screws to be loosened.

There may be up to three cables connected to the back of the socket. They should be plastic-covered and in good condition, with earth cores. If they are not, call in a qualified electrician.

A straight replacement merely calls for connecting the cable cores to the correct terminals at the back of the new socket: red (live) to L; black (neutral) to N; and the green-and-yellow (earth) to the E ⏚ terminal.

An option with a modern 'ring circuit' is to change old single sockets for doubles. Three plastic-covered cables wired into the socket signify a 'ring circuit'. Otherwise get a qualified electrician to confirm that it's permissible to convert.

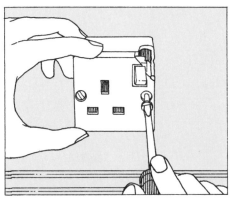

1 Damaged sockets are dangerous and must be replaced. **SWITCH OFF AT THE MAINS**, then unscrew the damaged cover.

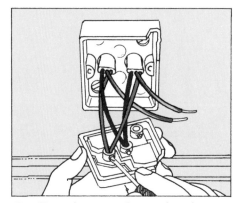

2 Ease the cover forward and use an electrician's screwdriver to loosen the terminals holding the cable cores.

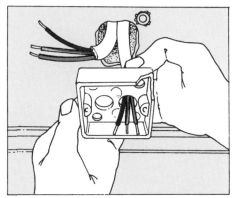

3 If a surface-mounted socket box gets damaged, it must be replaced. Remove its fixing screws.

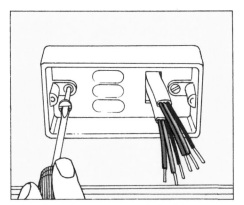

4 A surface-mounted double box can be fitted in place of a single surface box or to the lugs of a flush one. First, have the circuit tested for suitability.

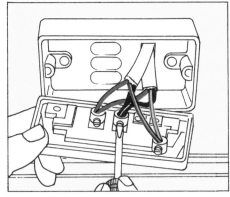

5 Pull the cables through the new box (they should be long enough for this) and connect the cores to the terminals of the double socket.

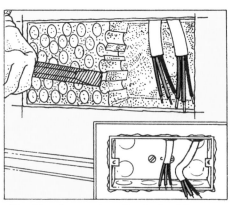

6 To change to a flush double outlet, drill wall repeatedly and chisel away masonry so metal double box can be fitted. Fit rubber *grommets* in the cable entries.

CENTRAL HEATING

If professionally serviced once a year, modern central heating systems rarely give problems. However, some simple things occasionally go wrong, and you may be able to save money by dealing with them yourself.

Radiators that are cold at the top may require only *'bleeding'* of air trapped inside.

Sometimes, no matter how the radiator valves are adjusted, some radiators get hotter than others. They may need to be 'balanced' by adjusting the lockshield valve on each one, at the opposite end to the adjustable hand valve. Start at the radiator farthest from the boiler. Take off the valve cover. Use a spanner to adjust the valve to give a temperature difference of about 11°C (52°F) between the water entering the radiator and the water leaving it. You will need a couple of clip-on thermometers for this.

The feed and expansion tank, which automatically tops up the system with water, is shown in the drawings. This tank will be in a high point – in the loft or airing cupboard – and should be checked annually for cracks, leaks or corrosion and to ensure the correct level of water is maintained.

1 To bleed a radiator, turn off the heating and open the vent valve by turning the key anticlockwise. When water starts to trickle out, turn key clockwise.

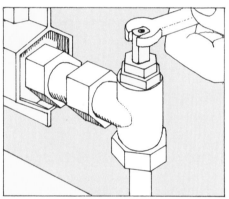

2 If temperatures in house are uncomfortable because some radiators are hotter than others, adjust lockshield valves to balance them.

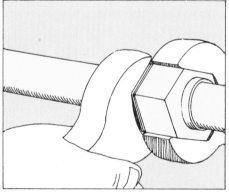

3 Leaks from joints with nuts (compression joints) may be cured by tightening the nuts slightly. One spanner holds the fitting while another tightens the nut.

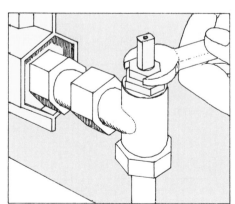

4 A leak from a radiator valve can sometimes be cured by tightening the gland nut gently. If it continues, the valve seals need replacing.

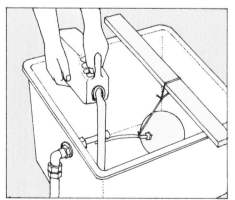

5 Corrosion inhibitor will keep the system in good condition. Add this to the feed and expansion tank after temporarily tying up the ball valve.

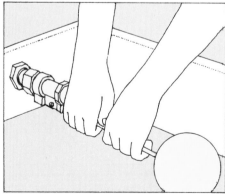

6 Feed and expansion tank should contain only a small amount of water. Bend down the arm of ball valve if system overflows occasionally.

INSULATION

A poorly insulated house will be uncomfortable and expensive to run. Its plumbing system will also be prone to freeze in winter, which could be very damaging.

Insulation is an excellent financial investment; because it helps to prevent heat loss through the roof, walls, floors, windows and doors, the heating system needs to generate less warmth and so is cheaper to run. In the long term, the money saved will recoup the cost of the insulation materials completely.

By and large, insulation materials are very easy to use. The starting point is the loft. If winter is approaching, first check to see if plumbing pipework is *lagged* thoroughly; pay special attention to bends and any pipes that run near outside walls. Pipe bandages or foam tubes are easily fitted.

Wrap water tanks in a glass-fibre blanket or enclose them with slabs of 25mm (1 in) thick polystyrene. Cover the lid of the tank, but not the loft floor below the tank – heat coming up from the room below will help prevent freezing.

Insulate the loft floor with rolls of glass fibre blanket or vermiculite pellets. Insulating an old loft can be dirty work, so wear a dust mask. Also wear gloves when handling glass fibre – it can irritate the skin.

Wrap the hot water cylinder in a purpose-made jacket available from any good d-i-y store. It is cheap and will pay for itself in weeks.

Draughts that come whistling through windows and doors can be stopped with any of the selection of excluders available. Self-adhesive foam strip is the cheapest and simplest to fit – just clean the frame and stick the strip in place so that the window or door closes against it and compresses it. For windows or doors that are used all the time, fit a more durable type – a V-shaped strip of plastic, copper or bronze. These are either pinned or stuck to the frame.

Seal gaps below doors with *self-adhesive* plastic strips, brushes fixed to a plastic bar or two-part devices – one half fixed to the door, the other to the threshold – that interlock when the door is closed.

Cavity walls can be filled professionally to stop heat loss; solid walls can be insulated with thermal plasterboard, cladding or panelling.

Good floorcoverings insulate floors, and double glazing cuts heat loss through windows by half.

Finally, make sure that all fuel-burning appliances have an adequate air supply to operate safely and efficiently.

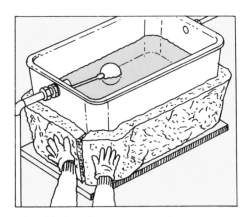

1 To insulate water tanks use glass-fibre blanket.

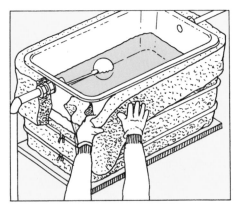

2 Wrap overlapping lengths around the tank and tie them in place with string.

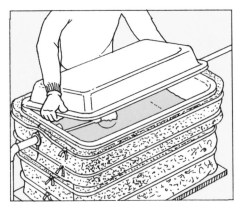

3 A tank must have a lid. It may be purpose-made or cut from exterior grade plywood.

4 Cover the lid with glass-fibre blanket tied in place with string taken around the lid. The lid must remain removable.

5 Unroll a length of glass-fibre matting from the eaves at one end of loft. Pass it under any cables.

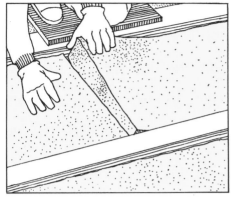

6 Unroll a length from the other end and butt-join in the middle. Don't block ventilation at eaves.

7 Alternatively, use vermiculite pellets poured between the joists. First cover pipes close to the ceiling below with building paper.

8 Use a T-shaped spreader, made from hardboard, to level off pellets to a minimum thickness of 100mm (4 in).

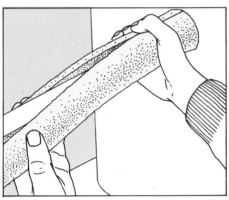

9 Foam tubing is supplied with a split so that it can be slipped on to pipes.

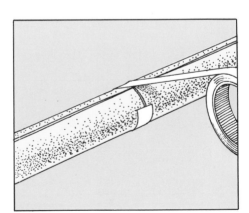

10 Tape it at intervals, joins between lengths and at corners.

11 A hot-water cylinder jacket is purpose-made to fit in place neatly. Measure the height and diameter of the cylinder before buying.

12 Seal gaps around exterior door and window frames and house wall with a non-hardening, purpose-made mastic.

DRIPPING TAPS

If a tap drips when it is shut off, the problem is a faulty washer. If it leaks from around the handle when it is turned on, the problem is faulty gland packing or a faulty O-ring seal.

DRIPPING TAPS

There are three types of tap: old-style, with crosshead handle (see diagrams); new-style, where the handle covers the workings of the tap; and mixer types, where two new-style taps are connected to a single spout. Once you have exposed the headgear, or workings, replacement of the washer is the same in all cases.

With all types, start by turning off the water supply to the tap.

Old-style taps   Open the tap, wrap a cloth around the chrome tap cover and, with a large spanner loosen the cover by turning it anticlockwise. If it is tight, steady the spout of the tap by hand or with another spanner to prevent the tap from twisting and perhaps breaking the fitting to which it is connected.

Lift the cover to expose the headgear body nut. Turn the nut anticlockwise with a large spanner. It is almost certain to be tight, so use a second spanner on the spout of the tap to prevent it from twisting.

Lift the headgear out of the tap body and take out the jumper unit, which carries the washer.

New-style taps   The handle of the tap covers the headgear. The handle is usually secured with a screw inserted centrally through the top and hidden under the small plastic disc marked 'hot' or 'cold'. Prise out the disc with a thin blade.

Mixer taps   Treat as individual new-style taps.

SPINDLE LEAKS

These are more of a problem with old-style taps, which have hemp gland packing, than with the new-style taps, which have O-ring seals.

With old-style taps, there is no need to turn off the water supply. Just remove the handle and cover to expose the gland nut. Gently tighten this. If it does not cure the problem, repack the gland with greased wool or purpose-made graphite-impregnated string twine.

With new-style taps, the water supply to the tap must be cut off, and headgear removed as for re-washering so that O-rings can be changed.

AIR LOCKS

If a tap splutters or totally fails to work, it could be air locked. Link the kitchen cold tap with a length of hose to the affected hot tap. Turn on first the kitchen tap, then the hot tap to blow out the trapped air. Turn off in reverse order.

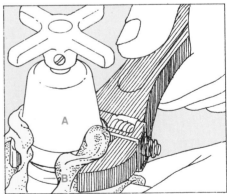

1 **Dripping taps:** Turn off water. With old-style type, unscrew cover (A) (anticlockwise). Loosen headgear (B) while holding spout steady.

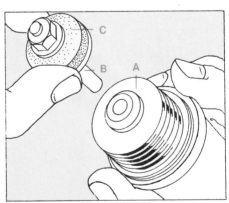

2 The headgear, handle and cover (A) will unscrew from the tap body. The 'jumper' unit (B), which carries the tap washer (C), can now be pulled clear.

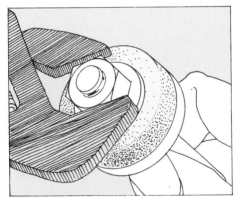

3 The washer will probably be fixed to the jumper with a small nut, which must be unscrewed. If held by a peg, simply prise off.

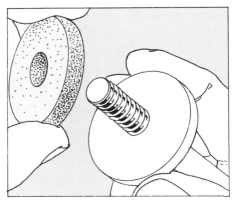

4 Fit a new washer on to the jumper, smear the threads with grease and reassemble. As temporary repair, turn washer over.

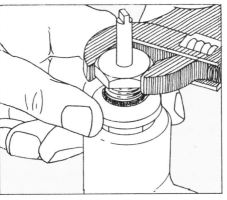

5 **Spindle leaks:** With old-style tap, remove handle and headgear cover. This will reveal headgear with gland nut at the top of the gear.

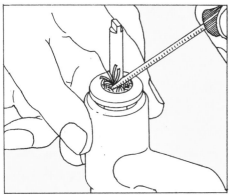

6 Tightening the gland nut may stop the leak. If not, remove the gland nut and dig out packing material from around the spindle.

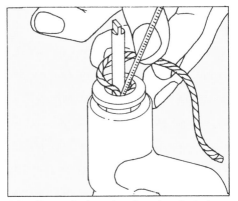

7 Repack the gland, using knitting wool or garden twine impregnated with petroleum jelly. Wind this clockwise round the spindle; press down.

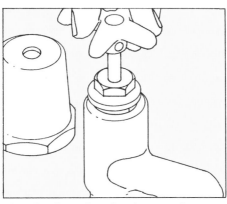

8 Replace the gland nut and tighten it. Refit handle and check that tap operates before refitting cover and handle.

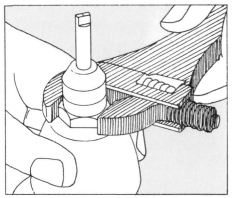

9 With new-style tap, turn off the water supply to tap and remove screw under coloured disc to release handle. Remove the headgear.

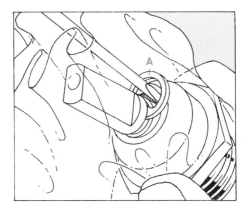

10 Release the spindle from the headgear by prising out the circlip (A). It is a good idea to do this with headgear in a plastic bag.

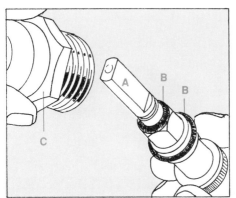

11 The bag will catch the circlip if it flies off. Pull the spindle (A) from the headgear (C) and lever off the damaged rubber O-ring seals (B).

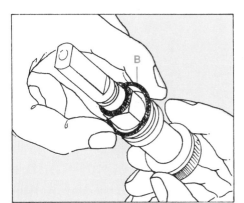

12 Buy new O-rings (B) of correct size, fit on spindle and refit spindle in headgear, securing it by replacing the circlip, which clicks home.

FAULTY WC

Water coming from the overflow pipe indicates either that the ball-valve washer needs replacing (see facing page), the ball float needs replacing, or the float arm needs adjusting.

If the cistern needs repeated, rapid operation of the handle to make it flush, the flap valve needs to be replaced. If the handle becomes disconnected, probably the metal link joining the handle arm to the siphon assembly has broken.

CURING FAULTS

Lift the cistern cover off carefully. If the water level is too high, check if the ball-valve washer is leaking by lifting the float arm and watching for drips. If lifting the arm stops the drip, in the case of an old-style metal valve, bend the arm downwards to lower the water level shut-off point. A modern plastic diaphragm valve may have an adjusting screw on the float arm, or the float may be fitted with a pegged arm, which allows the level to be adjusted.

Replace broken metal link with a new link or a chain sold for the purpose.

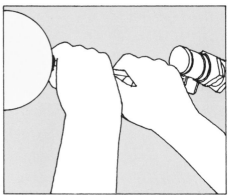

1 To adjust water level, with old-style metal valve, bend the float arm downwards to reduce level, or upwards to raise the water level.

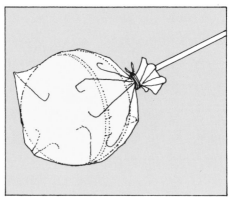

2 Old floats sometimes crack, so the float sinks and water keeps flowing into the cistern. As a temporary repair, empty float and wrap in a plastic bag .

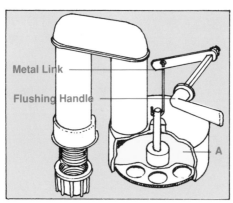

Metal Link

Flushing Handle

A

3 If the cistern needs repeated attempts to flush it, replace the flap valve (A) in the siphon assembly. This is simply a plastic disc.

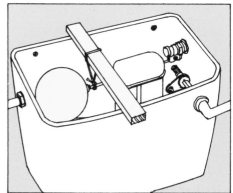

4 Remove the cover of the cistern and tie float arm to scrap of wood to stop the water flow. Flush the cistern and mop up to empty it.

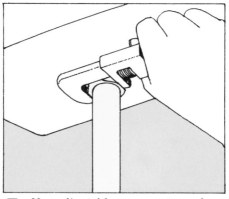

5 Use adjustable spanner to undo (anticlockwise) the flush pipe nut under the cistern, and the slphon assembly securing nut above it.

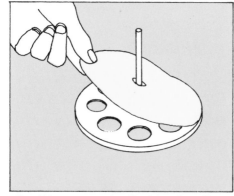

6 Disconnect the flushing handle metal link to the flap valve plate and lift the siphon assembly up so flap valve can be replaced.

BALL-VALVE WASHER

There are two types of ball valves: the older metal type, called the Portsmouth valve, and the modern plastic type, called a diaphragm valve. Before either can be repaired, the water supply to the valve must be turned off.

PORTSMOUTH VALVE

Corrosion can make this type of metal valve difficult to dismantle, particularly separating the piston assembly to make washer removal easy.

Rather than damage the piston, it may be better to dig the washer out with a screwdriver. Press a new one into place with a screwdriver, being sure to tuck the edges of the washer carefully under the rim. Before replacing the piston, rub it with wire wool to remove corrosion, and smear the body with petroleum jelly.

DIAPHRAGM VALVE

The retaining cap should come off by turning it by hand. If it is stiff, use a self-grip wrench, but be careful not to damage the unit.

Be sure to buy a replacement diaphragm of exactly the right type and to fit it the correct way round.

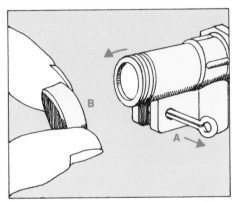

1 Portsmouth valves: Turn off the water to the valve. With pliers, close the ends and remove split pin (A). Unscrew valve end cap (B).

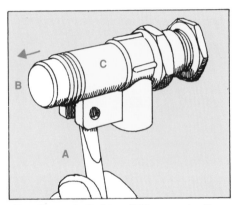

2 If cap is tight, a little penetrating oil may ease it. Use a screwdriver blade (A) to slide the piston (B) out of the body of the valve (C).

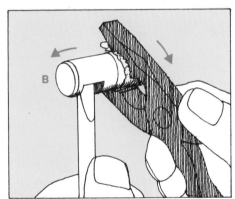

3 The washer is in the end of the piston assembly (B), which is in two parts. Separate the parts by holding end while turning the body.

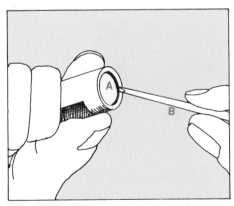

4 If piston will not undo, pick out the old washer (A) using a small screwdriver (B). Carefully press a new washer in place and reassemble the unit.

5 Diaphragm valves: Unscrew the large knurled nut (A) at the front of the valve body (B). Remove it complete with the arm (C) and float assembly.

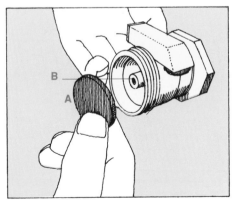

6 Lift out the rubber diaphragm (A). Use a fine wire to check that the nozzle (B) is clear. Fit a new diaphragm of exactly the same type.

BLOCKED SINKS

Clearing a blockage in a sink or drain may be an unpleasant task, but it often takes only a minute or two. Outside waste gullies are usually easily cleared, too.

A blocked wc pan may be more difficult, depending on the nature of the blockage. If it can be cleared in seconds using the mop technique (see diagram), it is worth tackling the job, but be careful not to force any foreign object in the pan, like a child's toy, into soil pipe. If the drains themselves are blocked, indicated by leakage from the drain-inspection covers, call in a specialist drain clearer.

Kitchen sink and shower tray drains are the most commonly blocked, and also the easiest to clear.

If possible, tackle drain clearing before the drain becomes totally blocked. While wearing rubber gloves and safety spectacles, try to clear the drain using a chemical drain cleaner based on caustic soda. You may be able to hook debris out of the waste trap through the drain outlet (plug hole) with a flexible drain-clearer wire.

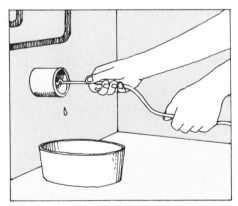

1 You can often clear a blockage in a sink by using a rubber plunger. Plunge up and down over outlet with a wet cloth held tightly on overflow.

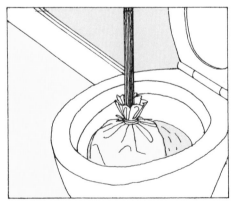

2 The blockage is likely to be in the waste trap. Probe trap with wire or, if plastic type, undo knurled nuts to disconnect the trap.

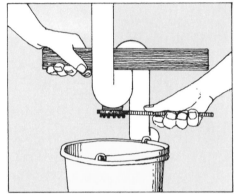

3 With an old lead trap, undo drain plug with a spanner while steadying the lead pipe with scrap of wood. Lead pipe is easily damaged.

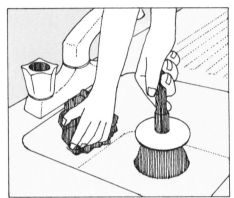

4 If the blockage is within the waste pipe you may be able to remove it with a flexible drain-clearer wire.

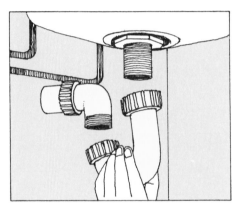

5 A blocked toilet pan may be unpleasant, but it is often easy to clear. Wrap a mop head in a plastic bag and plunge it up and down.

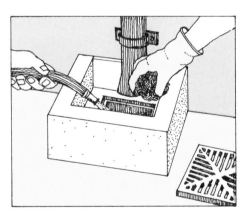

6 To unblock an outside gulley, wear gloves and use a trowel or stick to break up sediment in trap. Remove sediment and flush clean.

BURST PIPES

When pipes burst they must be dealt with quickly.

Before there is an emergency, learn where the stopcocks are and operate them two or three times a year to check they work. The main stopcock is on the rising main, which brings water into the house to the kitchen sink and the storage tanks. There should be cut-off valves on the pipes that distribute the water round the house. If you cannot find them, get a plumber to show you before an emergency occurs.

To make temporary repairs with tape or epoxy putty, the pipe must be clean and dry. Special waterproof repair tape is available, but plastic insulation tape can be used if it is reinforced with a length of split hosepipe held with wire twists or pipe clips and covered with more tape.

If a compression fitting (one with nuts) has pushed apart, push the pipe back and re-tighten the nuts.

If a pipe has split, cut out the damaged section and fit a new length of pipe. Plastic push-fit fittings are very easy to use with semi-flexible plastic pipe, which should have enough 'spring' to be flexed between the fittings.

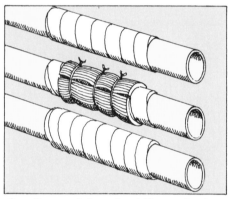

1 Do a quick makeshift repair of a burst pipe by draining it and wrapping it with insulation tape, hose pipe held with wire, and more tape.

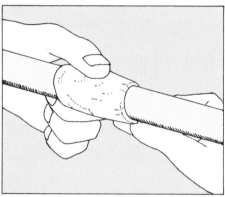

2 Make a more permanent repair with rapid-hardening two-part epoxy putty. Mix the putty and press round the drained and dried pipe.

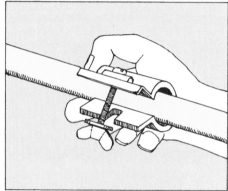

3 Be prepared for a burst by keeping a proprietary repair clamp in the tool kit. Its hinged body has a rubber pad that covers holes.

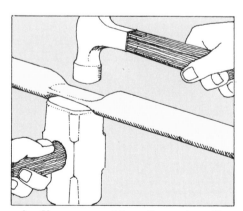

4 If you cannot turn the water off, hammer the pipe flat on either side of the burst as a temporary measure to stop water flow.

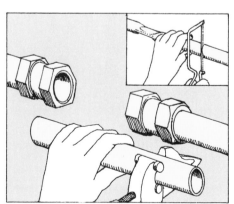

5 To repair permanently, turn off the water and cut out damaged pipe with hacksaw. Fit push-fit connectors on each side and spring semi-flexible plastic pipe into them.

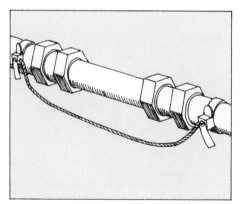

6 **SAFETY** Where a plastic joint or pipe is fitted between lengths of metal pipe, an earthing strap must be fitted to each pipe, linked by 10mm^2 ($\frac{3}{8}$ in^2) earth wire.

PLUMB-IN WASHING MACHINE

It is very convenient to have a permanently connected automatic washing machine or dishwasher. The easiest way to connect one is with self-boring washing-machine connectors, which clamp on to the water supply pipe and cut out a section as the tap (called a stop-valve) is screwed into place. There is no need even to turn off the water supply. These connectors will work on 15mm or ½ in diameter copper or plastic water pipe. As long as the machine has built-in anti-back-siphonage devices (check with the manufacturer), the appliance supply hoses can be connected direct to the stop-valves. If the machine is not so equipped, fit an in-line non-return, or check, valve to the stop-valve, and then connect the supply hose to the check valve.

If there is a plastic waste pipe nearby, fit a fast-flow outlet, incorporating a non-return valve, as shown in the diagrams.

If the waste pipe is some distance from the appliance, or you want conventional tap connectors, get a plumber to carry out the installation.

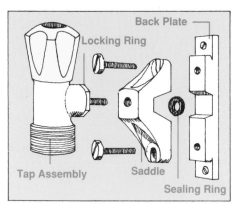

1 If using a self-boring fitting, the supply pipe to which the appliance will be connected must be 15mm or ½ in. First separate the parts.

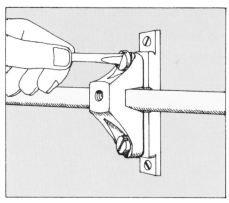

2 Copper or plastic pipe is suitable. Mount backplate on the wall behind the pipe. Tighten the sealing ring and saddle over backplate.

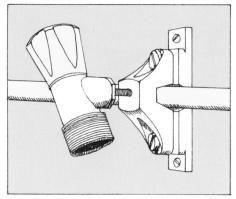

3 Insert the tap assembly, in the 'Off' position, into the saddle clamp. Turn body of tap clockwise until it penetrates wall of pipe.

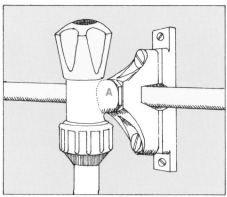

4 Turn the tap until it is in the required position, then tighten the locking nut (A) against the clamp to hold tap steady. Connect hose to tap.

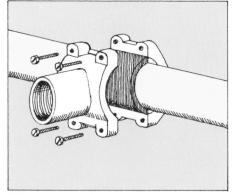

5 Connect the waste to plastic pipe with a fast-flow drain kit incorporating a non-return valve. Clamp it around the pipe.

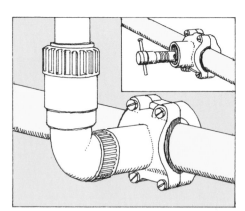

6 Use the cutting tool supplied to make a hole in the pipe (inset), then screw in the coupling and connect the appliance drain hose with a clip.

WINDOW & DOOR FAULTS

Painting doors and windows regularly will stop them from rotting and from swelling, which causes them to stick.

If a window or door sticks, open it, and try to lift the open edge while looking for worn or loose hinges, or weak joints.

If you can not tighten the hinges because the screw holes are enlarged, remove the screws, drill out the holes and glue wood dowels (rods) in them. When the glue has set, trim the dowels flush with the surface and drill *pilot holes* into them for the screws.

Reinforce loose joints by screwing metal corner plates over them. They do not look very neat, but may extend the life of a door or window for a few years.

If sticking is caused by a build-up of paint, plane off the high spot. If possible, let the wood dry out before repainting.

Frequently, window rattle can be cured by fitting draught excluder in the frame. Refitting window catches can also help.

Window rot can often be cured by applying proprietary wood hardener solution and filling the damaged area with a two-part glass-fibre wood filler. In serious cases cut out the rot and fit new wood as shown here.

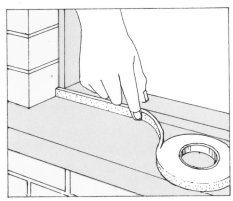

1 Cure window rattle in hinged windows by fixing self-adhesive foam draught-excluder strip where window closes against frame.

2 Look for rub marks on the edge of a frame to show where a window is sticking. Plane off high spot, allow the wood to dry, then repaint.

3 A sticking door or window may be the result of loose hinges. Remove the screws, drill out the holes and glue hardwood dowels in place. Drill pilot holes in dowels for screws.

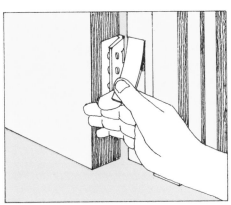

4 If a door is hard to close because it binds against the door frame on the hinge side, the hinge flaps may need to be packed out with card.

5 To repair a rotten windowsill, make angled cuts beyond the rotten part. Chisel away damaged timber, leaving straight sides.

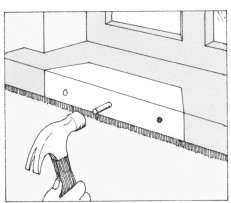

6 Cut a block of timber to fit into the gap. Drill the block and sill for dowels. Apply glue, hammer in dowels and plane smooth.

MAINTAINING · THE HOME

REPLACING PANE OF GLASS

When a window gets broken, quickly clear away any glass fragments. Wearing thick gardening gloves, collect pieces on the ground and place in newspaper. Remove loose pieces still in the frame. With a hammer tap out any that cannot be pulled away. If all the glass remains but is cracked, cover it with strips of adhesive tape to hold in place while you tap it to break it up into small pieces for removal. Put all the glass in a thick wrapping of newspaper for disposal.

If you cannot buy new glass immediately, fix a sheet of thick polythene to the inside of the window frame with double-sided adhesive tape. If the window is a security risk, screw to it a piece of 12mm (½ in) board. Measure the window and buy new glass and putty that is suitable for a metal or wood window frame. You also need primer paint for wood or metal. The glass is held in a wooden frame by small nails called glazing sprigs. In a metal frame special clips are used. If you prise out the old ones carefully, they can be re-used. Glass in hardwood frames may be set on a bead of mastic and held by beading screwed to the frame.

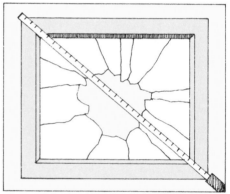

1 Measure height and width of window; deduct 3mm (⅛ in) from both dimensions. Measure diagonals to check frame is square. If not, make template.

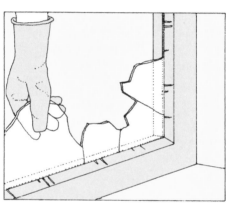

2 Remove all glass, wearing strong gardening gloves. Use a hammer to tap out stubborn fragments.

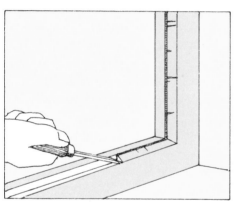

3 Hack out old putty with chisel. Remove sprigs or clips. Paint rebates with primer, allow to dry.

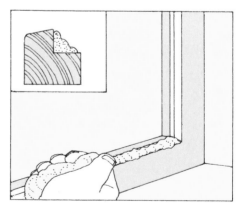

4 Press 3–4mm (⅛ in) of putty around rebate. Position matchsticks to support glass in right position temporarily.

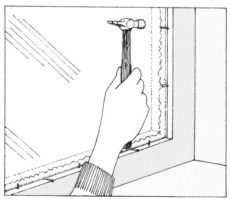

5 Press new glass in place, using pressure on edges, not middle. Tap in sprigs every 150mm (6 in) or replace clips.

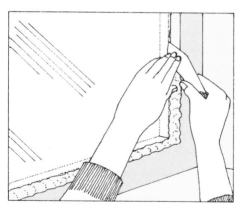

6 Add another layer of putty outside the glass, then angle it with putty knife.
Allow two weeks before painting.

PROJECTS

Even if you are a complete beginner,
all of the projects in this section will be
within your capability to construct
successfully. Each one has been specifically
designed to be made using the simplest
woodworking techniques without
sacrificing the required constructional
strength. If you want to gain
confidence, then start with one of the simpler
projects before progressing to greater
things. In the reference sections
at the back of this book you will find
complete guidance on tools, materials and
woodworking techniques.

Precise measurements are not given
for the items since, for fitted items,
dimensions will vary from house to house;
free-standing projects can be adapted in
size to suit personal preferences.

MODULAR STORAGE UNITS

Every room in the house needs storage space but almost as soon as shelves or cupboards are provided they seem to fill up. Too often, adding extra units produces a totally uncoordinated effect, as different styles and shapes are likely to be introduced into the room.

The advantage of building your own furniture is that you can design it to allow it to be extended as storage needs grow over the years. By using the same construction technique and materials, you can increase the height or length of your storage furniture whenever you choose while the room continues to enjoy a unified look.

It is important to choose a classic design. Avoid anything too modern or elaborate, which is likely to pass out of fashion or will lose its sparkle in a couple of years.

If you decide to paint the units it will be easy to redecorate the entire unit after it has been extended, either to ensure a perfect colour match or to introduce a new look.

The modular storage units shown here are deliberately plain, although you can make them more elegant by simply adding beading to the sides, as

- **Can be adapted to suit any room**

- **Possible to rearrange at any time**

- **Extra units can be added in future**

- **Stores a wide range of items**

- **Attractive, neat appearance**

- **Size of units is optional**

has been done with other projects in this book. You could also use them for occasional seating by placing attractive scatter cushions on them.

The hand grips in the sides allow the units to be moved around easily. This is necessary, of course, to get at the contents of the middle and bottom ones. And since all the units are of

exactly the same dimensions, they can be arranged and rearranged at will to ring the changes in the room.

There are two important points to bear in mind concerning the size of the units. First, they should not be too wide – just enough to be comfortable for one person to handle. Second, the deeper they are, the more they will contain and, therefore, the heavier they will be. If you are going to fill any of them with heavy items, it is best to reserve these as base units.

A useful size for the units is a maximum of 900mm (3 ft) square and 300–450mm (12–18 in) in height. You could then stack them three or four high and have space for at least two or three side by side. The fact that they are designed to stack one inside the other means that they are stable when stacked as well as

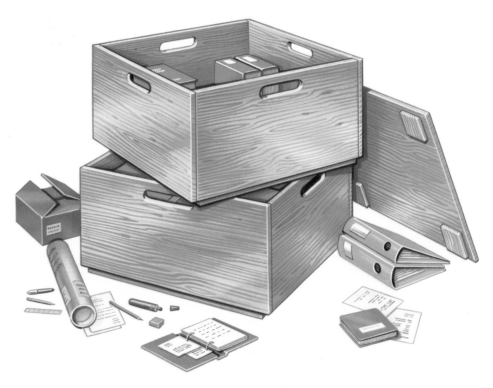

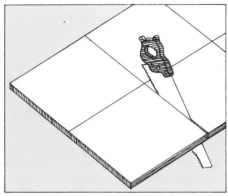

1 Mark, then cut out 18mm (³/₄ in) blockboard for the sides with a handsaw.

2 Smooth the edges of the blockboard with a smoothing plane; a block plane is better for the end grain.

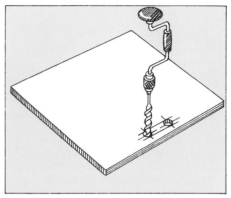

3 Mark the positions of handle holes 50mm (2 in) from edge. Drill hole either end using a 25mm (1 in) diameter auger bit in a swing-brace.

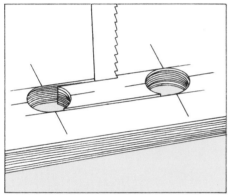

4 Use a jigsaw or padsaw to cut out the remainder of each hole between the guidelines.

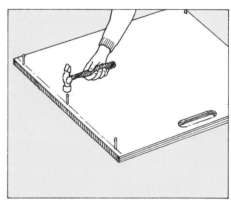

5 Use medium grade glasspaper wrapped around a wooden dowel to sand smooth the slots.

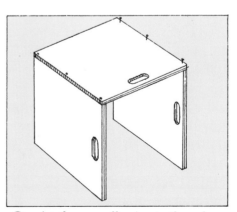

6 Drive three 50mm (2 in) oval nails 9mm (³/₈ in) from the edges, as shown, on two of the sides. The nails should just protrude through the board.

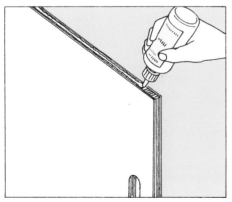

7 Apply *pva* woodworking adhesive to the edge of one adjoining side.

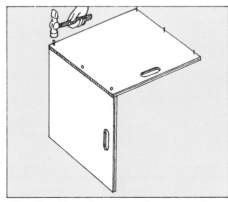

8 Position the two sides squarely and drive home the nails. Complete the side assembly in this way.

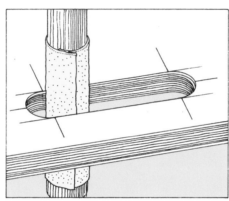

9 Apply *pva* adhesive to the edge of the third side, position it and drive home the nails.

easy to quickly rearrange.

To keep the weight of the unit itself to a minimum without sacrificing strength, we suggest you use 18mm (¾ in) blockboard throughout.

The vital aspect is that each unit is made to precisely the same dimensions. If you get the sizes even fractions out, the units will not stack correctly and quickly. Remember the system works well only if every unit fits next to, on top of or underneath any other one.

Each unit serves as the lid for the one below. Only the top unit is fitted with an independent lid.

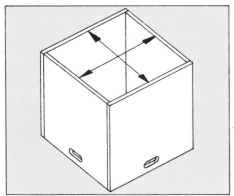

10 Hold the fourth side in place and measure inside open frame. Cut base to this size.

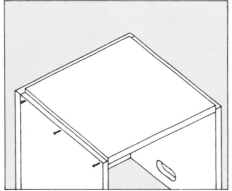

11 Position base so that 9mm (⅜ in) of its depth is inside box and 9mm (⅜ in) protrudes. Glue and pin in place between three sides.

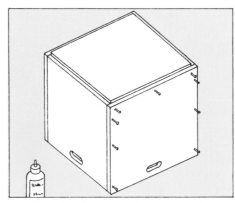

12 Apply *pva* adhesive to edges of two sides, position fourth side and drive home the nails.

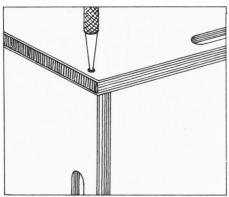

13 Use a nail punch and hammer to drive all the nail heads below the surface.

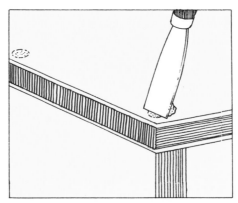

14 Fill the nail holes with wood stopping or filler. Sand smooth with medium grade glasspaper when dry.

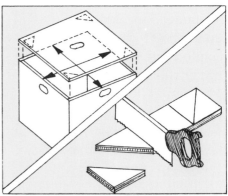

15 Cut lid to fit over box, and cut handle in centre. From spare blockboard cut four triangular locating blocks, with sides 75mm (3 in) long and glue into corners of lid.

CUPBOARD & SHELVES

Freestanding furniture has the single great advantage that it can be moved from room to room when you so desire and, perhaps more important, it can go with you when you move house.

The cupboard or shelf unit shown here is a very functional design. The beading giving a panelled effect is optional, but it certainly gives the cupboard greater character. You can, of course, use the beading to produce other design effects, for example, a narrower panel or even two panels per door. The handle design is according to personal preference – all screw-fixed types are equally simple to fit.

A classic size cupboard is about 750mm (2 ft 6 in) high and 375mm (15 in) deep. A width of up to lm (3 ft 3 in) allows for two comfortable size doors. The upper shelf unit should be about 1125mm (3 ft 9 in) high and 225mm (9 in) deep.

Inside the cupboard, the shelf layout is optional, although two shelves in a cupboard of this height is about right. You don't have to have shelves at all or you could have four if you need to store child's games, small ornaments, glassware or perhaps table linen.

- **Ideal for any room**
- **Simple to build**
- **Adaptable interior arrangement**
- **Freestanding, so is easily moved**
- **Designed to blend with any furnishing style**
- **Overall size optional**

Another possibility is to add a central partition, with shelves on one side and none on the other. The central partition would be fixed to the top and bottom using plastic joint blocks.

The material suggested for the cupboard is a veneered blockboard (*see* 'Materials') although you can use plain blackboard and paint or stain and varnish it later. All sawn edges that remain exposed are covered with edging strip, which is ironed into place and trimmed neatly

with a plane. This is a simple way to get a quality finish.

The upper shelf unit is made in the same way as the cupboard except that it does not have doors or a base – the latter is provided by the cupboard top. It is assembled and secured to the base unit with plastic joint blocks.

Because the assembly is freestanding, a back panel is necessary for both the cupboard and shelf unit to keep them rigid. The upper panel is pinned to the sides, top and second shelf up.

The bottom shelf simply rests on its joint blocks to allow access to the blocks that connect the shelf unit to the cupboard.

If the stability of the unit is in any doubt, for example, if it is standing on a thick pile carpet, it should be screwed to the wall using the appropriate wall fixings. Drill through the back panel behind one of the upper shelves, insert spacers to the thickness of the skirting, screw in position and replace the shelf to hide the screws.

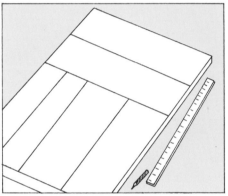

1 Mark out 18mm ($^3/_4$ in) blockboard for the top, base, sides, shelves and plinth. Cut with cross-cut handsaw.

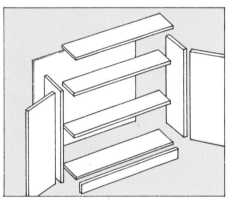

2 The top, base and shelves are the same size and fit between the sides. The plinth fits below the base.

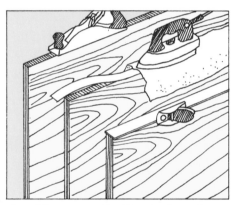

3 Plane smooth all cut edges. Iron on matching edge veneer to all edges that will be exposed. Trim flush when cool.

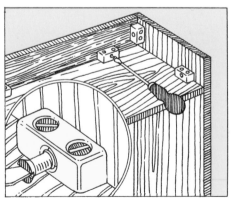

4 Use joint blocks to assemble the carcass, shelves and plinth.

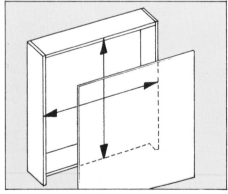

5 Mark out, then cut a piece of 4mm ($^3/_{16}$ in) plywood for the back panel. This should extend completely across the back.

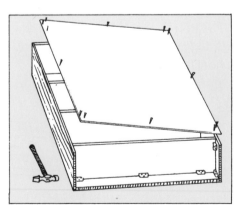

6 Square up the carcass and fix the back panel in position with 18mm ($^3/_4$ in) panel pins – three to a side.

7 Mark out, then cut the doors. Plane smooth all edges and fix edge veneer.

8 Measure to length 18mm (³⁄₄ in) *ovolo* moulding to make the door 'panels'.

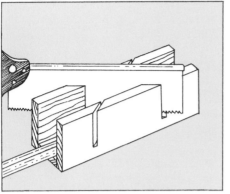

9 Cut the ovolo using a mitre block and tenon saw. Ensure that all lengths are the same way round.

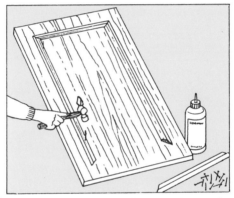

10 Following pre-marked pencil guidelines, fix the moulding with pva adhesive and 25mm (1 in) veneer pins. Tap heads below surface with nail punch.

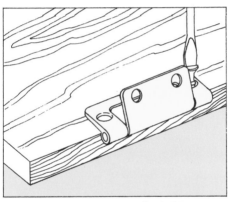

11 Fix 75mm (3in) flush hinges to the doors and then to the cupboard. Use two hinges for each door.

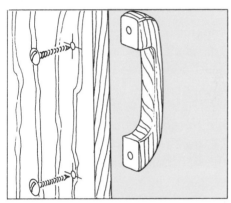

12 Mark out, then drill holes for handle fixings 25mm (2 in) from edge of door. Fit the handles using screws provided with them.

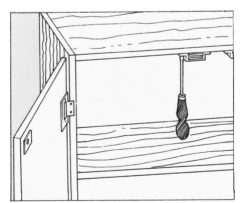

13 Fit a magnetic catch under the top of the cupboard for each door. Fit a corresponding catch plate to each door.

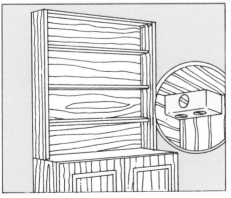

14 The upper unit and back panel are assembled in the same way. The middle shelves are cut about 75mm (3 in) short of the front.

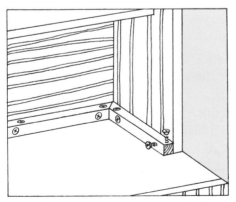

15 Join the upper unit to the base unit with 25mm (1 in) square battens, mitred in the corners.

BREAKFAST BAR

A breakfast bar ensures that you make the most of precious space in the kitchen. As long as it is carefully positioned, it can function as a food preparation area as well as an eating place.

In the design featured the main support is inset from the sides and end to allow seating all round. Most people use bar stools, which tuck under the bar when not in use. In this case the height of the bar top should be about 960mm (38 in) above the floor. The size of the bar top must depend on the space available and the number of people seated at any one time.

As a guide, the minimum width would be about 460mm (18 in), and there should be knee space of at least 250mm (10 in) underneath. When attaching the support to the floor, first determine whether the floor is timber or concrete. Screw the support to a timber floor with 38mm (1½ in) No 8 screws; on a concrete floor, glue the support with contact adhesive. For the bar top use 25mm (1 in) *m.d.f.* faced with ceramic tiles. Choose glazed-edge tiles and seal between them with epoxy grout. Alternatively, buy ready-laminated chipboard kitchen worktops that make ideal breakfast bars.

- **Doubles family dining facilities**
- **Simple to build**
- **Hygienic**

- **Adaptable to any dimensions**
- **Can be used as an extra worktop**
- **Designed to blend with any decor**

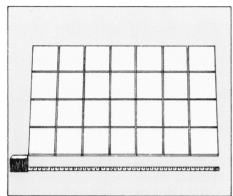

1 To fix the size of the top, lay out the tiles and select a size that avoids tile cutting. Mark the outline of the top and cut with a jigsaw.

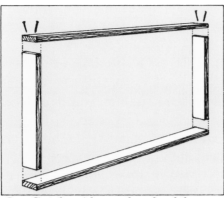

2 Cut the sides and ends of the frame from 75 x 25mm (3 x 1 in) softwood. Glue and nail the frame together.

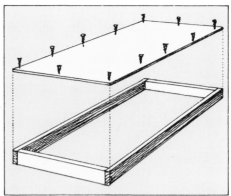

3 Before frame sets, apply glue to its top edge, then lay top of bar on frame and fix using 50mm (2 in) No 8 countersunk screws.

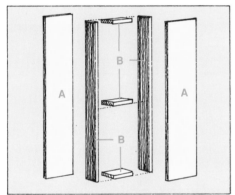

4 Cut the central support frame (B) from 75 x 25mm (3 x 1 in) softwood. Mark and cut out the two facing panels (A) from m.d.f.

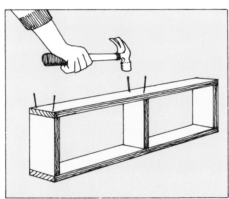

5 Apply adhesive to ends of cross pieces of the support frame before nailing on the main uprights. Use 50mm (2 in) oval wire nails.

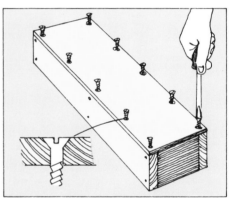

6 Keep the support frame square by gluing and screwing one of the facing boards to it while the frame is resting on a flat surface.

7 Mark position of support frame on underside of bar top. Spread adhesive on top of frame and from above screw the top to it using 38mm (1$\frac{1}{2}$ in) No 6 screws.

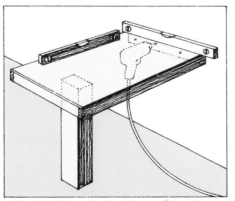

8 Drill two holes through bar frame for screws. Position the bar; use a spirit level to ensure it is level. Mark fixing holes on wall.
Drill fixing holes and insert wall-plugs. Screw or glue

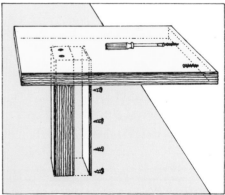

9 support to floor, while supporting wall end of bar, and fit second facing board. Finally fix bar to wall with 75mm (3 in) No 8 screws.

BATH PANELS

This is a job that involves simple construction and is enormously effective. A basic 50 x 50mm (2 x 2 in) timber framework is assembled at the side and end of the bath, and screwed to the walls and floor. Panels are screwed to the framework, using decorative dome caps to cover the screws. Thus the panelling can be removed quickly if access to the plumbing is necessary. The result is a fitted bathroom look.

Although a paint or varnish finish is suggested here, you could fix ceramic tiles to the panels. Then you would drill screw holes through the tiles and fix the panel after tiling it.

- **Ideal beginners project**
- **Hides bath plumbing**
- **Gives bathroom fitted look**
- **Can be decorated to match any decor**
- **Easily removable when necessary**
- **Cheap to make**

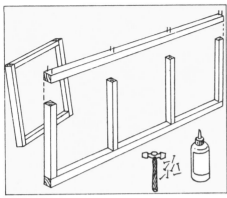

1 Cut the supporting framework from 50 x 50mm (2 x 2 in) softwood. Glue and nail together at corners.

2 Drill clearance holes for No 8 screws through those uprights to be fixed to the wall.

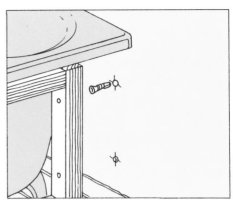

3 Mark hole positions on wall, drill holes and insert wall-plugs.

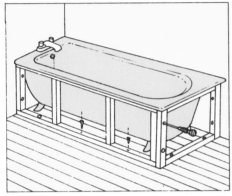

4 Screw the framework to the walls and screw the end frame to the long side frame using 75mm (3 in) No 8 screws. Screw side frame to floor with 63mm (2½ in) screws.

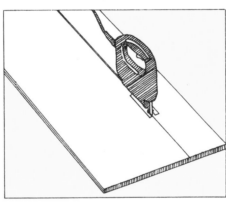

5 Measure and cut the 12mm (½ in) plywood panels using a power jigsaw or handsaw. The side panel overlaps the end panel. Smooth the exposed edge with glasspaper.

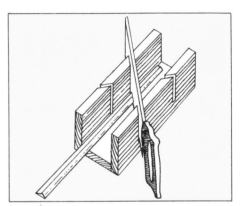

6 Cut decorative moulding to length using a mitre box and tenon saw.

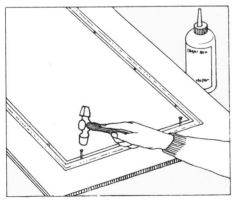

7 Use 18mm (¾ in) panel-pins to fix moulding on pre-marked guide lines. Sink heads below surface with a nail punch.

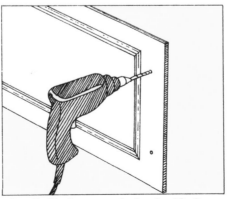

8 Drill clearance holes for No 8 screws in panels – two each end and two in the middle at the top and bottom. Countersink them as necessary.

9 Fix to framework using 25mm (1 in) No 8 screws and either screw caps or domed caps. Finish panel with paint or varnish.

VANITY UNIT

A vanity unit can bring tremendous benefits to a home. By installing one in a bedroom and thereby adding extra washing facilities, you can considerably ease the early morning congestion in the bathroom. Fitted with good overhead lighting and a mirror, a vanity unit is an ideal centre for personal grooming, such as hair styling and make-up. The cupboards below the basin are ideal for storing towels and toiletries, which will help to keep the bedroom looking neat, while hiding the plumbing pipes. And the unit can be painted or stained to match other furniture in the bedroom.

ESSENTIAL PLANNING
Of course, a vanity unit can be fitted in a bathroom where its towel and toiletry storage benefits could be valuable, but in the majority of cases the unit will be required for extra washing facilities in a bedroom.

The first thing to consider is where the vanity unit will be sited. You must have enough space around it to be able to use it for washing, and you must be able to open the cupboard doors: the minimum comfortable area is 1100mm (43 in) wide by

- **Enclose basin pedestal and plumbing**
- **Adaptable to suit any basin shape**
- **Adds extra washing facilities when fitted in bedroom**
- **Ideal storage for toiletries**
- **Attractive appearance**
- **Size of units is optional**

1 Carefully mark out blockboard for the sides, fascia, front and back plinths, and footboard, doors and middle and lower shelves. Cut out using a cross-cut handsaw.

2 Cut just to the outside of the cutting line, then use a smoothing plane to trim the edges of the boards back to the line.

3 On the edges that will show, iron-on matching edge veneer, protecting it with brown paper. Trim off overlap with block plane when completely cooled.

4 On inside faces of cabinet sides mark and drill holes for adjustable shelf supports. Use tape to mark drilling depth 10mm ($^3/_8$ in), on drill.

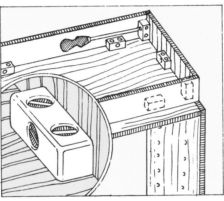

5 Assemble unit by screwing panels together using plastic joint blocks. These hold the top, sides, lower shelf, fascia and plinths.

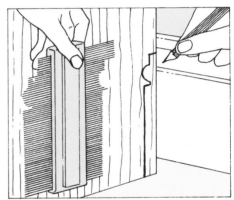

6 Place the carcass (body) of the cabinet against the wall. Press a *profile gauge* against skirting and mark outline in pencil on side.

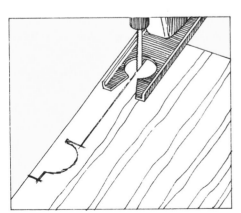

7 Fit an electric jigsaw with a fine-tooth blade and cut out the shape of the skirting in the bottom corner of each side panel.

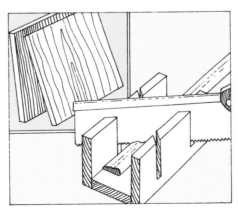

8 Iron on edging all round doors and plane off surplus. Mitre cut the lengths of wood moulding at 45° for centre panels.

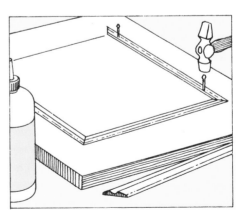

9 Glue and fix moulding to door fronts with veneer pins. Use nail punch and hammer to drive pins below surface. Fill and sand down.

700mm (28 in) deep. Most important of all, you must be able to plumb it in.

Laying on a hot and cold water supply to the new basin is usually easy, because hot and cold water can be run quite neatly in 15mm ($\frac{1}{2}$ in) copper or plastic tube. Running the waste pipe might be more difficult. It must be in 32mm ($1\frac{1}{4}$ in) diameter plastic pipe, which should be as short as possible – no more than 3m (10 ft) long – and slope at 6mm ($\frac{1}{4}$ in) per 300mm (1 ft) of pipe run to an outside drain.

The ideal place to site the vanity unit is on a wall adjacent to the bathroom so it is an easy matter to bring the supply and waste pipes through the wall as branches from the existing pipes.

It is a good idea at this stage to talk to the plumber who will be doing the installation and tell him what you propose. He will soon say whether or not your plan is feasible, and, if necessary, propose an alternative based on his experience.

SIZE OF UNIT
The size of the unit will depend to a large extent on the size of the washbasin that is to fit into the top. The unit is designed for an inset basin, so buy this first and build the cupboard unit to suit it.

For the average person, a rim height of about 800mm ($31\frac{1}{2}$ in) from the floor is about right. As a vanity unit is likely to be used by only one or two members of a family, you could increase or decrease the height to suit them.

Beware, however, of making a low unit for small children: childhood years pass in a remarkably short time, and children grow very quickly.

The width of the unit will also depend on the size of the washbasin you buy and the amount of space available. It is a good idea to have at least 100mm (4 in) of countertop on each side of the basin for bottle storage. About the minimum acceptable width of the unit is 600mm (2 ft).

The depth of the unit will depend on the depth of the washbasin. You do not want the basin set too close to the rear wall or it will be difficult to operate the taps. Have a minimum of 50mm (2 in) at the front and back of the basin. A typical minimum depth for a vanity unit is 500mm (20 in).

Once you have settled your plans, tell the local authority planning department what you have in mind, as Building Regulation approval may be required.

MATERIALS
We suggest you make this unit using 18mm ($\frac{3}{4}$ in) blockboard. Standard blockboard is faced with birch, which is quite a plain timber, but attractive after staining. You can also get blockboard veneered on one face with a high-quality timber, such as oak, sapele, mahogany or teak, and you might want to choose one of these to match other furniture in a bedroom.

With blockboard you can glue on strips of decorative wood

mouldings, as we show here, to simulate wood panels, which gives the effect of very high quality furniture.

The unit is certain to be splashed with water, so, after staining or painting, finish it with three coats of exterior-quality polyurethane varnish, rubbing down with fine abrasive paper between coats to produce a tough water-resistant surface.

To prevent any water getting under the rim of the basin, before installing it in the top spread a continuous band of clear silicone rubber mastic under the basin rim. Then install the basin, holding it down from the underside with the metal clips supplied.

If a very hard-wearing and easily cleaned top is required, fix ceramic tiles to the countertop before the basin is fitted. Check with the tile supplier that the tiles are strong enough to be used on a worktop.

CONSTRUCTION
Construction is very easy following the stages shown in the drawings. The unit is basically a box screwed together with plastic joint blocks. Cut all the parts accurately and square, and the unit will go together very easily.

After installation of the unit, the final plumbing connections can be made.

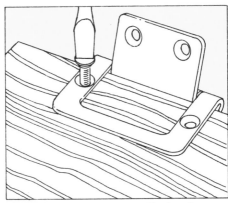

10 The easy way to fit the doors to the cabinet is with flush hinges. Simply screw them to the inside of doors and edges of sides.

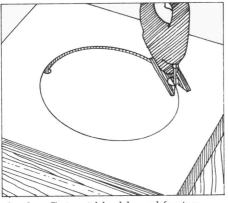

11 Cut out blockboard for top. Use the template supplied to mark cut-out for basin. Drill hole for blade and cut out using a power jigsaw.

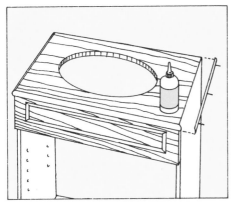

12 Fix the top of unit to the sides using six plastic joint blocks. Glue and pin a decorative wood *nosing* to front and sides.

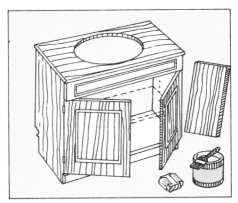

13 Rub down unit with a finishing sander and apply three coats of exterior polyurethane varnish, sanding down between coats.

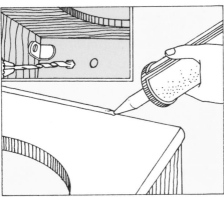

14 Fix angle brackets to inside rear edges of unit. Mark holes for screws and drill wall with masonry bit. Screw into wall-plug to fix unit.

15 Apply silicone rubber to top where it meets wall. Also apply to underside of basin rim. Fit basin; wipe away excess silicone.

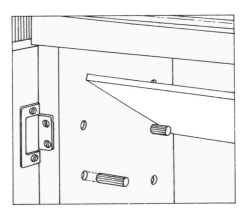

16 Connect services to the basin. Fit the four support pegs or dowels into side panels for the adjustable shelf and fit the shelf.

17 Carefully measure for the door handles so they are inset by the same amount on each door and are level. Drill for the fixing screws.

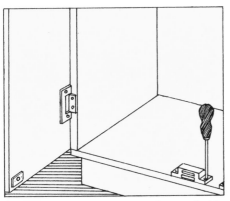

18 Use magnetic catches to hold the doors closed. Screw catches to front edge of fascia shelf; metal plates to inside faces of doors.

WINDOW SEAT

Abay offers the opportunity to install a window seat, which is an effective way of utilizing space. Apart from having a charm of its own and providing extra seating it also creates a valuable storage area underneath.

Bays can be draughty and uncomfortable places if windows are old and badly fitted, so first make sure openable casements or sashes are well

- **Adds additional seating**
- **Suitable for any square-sided bay**
- **Can be finished to match room's decor**
- **Provides valuable storage place**
- **Makes use of wasted floor space**
- **Simple yet strong construction**

draughtproofed or double glazing is fitted.

This project is designed for a bay with right-angled corners and is very straightforward; the only tricky part is shaping the front of the seat to follow the profile of the skirting-board.

However, if the skirting is ornate, you can use a profile gauge (see 'Tools') to transfer its outline to the wood. Then you need to cut it carefully with a jigsaw or padsaw.

The seat has to extend to the full width of the bay, but its depth and height have to be determined. Normal seating is about 375–400mm (15–16 in) above ground level and around 450mm (18 in) deep. Check existing armchairs and sofas to establish the dimensions.

Although vertically fixed tongued-and-grooved cladding has been selected to enclose the framework in this design, it could easily be fixed horizontally. If that is what you prefer, you need to add vertical supports to the front frame. Make them from

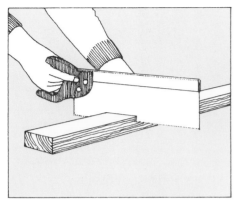

1 Measure the width of the bay. Calculate height of seat. Cut battens for front support frame from 50 x 25mm (2 x 1 in) softwood.

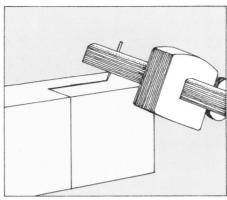

2 Use a *marking gauge* to mark out halving joints (*see* 'Techniques') for all four corners of the frame.

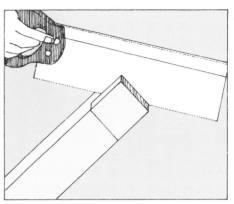

3 Use a tenon saw to cut out the joints.

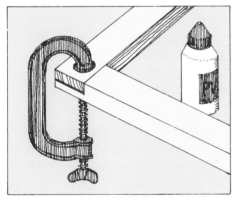

4 Apply woodworking adhesive and assemble the frame. Check that the corners are square, clamp each joint and leave for 24 hours to set.

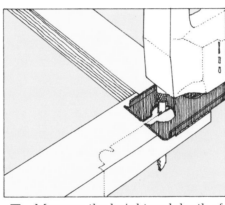

5 Measure the height and depth of the skirting and remove that amount from each side of the frame, using a power jigsaw or padsaw for curves.

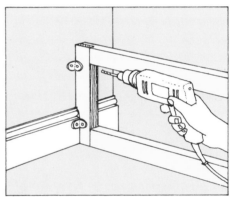

6 Use steel angle brackets to fix each side of frame to wall and skirting with 37mm (1½ in) No 8 screws.

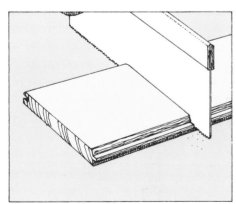

7 Cut lengths of tongued-and-grooved board to cover the front of the frame. Plan to have cut boards of equal width at the ends.

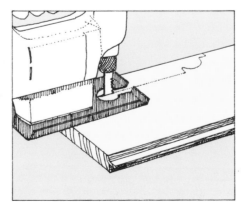

8 A *profile gauge* is used to transfer the exact skirting shape to both end boards. Cut out with jigsaw or padsaw.

9 Use 18mm (¾ in) panel pins and adhesive to fix the boards to the frame. Remove the tongue of the last board and pin through the face.

50 x 25mm (2 x 1 in) softwood and set them at 600mm (2 ft) intervals. Use plastic joint blocks to fix them.

If you prefer a flat surface, then fix 12mm (½ in) thick board (for example, M.D.F. or blockboard) to the basic framework – intermediate vertical uprights are not needed. You can paint the board and perhaps add moulding to give a panelled appearance, as has been done with some of the other projects in this book.

The seat is made from 18mm (¾ in) blockboard and it has to be fixed using a long single hinge called a *piano hinge*, which is screwed to a batten on the front wall of the bay. It rests on the front framework and, optionally, on battens screwed to the side walls, flush with the top of the front panel. At the front a round edge is created by pinning on a moulding, called nosing.

If you wanted the seat to be tongued and grooved to match the front, you can fix the boards to the blockboard.

For cushioning, you can use scattered cushions or cover blocks of foam for the seat, cushions, backrest and arms. In order to give access to the storage space below the seat, the cushioning has to be removable, so use any simple fixing method. If the windowsill projects out from the wall and the backrest reaches to that level, fill out beneath the sill by using thicker foam for the cushions.

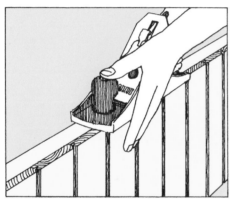

10 Use a smoothing plane to trim the top of the boards flush with the frame.

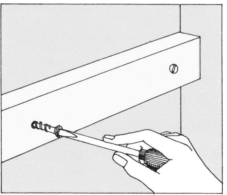

11 Cut a 50 x 25mm (2 x 1 in) batten to full width of bay. Screw to wall with 75mm (3 in) No 8 screws, 18mm (¾ in) higher than front frame.

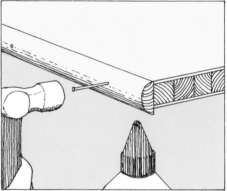

12 Mark out and cut the seat from 18mm (¾ in) blockboard, to reach from front of wall batten to front of panelling. Glue and pin nosing to front edge.

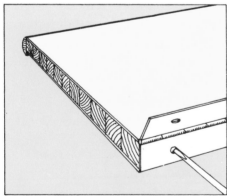

13 Cut piano hinge to length of seat with hacksaw. Fix to back edge of seat using 19mm (¾ in) No 6 screws.

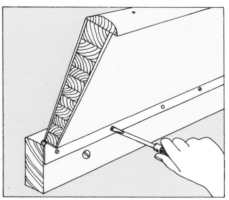

14 Using similar screws, attach hinge to wall batten.

15 Sand down the tongued-and-grooved boards. Finish with paint or varnish.

LAUNDRY STORAGE

The bathroom is the customary place for laundry storage – usually a wicker basket that might not blend with the room or is kept out of sight in an airing cupboard.

Why not regard the laundry basket as a piece of furniture? It can be tailor-made to suit any situation and decorated to blend with the room. You could also combine it with a bath side panel to give the room a fully-fitted look. Just use the same moulding as on the bath panel – see p. 122.

Size is the first consideration. The unit shown here is about 500mm (20 in) square and approximately the same height,

- **Simple to make**
- **Can be adapted to any length**
- **A matching pair is optional**
- **Makes dealing with laundry convenient**
- **Ideal for any bathroom**
- **Any finish is possible**

but there are no hard and fast rules to follow. You could make one about the same height and depth but a greater length if you have a larger space to fill or if your family washload is likely to fill a smaller unit quickly.

Keeping coloured and white fabrics separate makes washdays a little less troublesome, so you could partition the laundry storage unit by adding a centre panel or make two separate units. A dustbin liner placed inside a unit makes it easier to transfer the laundry to the washing machine.

Although you can make simple square boxes, it is easy to create a decorative shape by cutting out recesses at the top and bottom of the front and side panels. The rear panel, to which the lid is hinged, is not cut out at the top. Cut-outs can be made to any configuration you like.

A hinged lid has been suggested here, but you could fit a simple lid that will just lie in position instead. However, a loose lid is likely to be left off from time to time, leaving laundry on display and defeating the object of the unit.

You can decorate the top with cork tiles or you could paint it. If you like the idea of cork tiles, then design the size of the lid around four full-size tiles or almost full-size ones to avoid being left with narrow pieces at the edges. The tiles should all be the same size.

To protect the edges of the cork tiles, narrow beading must be pinned to the edge of the lid. The height of beading is the total

thickness of the plywood plus the cork tiles including adhesive. 21 mm ($^7\!/_8$ in) should be adequate, and a thickness of 9 mm ($^3\!/_8$ in), but you may need to buy the next larger width and plane it flush with the underside of the lid. Without this beading the continual handling of the lid would eventually cause the tiles to wear and lift at the edges.

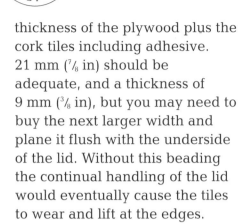

1 Mark out a length of 18mm ($^3\!/_4$ in) plywood for all four sides.

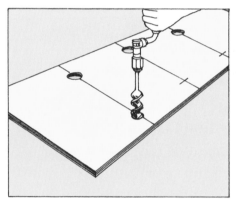

2 Use a swing-brace and auger bit to drill two holes on each line. The hole centres are about 75mm (3 in) from the edge.

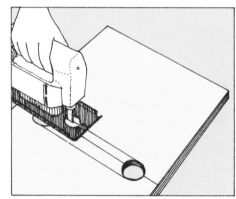

3 Join the edges of the holes with pencil line and cut along the line with a jigsaw or padsaw.

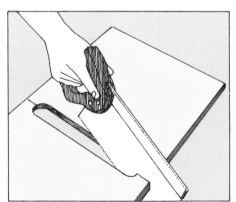

4 Cut out the four sections and sand down the cut edges to make smooth.

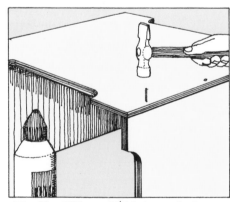

5 Use 370mm ($1^1\!/_2$ in) panel pins and woodworking adhesive to join the four sides. The front and back overlap the side panels.

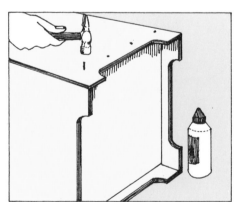

6 Measure interior of unit, then cut a a sheet of 18mm ($^3\!/_4$ in) plywood for the base. Glue and pin in place 25mm (1 in) above the cut-outs.

7 Cut lid from 18mm (³⁄₄ in) plywood to overlap all edges by 18mm (³⁄₄ in). Apply cork tile adhesive.

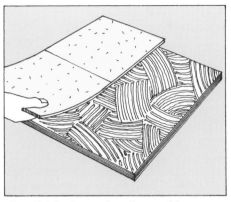

8 Stick down the tiles and leave to dry according to adhesive instructions.

9 Turn lid over on to a flat worksurface, protect if necessary and trim tiles using the lid to guide the knife.

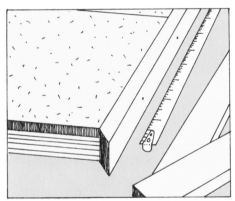

10 Mark out, then cut 9mm (³⁄₈ in)-thick beading to cover the edge of the lid. Mitre the ends with the longer dimension vertical.

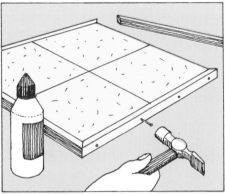

11 Glue and pin beading to lid, flush with surface of tiles, using 18mm (³⁄₄ in) panel pins. Plane underside flush if necessary.

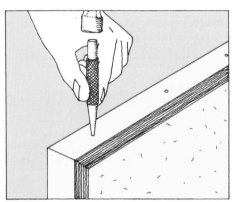

12 Use a nail punch and hammer to drive pin heads below the surface.

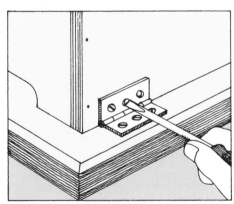

13 Fit two 75mm (3 in) butt hinges to the lid and then to the back of the unit.

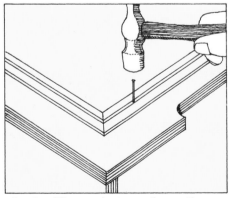

14 Glue and pin on decorative moulding following pre-marked pencil guidelines. Sink heads below surface.

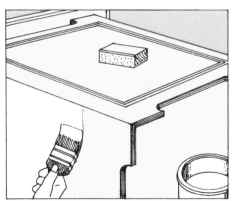

15 Fill nail holes, then sand down and paint with primer, followed by undercoat and gloss. Painting the inside is optional.

PROJECTS · STEP-BY-STEP ·

FRAMES & SKIRTINGS

Ｎew skirting-boards and architraves can be used for restoring an old house or adding traditional style to a new one.

Fitting a new architrave is easy; just remember that it is nailed to the wooden part of the frame, not to the wall.

Skirting-boards are nailed to blocks of wood that are nailed or screwed to the wall.

It is best to fit skirtings in continuous runs between doors and corners. If you have to join lengths, cut parallel mitres with a power saw set to 45°.

Glue and pin external corners after fixing. Pin internal corners joints before fixing.

- **Helps re-style a room or hallway**
- **Simple skills involved**
- **Traditional or modern appeal**
- **Can be finished with varnish or paint**

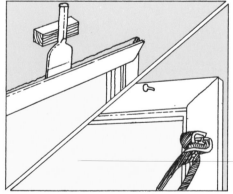

1 Prise off the existing architrave with a bolster chisel over a wooden block to protect the wall. Pull out nails with pincers.

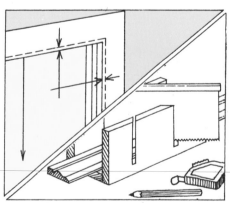

2 Allow about 6mm ($\frac{1}{4}$ in) set-back from edge of door and measure internal length of architrave moulding. Cut in mitre block.

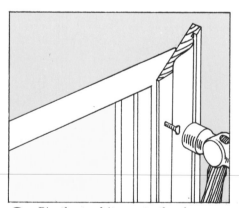

3 Pin the architrave to the door frame using slim 25mm (1 in) oval nails. With a hammer and nail punch, drive the heads below surface of wood.

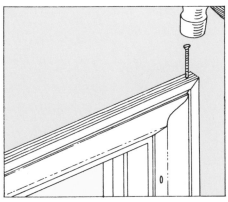

4 Cut and fit a moulding at the head of the frame, making sure mitre joints fit snugly. Drive pin into joint to ensure alignment.

5 **Skirtings:** To make a straight cut when butting a skirting up to an architrave, mark square with pencil and cut with a power saw.

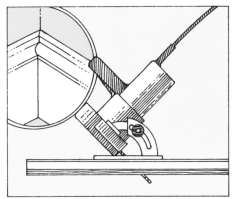

6 For corner joints, set the saw blade tilted at 45° to cut an exact mitre angle. Test joint on scrap timber.

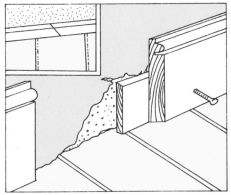

7 Skirtings must be well supported at the back by nailing to wood blocks that are securely fixed to wall. Mitre-join adjacent lengths.

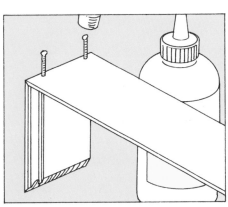

8 Join short pieces of skirting to long pieces before fixing to the wall. Glue the joint and nail from back.

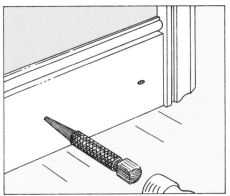

9 Before fixing, mark the floor or wall to indicate positions of the fixing blocks. Use oval nails and punch nail heads below surface.

10 Fill the nail holes with coloured wood stopper if the boards are to be finished with varnish. Use ordinary filler with paint.

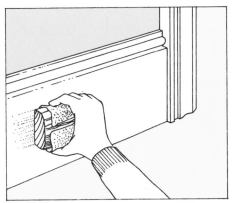

11 When the stopper or filler has dried, rub down with fine abrasive paper to leave a smooth surface ready for finishing.

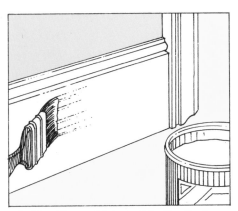

12 If varnishing, thin the first coat of varnish with 10% white spirit as a base coat. If painting, apply wood primer as first coat.

WORK DESK

- **Adaptable design to suit any need**
- **Optional drawer arrangement**
- **Neat, functional appearance**
- **Handy for study, hobby or business use**

One of the problems with mass-produced furniture is that it is manufactured to a design that will do a reasonable job for most people. Sometimes it is perfect for an individual, but more often it would be much more convenient and enjoyable to use if details were altered.

People like to work in different ways and the design needs to reflect that and to be specific to the work or hobby being pursued. For example, someone who needs to study large plans – an architect or surveyor – needs a surface of sufficient proportions to be able to lay out flat a complete plan. A hobbyist, collecting stamps, for example, might need drawers on both sides in which to store treasured albums.

The beauty of building a work desk is that you can tailor it specifically to your exact requirements.

The design shown here, using

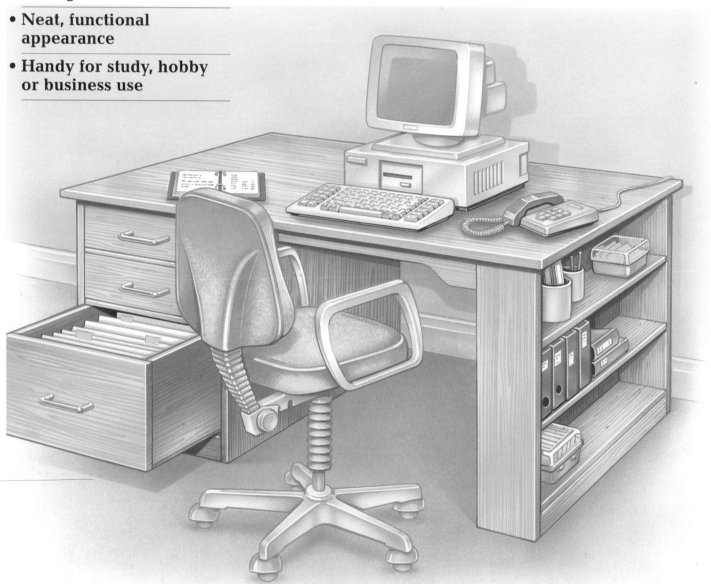

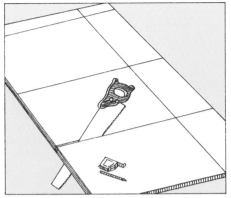

1 Mark out then cut the panels for the drawer housing unit from 18mm (³⁄₄ in) veneered blockboard.

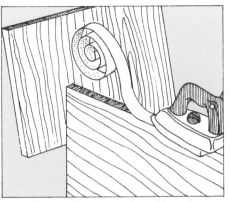

2 Plane the front edges flat with a smoothing plane. Iron on edge veneer to exposed edges and trim when cool.

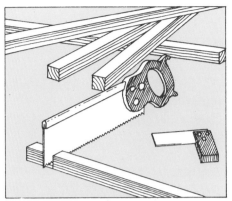

3 Cut to length 25 x 25mm (1 x 1 in) softwood battens to make the drawer slides and top frame (for fixing the housing to the top). Ensure cuts are square by using a try-square.

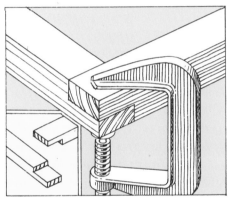

4 Cut corner halving joints (*see* 'Techniques') and assemble with pva woodworking adhesive. Check for square and clamp each joint for 24 hours.

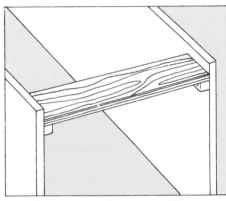

5 Cut a plinth from 75 x 25 mm (3 x 1 in) softwood and fix 25mm (1 in) in from front edge of housing sides with joint blocks.

6 Drill slides and top frame and fix to housing side panels with 37mm (1¹⁄₂ in) No 8 screws. Bottom slide rests on plinth; top frame is flush at top.

7 Cut a sheet of 4mm (³⁄₁₆ in) plywood to cover complete back of housing unit. Fix in place with 18mm (³⁄₄ in) panel pins.

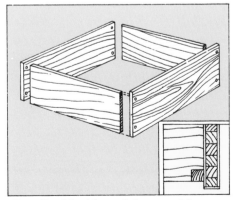

8 Cut blockboard drawer sides, backs and fronts. Fronts are 4mm (³⁄₁₆ in) deeper to hide plywood base. Glue and pin 12 x 12mm (¹⁄₂ x ¹⁄₂ in) beading to front supports to front of base.

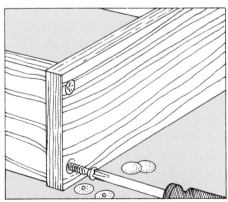

9 Veneer exposed edges. Drill holes in fronts and backs and glue and screw to sides with 37mm (1¹⁄₂ in) No 8 cappable screws.

18mm (¾ in) veneered blockboard, is very adaptable. The only governing feature is the height, which should be around 600mm (24 in) – a working level that suits most people. If you want it slightly higher or lower, then just increase or decrease the height of the support panels accordingly.

Although three drawers have been indicated here – a larger one at the bottom occupying half the depth of the housing unit and the other two each half that size – you may prefer four drawers or two large ones. In this case you simply increase or decrease the number of drawer slides in the housing unit.

It is very important that the drawer slides are set in exactly the same positions. Making up a square frame for each slide and then fixing it to the side panels of the housing unit will ensure correct positioning.

Only if you were storing exceptionally long items would you need the drawers to run to the full depth of the unit. Normally a depth of about 450mm (18 in) is sufficient. With this design, the drawer action is not on proper runners, which means that the drawers are really slide-in boxes. This makes them perfectly functional, though less smooth in operation than you would expect from high-quality furniture.

To prevent the drawers from being pushed right inside the housing some form of stop is necessary. One method is to screw a 25 x 25mm (1 x 1 in) batten across the top of the slides

as a stop. The back of the drawer will meet the stop as it is pushed in, leaving the front almost flush with the front of the housing unit.

You will have to fix the stop in position as each slide frame is constructed. Just measure the complete depth of each drawer and fix the stop that exact distance from the front of the housing unit. Make sure you measure from the front rather than the rear of the housing.

The alternative method is to use the front edges of the housing unit as a complete drawer stop. To do this, measure and cut the drawer fronts to the width of the opening plus just under twice the thickness of the housing panels. So if the drawer opening is 450mm (18 in) wide and each of the side panels is 18mm (¾ in) thick, the door fronts would be 450mm (18 in) plus twice 18mm (¾ in) – less about 10mm (½ in). That gives a figure of 476mm (19 in). When fixed centrally to the sides of the drawer, this front will close to leave a slight margin on either side.

The open shelves forming the other support can be enclosed on one side if you prefer, by adding a panel of 4mm (³⁄₁₆ in) plywood to the inside face. Secure it around the edges using 18mm (¾ in) panel pins driven into the blockboard. You should not enclose the outside face of the open shelves, since that would make access possible only from the inside, which would not be practical.

If the work area needs to

accommodate a word processor or computer, then, provided space is available, a second desk could be added at right angles to the first. This would give the best of both worlds – an immediately accessible word processor or computer desk and a separate work area.

The second desk could be designed in much the same way as the first, with drawers or a shelf unit as a support at one end. The other end support would be a plain sheet of blockboard, since neither drawers nor shelves would be accessible. It would have to be fitted at the drawer end of the main desk, otherwise it would prevent access to the shelves. The plain end could be attached to the drawer housing with joint blocks to keep it rigid.

Although the two work surfaces could be a single complete L-shaped piece, making the double desks one unit, in many cases it would be more convenient and flexible to have two units – in case you ever want to rearrange the room or move house, for example.

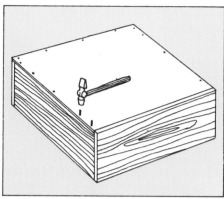

10 Cut 4mm (³⁄₁₆ in) plywood bases 18mm (¾ in) less than drawer length. Check for square and fix with 18mm (¾ in) panel pins.

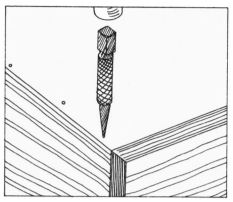

11 Use a nail punch to sink heads of pins below surface. Smooth edges of base with glasspaper.

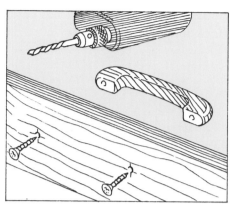

12 Drill holes in drawer fronts and fix on the handles. Rub beeswax on drawer slide to ensure smooth operation.

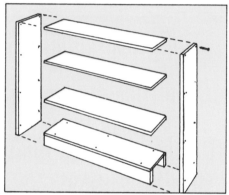

13 Cut shelf-unit sides, shelves and plinths. Assemble with 37mm (1½ in) No 8 cappable screws. Apply edge veneer before assembly.

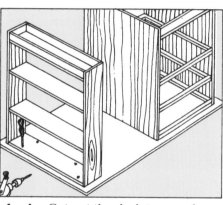

14 Cut out the desk top, apply edge veneer and screw to drawer and shelf unit from underside using 37mm (1½ in) No 8 screws.

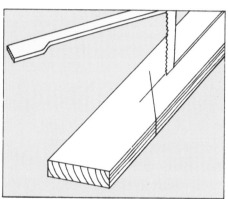

15 Cut the front and back fascia pieces from 75 x 25mm (3 x 1 in) softwood, using a jigsaw or padsaw.

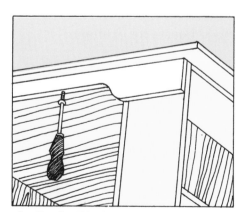

16 Drill holes through fascia edge, and glue and screw to underside of desk top. Use No 6 screws, long enough to go halfway into the top.

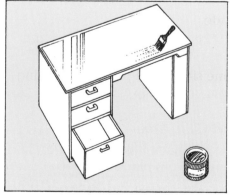

17 Sand down and apply three coats of chosen finish, sanding between each coat.

18 Fix push-in caps to all screw heads.

CORNER SHELVES

- **Makes use of 'wasted' corner space**
- **Attractive to look at**
- **No complicated joints**
- **Simple screw-together construction**
- **Will fit neatly in any corner**
- **Finish with clear lacquer, stain and lacquer, or paint**

The corners of a room are often bare-looking, wasted areas. However, you can enhance their appearance by making the shelf unit shown here.

One reason corner shelving is fairly unusual is that it can be quite difficult to get it to fit properly because even in new houses, the corners of a room are rarely square. If you were to make a corner shelving unit with the corner accurately made at 90°, when you came to fit it you would probably find that when one side was pressed against the wall, the other side would show an ugly gap.

Our design overcomes this problem by simply butt-jointed together, with no complicated mitre joints in the corner.

You simply decide how long you want the shelves to be, cut the two shelves to this length, then overlap them by 25mm (1 in) or so while holding each against its respective rear wall. Clamp them together in this position and mark the line where they overlap with a pencil. Cut the shelf with the mark to this line. The process is then repeated with the overlap of the shelves reversed. When the shelves are pushed together and

into the corner, they should be an exact fit, although they may not be exactly at right angles.

MATERIALS

We suggest that the shelving is made from planed softwood. Use 150 x 25mm (6 x 1 in) timber for the shelving and 100 x 25mm (4 x 1 in) for the back supports and support brackets. All these parts can be given curved corners by using cans, or lids as templates.

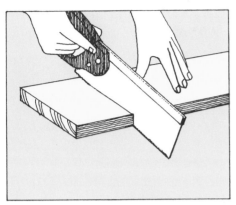

1 Decide on the length of shelves required. Using a pencil and try square, mark two pieces of planed softwood. Cut with a tenon saw.

2 The corner might not be square, so hold the shelf pieces in the corner so they overlap. Hold them with a *G-cramp*, and mark the line with a pencil

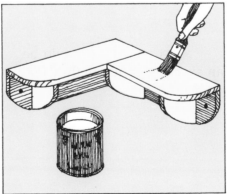

3 Cut accurately along this line using a tenon saw. Test the shelves for fit. On the outside corners mark curve using paint can.

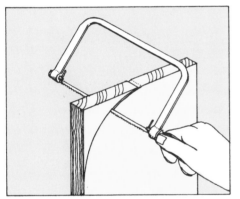

4 Cut out these curves using a coping saw if working by hand, or an electric jigsaw if using power tools. Smooth with abrasive paper.

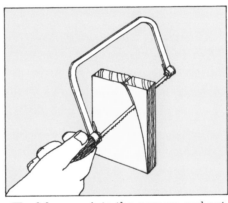

5 Measure into the corners and cut the back supports to length. Curve the corners as above. Mark and cut out the support brackets.

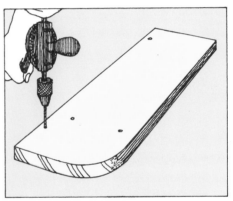

6 Drill 3mm ($\frac{1}{8}$ in) countersunk holes through the shelves and back supports for the 38mm ($1\frac{1}{2}$ in) gauge No 8 fixing screws. The central bracket should span the join between shelves.

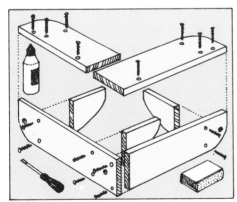

7 Sand all pieces using abrasive paper wrapped around a block. Apply woodworking adhesive to all joining edges, and screw together.

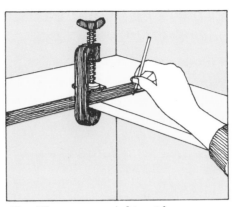

8 The corner shelves can be finished as desired. For a wood finish, stain as necessary and apply three coats of clear lacquer.

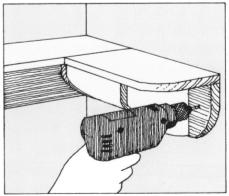

9 For wall fixing, screws should be 38mm ($1\frac{1}{2}$ in) from each end and at a maximum interval of 600mm (2 ft) between. Drill wall with masonry drill, insert wall-plug and screw unit to wall.

UNDER STAIRS STORAGE

- **Utilises existing storage space to full advantage**

- **Convenient to use**

- **Interior can be designed to suit any arrangement of shelves**

- **Design adaptable for any size of understairs cupboard**

- **Gas and electricity fittings remain readily accessible**

- **Houses items of all shapes and sizes**

- **Requires basic woodwork skills to construct**

When storage space is at a premium, it is wasteful not to take advantage of an opportunity to increase it. A classic example is the under-stairs cupboard.

The problem is that the useful space is really just the couple of feet around the door. Here you can stand up straight; delving down into the back means bending double. To reach items kept at the back invariably means first having to take everything out in order to get there. Eventually, only a few things are stored in it while several square feet near the back are ignored.

So here's the answer. Turn the problem around and enter the cupboard from the side. A number of doors are arranged to

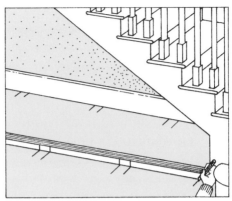

1 Calculate door width (see text) and mark on batten the positions of doors, fascias and clearances. Mark fascia positions on floor.

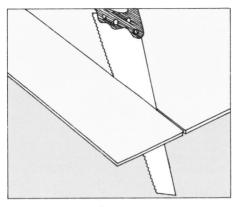

2 Cut 4mm ($^{5}/_{32}$ in) plywood to cover underside of stairs so that edge is flush with face of stair string.

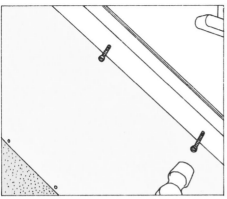

3 Pin plywood to stair strings. Cut top rail from 50 x 25mm (2 x 1 in) timber and temporarily pin to stair string. Mark top and bottom ends.

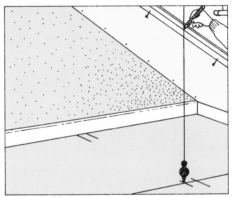

4 Using plumb bob line, mark fascia positions on edge of top rail and plywood from corresponding marks on floor.

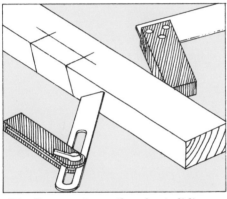

5 Remove top rail and set sliding bevel to angle of marks. Mark recesses for vertical fascias on both faces of top rail.

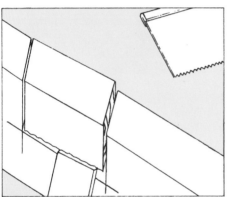

6 Cut to depth line with tenon saw and chop out recesses, parallel to cuts, with firmer chisel. Work from both sides.

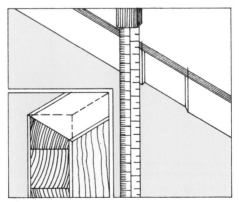

7 Fix top rail. Measure dividers from floor to top of recess and from back of recess to wall. Cut from 18mm ($^{3}/_{4}$ in) blockboard and bevel top edge.

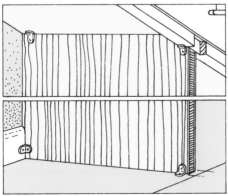

8 Notch divider to fit round top rail and skirting. Secure with angle brackets, bent open at top. On solid floor, screw to batten glued to floor.

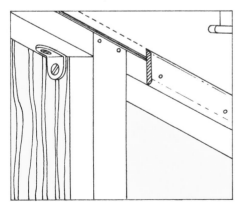

9 Measure and cut vertical fascias and glue and pin to dividers and top rail recesses. Pin D-moulding to top rail, flush with bottom edges.

give access to every square inch of the area. Inside each compartment you can arrange hooks, rails, shelves, drawers or pull-out boxes to suit whatever you want to store. Remember to leave electricity meters and so on readily accessible.

Understairs areas are primarily the same shape, but in different lengths and depths, so you will have to determine the number and width of doors (doors of equal width will give a uniform appearance). Assume a maximum width of 600mm (24 in), including fascias. For example, suppose the available length is 2100mm and a fascia width of 44mm. Deduct one fascia width: 2100 – 44=2056; divide by maximum width: 2056/600=3 (+ remainder) so 4 doors are needed.

2056/4=514, less the width of the fascia: 514 – 44=470, less clearance for hinge thickness and opening (say 5mm): 470 – 5=465. This is the door width.

Once you have determined these dimensions, make a gauge batten with fascia widths, doors and clearances all marked on, then transfer the fascia positions to the floor. One difficulty is that pieces have to be cut to an angle. The use of a sliding bevel to mark the dividers and fascias ensures accuracy. The doors are shorter than the openings to allow them to clear the top rail; the small resulting gap provides ventilation.

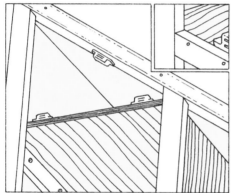

10 Fit shelf above rectangular cupboard on battens screwed to dividers. Pin fascia to front edge. Triangular panel is held by magnetic catches.

11 Cut doors from 19mm ($^3/_4$ in) blockboard, 25mm (1 in) shorter than heights of opening. Iron on edge strip to exposed edges.

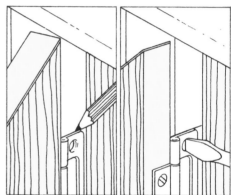

12 Screw flush hinge 75mm (3 in) from top and bottom of door. Prop open at 90°, clear of moulding, and mark hinge positions on fascia. Screw in place.

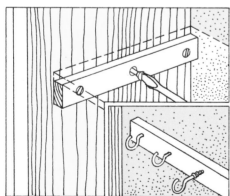

13 Fit remaining shelves using battens screwed to dividers. Screw batten for hooks to wall and screw in hooks.

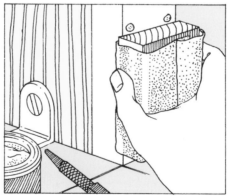

14 Punch all nail heads below surface and fill holes. Sand smooth and apply required finish to all surfaces.

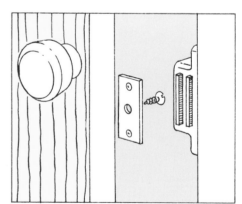

15 Fit a handle to each door and the triangular panel, and fit magnetic catches. Screw magnet to divider panel, adjacent to handle.

SCREEN

- **Lightweight and versatile**
- **Hides untidy corners**
- **Make to match room décor**
- **Make any size to suit your requirements**
- **Folds away flat when not in use**
- **Cheap to make from softwood and plywood**

The versatility and practicality of a folding screen makes it an invaluable asset. It is ideal for hiding an untidy corner, such as the toy storage area in a child's room, and for separating parts of a room that have different uses, such as the eating area in a living room, the kitchen part of a bed-sit, the home office and workstation.

The screen shown here is easy to make, lightweight and versatile. It has a softwood frame with plywood in-filling, and there are many ways of decorating it so that it blends in with the décor of the room in which it will be used.

STARTING WORK

Decide how high and wide you want the screen panels. Do not make the screen too big or it will be difficult to use. A screen about 1.5m (5 ft) high will be about right for most situations. The frame should be wide enough to take 600mm (2 ft) wide panels, so you will be able to cut two panels from a standard 1200mm (4 ft) wide sheet of plywood.

Use halving joints to join the timber framing pieces. Where the two pieces of framing timber cross each other, cut half the

thickness of wood from each piece so the two pieces are level when assembled. Saw exactly halfway through each piece. At the corners at the top of the frame cut the joints with just a saw. At the bottom of the frame you must form a T-halving in each side rail for the bottom rail. Cut the joint with a saw and then remove the waste wood using a chisel.

FINISHING TECHNIQUES

One of the easiest finishes is to sand down all the surfaces and apply three coats of clear wood lacquer. Alternatively, coloured stains can be used to match or contrast with existing furniture.

Another idea is to stencil a motif on the panel before lacquering it, which introduces paint but maintains the basic wood effect.

Of course, the screen can also be painted, with or without stencil décor. Wallpapered panels can look very effective, and in a teenager's bedroom a screen makes an ideal backing for posters, pictures and magazine cuttings.

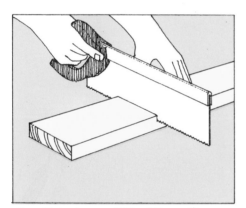

1 Cut pieces of 75 x 32mm (3 x 1¼ in) planed softwood for the uprights and bottom rail, and 150 x 32mm (6 x 1¼ in) softwood for the top rail.

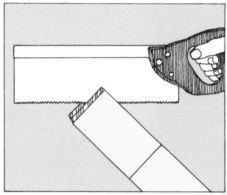

2 Join top rails with corner halving joints. Overlap the two pieces and mark width of overlap on each. Cut half the depth of wood to mark with a tenon saw.

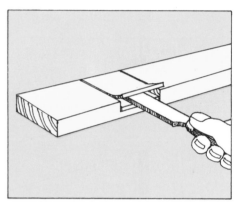

3 Join bottom rails to uprights with T halving joints. After cutting sides with tenon saw, chisel out waste with a firmer chisel.

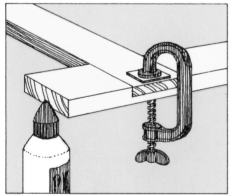

4 After preparing both parts of halving joints, apply adhesive to mating surfaces, assemble joints and hold with G-cramp.

5 After the glue has set (about 24 hours) trim the joints smooth and flat with a smoothing plane.

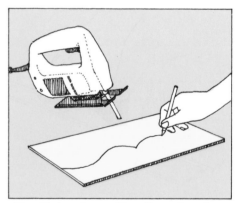

6 Cut a piece of hardboard to the width of the panel to make a template for the shape of the top of the screen. Cut out with jigsaw.

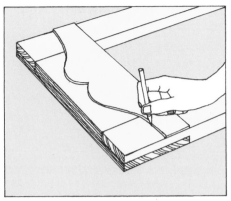

7 Position the template on the top rail and trace round the outline with a pencil.

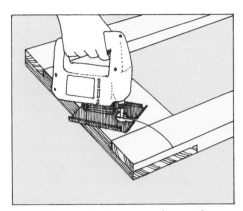

8 Clamp the frame to the work-bench, overhanging the end, and cut round the pencil outline with a jigsaw. Smooth with a plane followed by glasspaper.

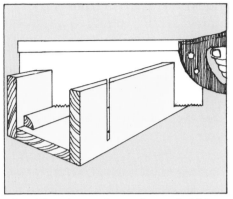

9 The plywood panels are held in the frame of the screen by 12mm ($\frac{1}{2}$ in) timber quadrant moulding on both sides. Cut the moulding in a mitre block.

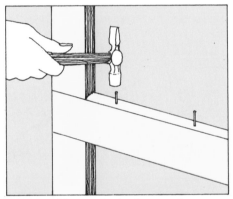

10 Glue and pin the quadrant moulding to the internal perimeter of the frame so that the screen panel will sit centrally in the frame.

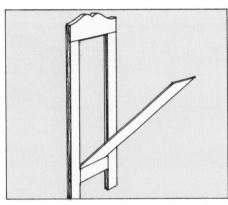

11 Measure and cut a sheet of 4mm ($\frac{3}{16}$ in) thick plywood to fit into the frame. Place it in the frame against the moulding.

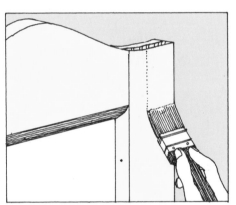

12 Hold the panel in place by pinning quadrant moulding to the other side of the frame perimeter. Sand down and apply finish.

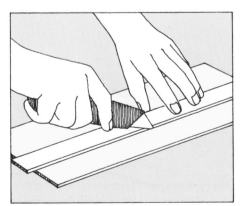

13 Make two-way hinges from strips of leather. Use a sharp craft knife to cut the strips. They should be about 125mm (5 in) long and 50mm (2 in) wide.

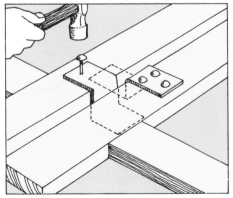

14 Each hinge is formed with two strips wrapped round the uprights in an S-shape. Fix strips to face of frame only with dome-head upholstery nails.

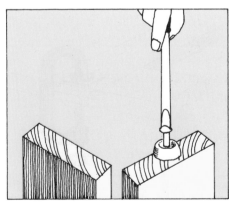

15 Finish off by screwing rubber feet to the bottoms of the uprights to stop the screen from slipping in use.

FITTED CUPBOARDS

Many houses have alcoves and recesses that are often wasted spaces. The fitted cupboards shown here – a lower section with a useful countertop, and an upper wall unit – not only provide useful storage for a range of items, but also enhance the appearance of the room.

The recesses on either side of a chimney breast are the obvious places to build them, but any alcoves can be used. Because the sides of an alcove are rarely flat and true, even in a new house, it is essential to build cupboards in the correct way.

Build the cupboard as a square, free-standing unit, fractionally smaller than the alcove. To fit it neatly into the alcove; join it to a fascia frame, which is made square to the width and height of the alcove. Make the frame very slightly over-size, then plane it to fit snugly into the opening with the top and bottom rails perfectly horizontal. You must check this with a spirit level.

At the planning stage think about how you will finish the cupboards. They can be painted, or stained and lacquered, or varnished. We suggest that in most cases the fascia frames are made from softwood, and the cupboard carcass, shelves and

- **Useful storage**
- **In two sections to combine storage and a counter-top**
- **Build into any alcove**
- **Simple construction using hidden battens**
- **Use a clear wood or paint finish**
- **Easy-to-make panelled door effect**

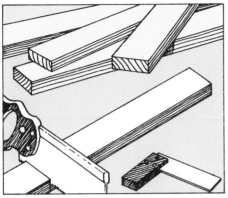

1 Measure and cut 25 x 75mm (1 x 3 in) softwood for upper and lower cupboard fascia frames. You can use hardwood if preferred.

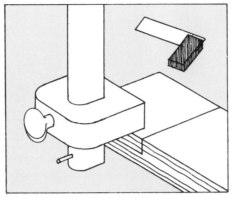

2 Mark out halving joints at corners of fascia frames using a try square and marking gauge, to half depth of timber and width of adjoining piece.

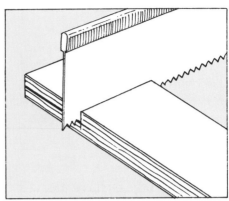

3 Cut down the shoulder to the centre line with a tenon saw, then remove the waste wood by cutting down from the end.

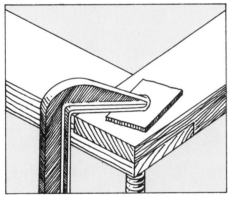

4 Check the joint for fit then apply adhesive to the shoulder and face of both parts. Clamp loosely, check corner with try square, then tighten cramp.

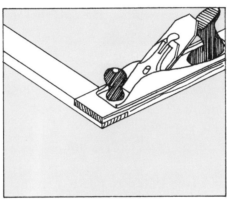

5 Trim all faces of joints neatly with a smoothing plane. Trim upper frame to fit alcove.

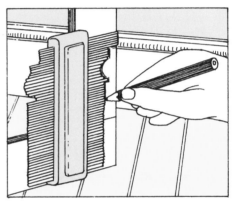

6 Set *profile gauge* to shape of skirting at height of lower frame and transfer outline to timber.

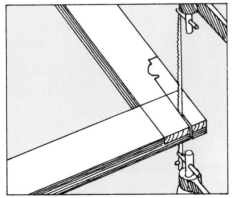

7 Now carefully cut out this skirting shape in the sides of the lower cupboard frame using a powered jigsaw or hand coping saw.

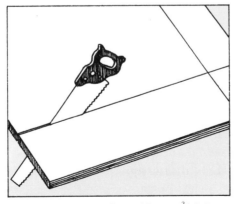

8 Measure and cut 18mm ($^3/_4$ in) thick blockboard for shelves, top board, doors and footboard. The top board should overlap and finish flush with the lower cupboard fascia.

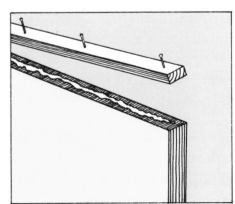

9 Glue and pin a strip of hardwood to the front edge of the lower cupboard top board.

doors from ordinary 18mm ($^3/_4$ in) blockboard. However, if the unit is to be given a clear finish the cupboards could be built with hardwood fascia frames and matching veneered blockboard doors and carcass components.

MAKING THE FRAMES

Make fascia frames from 25 x 75mm (1 x 3 in) timber joined at the corners with halving joints. These joints are simple to cut, but they must be marked out accurately. Each piece has exactly half its thickness cut away.

Mark the width of the adjoining rails at each corner, then using a pencil and *try square*, mark a line across the rail at exactly 90° at this point. Also mark down each side at this point. Draw a line at half the thickness of the wood down each side, and across the end of the rail, using a *marking gauge*.

Use a tenon saw to accurately cut the shoulder line down to the marking gauge line. Then remove the waste wood by cutting down from the end, again using a tenon saw. Cut to the waste side of the line.

FITTING THE FRAME

When the fascia frame has been assembled and the glue has set, hold the frame in position so it is horizontal, and plane its edges to follow the outline of the walls at each side of the alcove to give a neat, tight fit.

For the lower cupboard, use a *profile gauge* to copy the shape of the skirting board on to the edge of the fascia frame. Cut it

out with a power jigsaw or by hand using a coping saw.

Note that the carcass is assembled with battens on the outside edges to give a strong framework with no fixings visible inside the cupboards. Battens at the front outside edges of the carcass allow the unit to be fixed securely to the fascia frame. The fascia frame is fitted with the top edge of the rail, its lower flush with the bottom panel of the cupboard carcass (see diagram 12). This panel is supported by the footboard, which is screwed to the back of fascia board before the unit is installed (see diagram 15).

Fixing the back panel in place produces a very rigid unit, which is slotted into the alcove and screwed into the wall at the back through steel corner brackets.

MAKING THE DOORS

Cut the doors from blockboard, edge them with iron-on veneer strip, and give them the appearance of panelled doors by fixing decorative wood moulding strips to the surface. These decorative mouldings are made in exactly the same way as picture frames – the ends are cut in a mitre box to give accurate 45° mitre joints at the corners. The mouldings are simply glued and pinned in place on the door fronts, and the doors are hung on flush hinges which themselves are simply screwed to the back of the doors and the surface of the fascia frames.

If preferred you may be able to use ready-made cupboard doors on these units. A wide range of

these doors is available in d-i-y stores and by buying pairs of doors in suitable sizes before starting work on the carcases, the size of the fascia frames can be adjusted to suit the doors.

Some of these doors have attractively moulded frames and raised panels which would be very difficult to make at home, but make sure that the timber used is suitable if you intend to apply a clear finish as some of these doors are made from cheap timber specifically to be finished by painting.

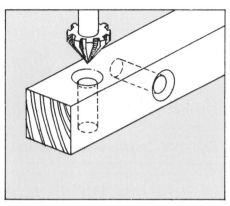

10 Use 25 x 25mm (1 x 1 in) battens to securely join the cupboard components. Cut them to length and drill for fixing screws.

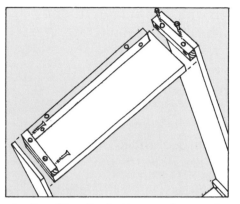

11 Glue the battens and screw to the outer edges of the top and bottom panels, and to the front edges of the end panels.

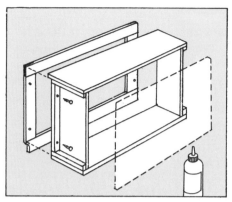

12 Assemble the cupboards and fascia frames by gluing and screwing through the battens on the outside.

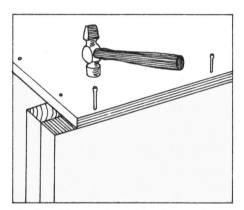

13 The cupboard backs are 4mm ($^5/_{32}$ in) plywood sheets, which are glued and pinned into position on the cupboard carcasses.

14 Screw steel corner brackets into the four corners of each cupboard for strengthening and fixing them. Drill the back through the fixing hole in each bracket.

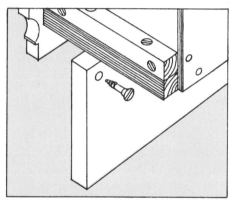

15 Cut foot board from 25mm (1 in) thick timber to fit between skirtings and to reach from floor to underside of bottom panel. Drill and screw to back of fascia.

16 Position each cupboard. Check for horizontal with spirit level. Mark through fixing holes, drill wall, and secure with 50mm (2 in) No 8 screws and wall fixings.

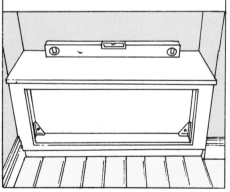

17 Mark wall through fixing holes in brackets. Remove cupboards and drill with masonry bit. Insert wallplugs and screw cupboards in place.

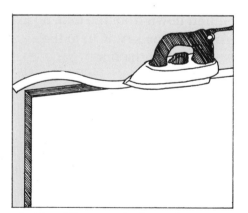

18 All exposed edges of blockboard on shelves and doors should be edged by applying a matching iron-on veneer.

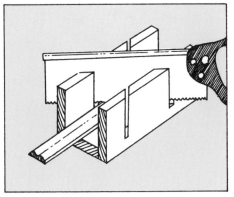

19 Doors can be given a panelled effect by fixing a decorative moulding to the front face. Corners of this moulding are mitre cut.

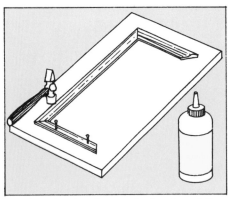

20 Apply glue to the backs of the moulding strips and pin them in place so that the mitred corners butt tightly together.

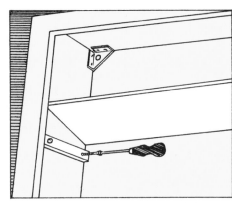

21 From 25 x 25mm (1 x 1 in) softwood, cut support battens for shelves. Drill and screw into position. Insert finished shelves.

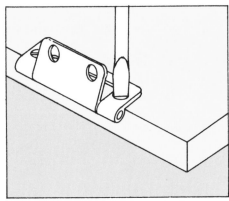

22 Screw flush hinges to the backs of the finished doors and hang the doors by fixing the flaps of the hinges to the fascia frames.

23 Drill the doors (with scrap wood held behind to prevent burst through) and fit the handles in convenient positions.

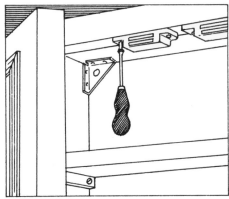

24 Finally, fit magnetic catches to hold the doors closed. Fit the magnet to the frame and the metal plate to the back of the door.

TOY BOX

- **Simple to build**

- **Handy for keeping toys tidy**

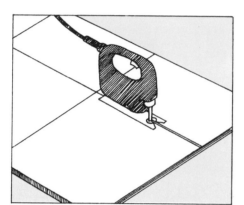

1 From 12mm ($\frac{1}{2}$ in) plywood, mark out the sides, lid, lid supports and base. Cut with a jigsaw or handsaw. Lid and base fit within sides.

2 Use a swingbrace and 25mm (1 in) diameter auger bit to drill holes at each end of handle area.

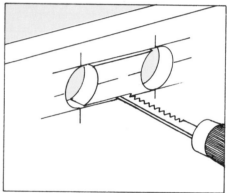

3 Use a jigsaw or padsaw to cut out wood between holes to create handle. Make similar handles in the lid.

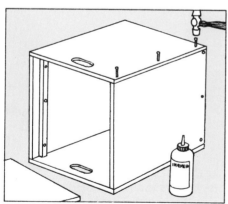

4 Use adhesive and 38mm (1$\frac{1}{2}$ in) panel pins to join sides and base; fix lid supports with 19mm ($\frac{3}{4}$ in) panel pins. Sink pin heads below surface with nail punch.

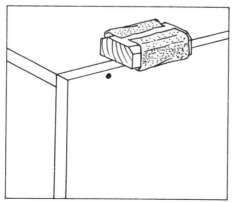

5 Fill pinhead holes, then sand down all parts until perfectly smooth.

6 Paint in lively colours. Simple shaped cut-outs from 12mm ($\frac{1}{2}$ in) plywood can be glued to sides.

DRINKS CABINET

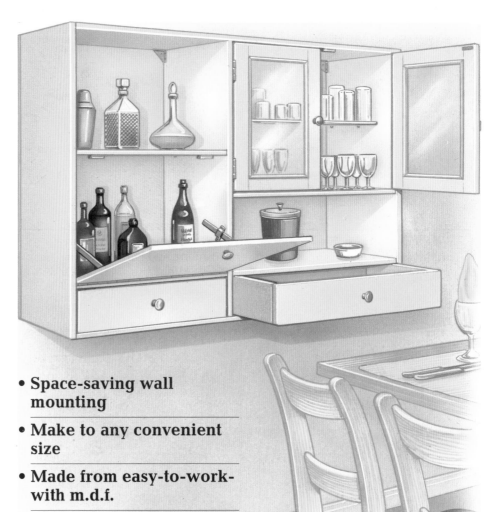

I t is often a problem to know where to store drinks and drinking glasses. Often they are relegated to a cupboard, and then serving drinks becomes a problem because there is nowhere to put down the tray, glasses and bottles.

The drinks cabinet shown here very neatly overcomes the storage problem without taking up valuable floor space. Fixed to the wall at just above waist height, it provides an attractive display for the glasses on glass shelves behind glass doors, while the bottles are neatly accommodated in a compartment behind a drop-down flap, which makes an excellent surface for serving the drinks.

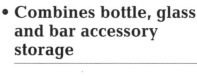

- **Space-saving wall mounting**

- **Make to any convenient size**

- **Made from easy-to-work-with m.d.f.**

- **Paint finish makes it easy to match room décor**

- **Attractive design with pull-down serving flap**

- **Combines bottle, glass and bar accessory storage**

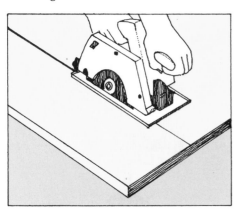

1 Mark pieces for the carcass on 18mm ($^3/_4$ in) m.d.f. Cut just outside the marked lines.

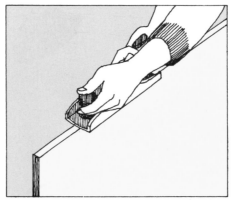

2 Trim the edges back to the lines with a smoothing plane to leave them smooth and straight.

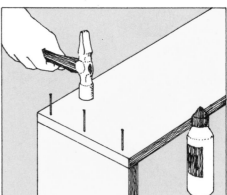

3 Assemble the carcass by applying glue to the joints, then nailing them with 38mm ($1^1/_2$ in) panel pins.

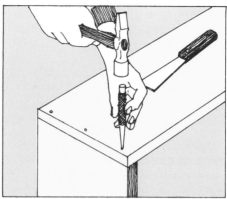

4 For a smooth finish in preparation for painting, use a nail punch to drive pins below the surface. Fill holes with stopping.

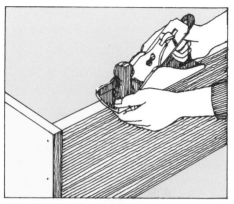

5 While glue sets, keep carcass square and lying on a flat surface. After about 24 hours, trim the joints with a smoothing plane.

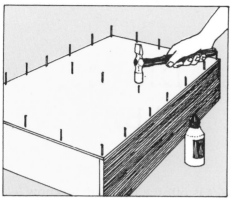

6 For the back, cut a sheet of 6mm ($^1/_4$ in) m.d.f. about 1mm ($^1/_{16}$ in) over size. Glue and pin in place, then trim excess with a plane.

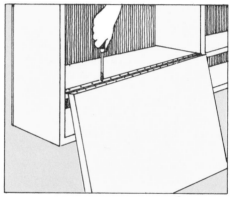

7 Measure and cut 18mm ($^3/_4$ in) m.d.f., for drop-down door, allowing for thickness of piano hinge. Cut hinge to length with hacksaw and fit to door first, then carcass.

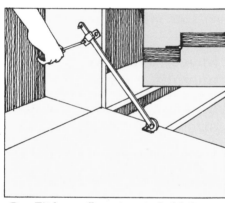

8 Fit brass flap stays to hold the flap open in a horizontal position. The stays must not hit the cabinet back when the flap closes.

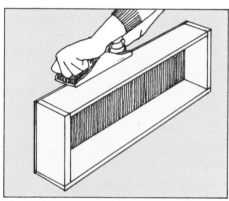

9 Cut drawer frames from 12mm ($^1/_2$ in) m.d.f. Glue and pin together, then fit 6mm ($^1/_4$ in) m.d.f. drawer bottoms. Trim with plane to fit.

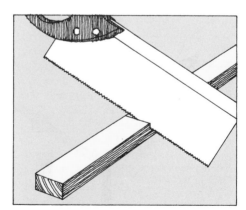

10 Make the door frames from 50 x 25mm (2 x 1 in) planed softwood. Carefully saw this to length after squaring ends with a try square.

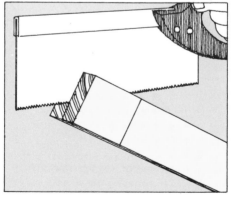

11 Accurately mark and cut corner halving joints for door frames with a sharp tenon saw (see 'Techniques').

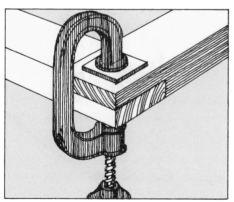

12 Loosely assemble the door frames to check fit of joints. Apply woodworking glue to each joint, holding it with a G-cramp.

There is shelf space for decanters, jugs and ice buckets, and two drawers for napkins, coasters, bottle openers, corkscrews and other bar accessories.

The best material to make this unit from is m.d.f., medium-density fibreboard. This board is particularly easy to work with, and produces an excellent result when it is finished by painting.

It will be easy to make the cabinet blend in with any room décor, as paint is available in an immense variety of colours, and you can choose a high gloss, satin or flat matt finish.

We also recommend a paint finish because this is quite an ambitious project for a beginner, and paint will camouflage any small mistakes.

If you prefer to have a natural wood finish, then make the cabinet from veneered blockboard. Blockboard is available with a wide choice of decorative wood veneers, and you can make the framing for the glass doors to match. (If the unit is made from m.d.f., the frames of the glass doors are made from 50 x 25mm (2 x 1 in) planed softwood.)

SIZE OF UNIT

The size of the unit will depend on the wall space available and the number of bottles and glasses that are likely to be stored. A good depth for the cabinet is about 300mm (12 in). When working out the length and height of your cabinet, measure the height of the tallest bottle to make sure it will go into the drop-down flap compartment, and ensure there will be enough shelf space to hold all the glasses.

Bear in mind the commonly available sizes of m.d.f. boards in d-i-y superstores and timber merchants when designing the unit. Using 900 x 600mm (3 x 2 ft) or 1200 x 900mm (4 x 3 ft) boards, for example, will avoid waste and obviate the need to buy expensive and difficult-to-handle full-size 2440 x 1220mm (8 x 4 ft) sheets.

SECURE FIXING

When loaded, this cabinet is very heavy, so secure fixing to the wall is essential.

If you are fixing to a solid wall (which sounds dense when tapped and produces red or grey dust when drilled), the size of the cabinet does not matter because the wall can be drilled more or less anywhere for plastic wall-plugs to give a secure fixing.

However, if the wall is a hollow partition construction (which sounds hollow when tapped and offers no resistance to a drill bit once the plaster layer has been penetrated), then adjust the size of the cabinet so it can be fixed into the timber studs, which are in the core of the wall about 400mm (16 in) apart, and to which the plasterboard or timber lathes are fixed.

To get a good fixing, use steel corner brackets in the upper inside corners of the cabinet. The brackets strengthen and square up the cabinet, while also providing a central hole through which a fixing screw can be passed. This fixing screw *must* be long enough to go through the back of the cabinet, through the plaster layer, and at least 38mm (1½ in) into the masonry or timber stud of the wall behind. Usually a 75mm (3 in) No 10 screw is sufficient. There will be four corner brackets at the top, giving four fixing points.

CUTTING OUT

It is best to cut out the m.d.f. panels with a power saw. To ensure a straight cut each time, clamp a straight batten parallel to the cutting line and run the base plate of the saw along it.

ASSEMBLING THE CARCASS

Assemble the carcass of the cabinet by simply butt joining, and gluing and pinning the panels. Make sure the carcass is on a flat surface and kept perfectly square while the glue sets. You can check it for squareness by measuring the diagonals, which should be equal.

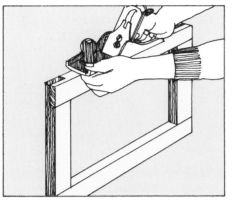

13 After the glue has set, trim each joint with a smoothing plane. Measure opening, cut doors to fit and smooth edges with plane.

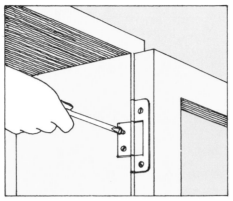

14 Hang the doors using flush hinges. Screw the hinges to edge of doors first, then doors to cabinet.

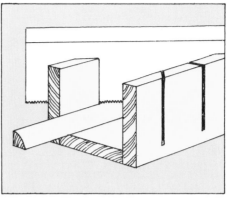

15 Use 8mm ($^5/_{16}$ in) quadrant moulding to hold the glass in place. Cut ends to 45° mitres.

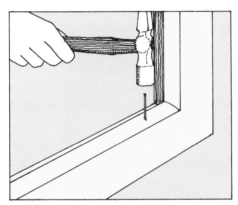

16 Glue and pin the quadrant moulding around the front inside edge of each door frame, setting it back from front face.

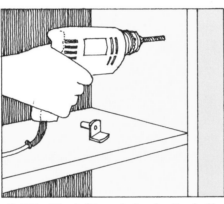

17 Next, fit push-in plastic shelf supports in the cabinet. Mark positions for these carefully; drill holes as required.

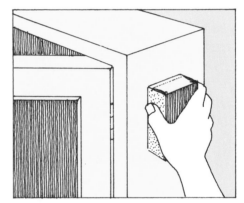

18 Temporarily remove any metal fittings and carefully rub down the entire cabinet, inside and out, with fine abrasive paper.

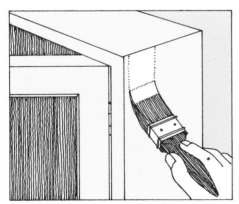

19 Finish the cabinet by applying a coat of primer, one or two coats of undercoat, and one coat of gloss, satin or matt paint.

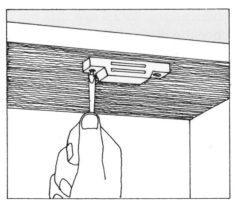

20 After painting, reassemble the cabinet. Fit each door with a magnetic catch, and the drop-down flap with two catches.

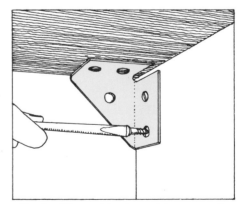

21 The cabinet must be securely fixed to the wall. Screw brackets for wall-mounting kitchen units to interior of cabinet.

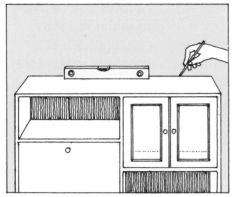

22 Drill the back panel through fixing hole of bracket. Align cabinet with spirit level and mark position and fixing holes on wall.

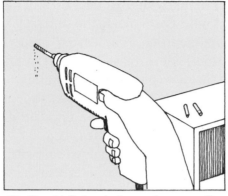

23 At fixing hole marks on wall, drill holes for wall-plugs, using a masonry drill bit. Make sure holes penetrate into brickwork.

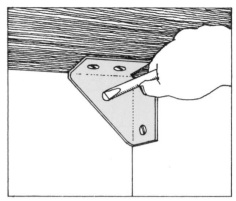

24 Reposition the cabinet, insert 75mm (3 in) No 10 screws through corner bracket fixing holes, then drive screws into the wall-plugs.

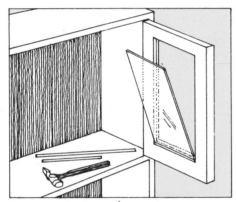

25 Cut 3mm ($\frac{1}{8}$ in) glass for doors 2mm ($\frac{1}{8}$ in) less than internal frame dimensions. Hold glass in place by pinning painted quadrant moulding to inside of door frames.

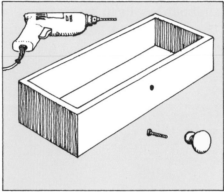

26 Measure carefully to position the door and drawer knobs centrally. Drill at these marked points for the knob fixing bolts.

27 Order polished-edge glass shelves from a glass merchant. Fit these by placing them on to plastic shelf supports.

UNDER-STAIRS WORKSPACE

- **Make use of 'wasted' area**
- **Ideal for homework and hobbies**
- **Easily constructed from blockboard**
- **Includes hat and coat store**
- **Provision for lighting and power points**
- **Paint to match hallway décor**

I n many houses the hallway, and particularly the under-stairs region, is a 'wasted' area. However, with a little replanning it is often possible to bring this part of the home into mainstream use by building an under-stairs workshop for hobbies, or a workstation for homework, word processing or computer use.

PREPARATION

Start by clearing out the under-stairs area. Usually it is used merely for storage and there may be some simple cupboard walls to knock down. The stairs will be self-supporting, but it would be wise not to remove any substantial timbers you may find under the stairs before taking the advice of a building surveyor or competent builder.

If the underside of the staircase is unlined, line it by nailing up some sheets of plasterboard, m.d.f. (medium-density fibreboard) or plywood. If the underside is already plastered but the plaster is cracked or falling away, pull it off and reline it as described above.

CONSTRUCTION OF THE UNITS

Make the basic units from 18mm ($^3/_4$ in) blockboard, which is easy

to work with and gives a good result. Blockboard comprises two sheets of plywood either side of a core of softwood battens. Buy iron-on self-adhesive edging veneer for blockboard and apply it to all the exposed edges after the units have been constructed.

There will probably be a skirting board on the rear wall under the stairs. You can either remove this and fix new pieces behind and between the units after installation, or you can shape the back panels of the

units to fit round the skirtings. A profile gauge, or shape tracer, makes it easy to draw the outline of the skirting board on the panel. The profile gauge has many straight wires sandwiched between two metal plates. When the wires are pressed into the skirting, they adopt its shape, which you then trace on to the wood. Alternatively, you can cut a cardboard template, or pattern, of the skirting by trial and error.

To allow for the wiring to the light, the back panel of the

pinboard is fixed about 25mm (1 in) away from the wall. If you will be using a computer or word processor at the workstation, it is a good idea to incorporate a twin socket outlet in the pinboard. Call in a qualified electrician to install the wiring before screwing the unit to the wall, and to connect the light and socket afterwards.

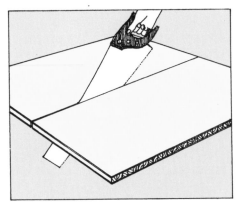

1 Make the carcass for the main workstation first. Measure, mark and cut it from 18mm ($^3/_4$ in) blockboard using a cross-cut panel saw.

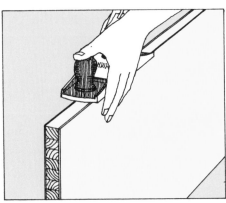

2 Cut just to the outside of the marked lines and then trim back to the lines using a sharp smoothing plane.

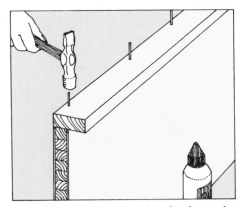

3 Glue and pin a strip of softwood to the front edge of the worktop. A 75mm (3 in) wide strip will add to its strength.

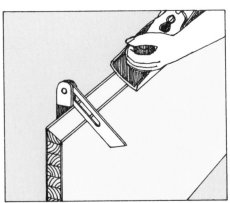

4 To get the vertical side panel of the small cupboard to fit, set a sliding bevel to angle of stairs and plane to this angle.

5 To get the vertical panels to fit against the wall, trace the silhouette of the skirting board on panels and cut shape with jigsaw.

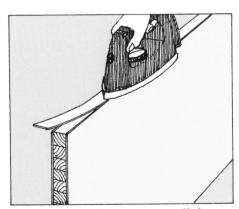

6 Iron-on edge veneer to all the exposed edges of the blockboard carcasses. Trim back excess with a plane when cool.

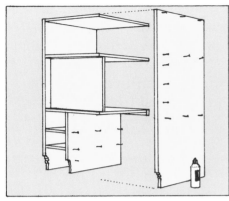

7 Glue and pin the components of the large unit together. Note allowance to set pinboard-back 25mm (1 in) from wall.

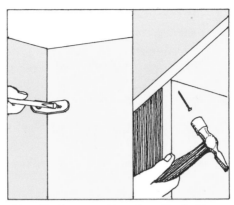

8 Fix large unit and vertical side of small cupboard into position with steel angle brackets. At top of small cupboard, nail through into stair strings (skirting at the side of stair).

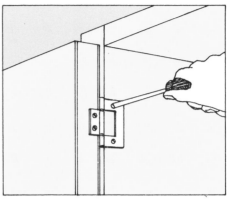

9 Cut out the doors about 1mm ($^1/_{16}$ in) undersize using blockboard. Fix flush hinges to door edges and fit in place. Angled door requires 15mm ($^5/_8$ in) clearance above it.

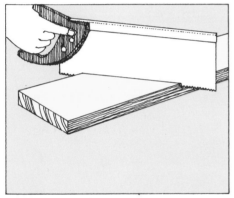

10 For the coat hooks, mark 100 x 25mm (4 x 1 in) softwood to length and cut at an angle. Screw to rear wall, fixing into wall-plugs.

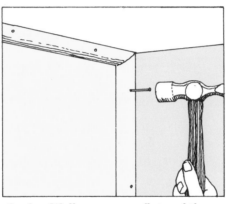

11 Walls are never flat and there are bound to be gaps at back of panels. Hide these by pinning quadrant moulding to the panels.

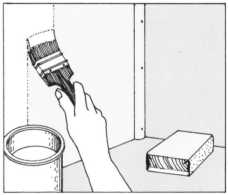

12 Sand all the boards smooth, especially the edges, dust down, then paint or varnish all the new wood, except the pinboard-back.

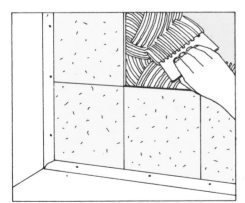

13 Mark and trim cork tiles for the pinboard and fix into position on the pinboard-back with cork tile adhesive.

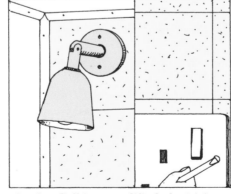

14 Call in a qualified electrician to connect the cables to the spotlight and socket outlet.

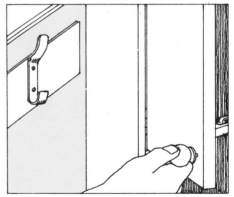

15 Finally, fix the coat hooks to the softwood batten, and screw the door knobs and magnetic catches to the doors.

PROJECTS
· STEP-BY-STEP ·

BEDHEAD UNIT

This bedhead is both attractive and practical: it is sturdy enough to lean against while reading in bed, is very easily fixed in place and takes only seconds to remove for redecoration. You can make it from blockboard veneered with a hardwood that matches the rest of the furniture in the bedroom, or you can use standard blockboard and paint it. To give the unit some style, decorative wood moulding is glued and pinned to the surface as framing.

- **Easily made from veneered blockboard**
- **Simply slots on to wall batten**
- **Easily removed for redecoration**
- **Can be made to match bedroom furniture**
- **Useful bedside compartments and shelves**

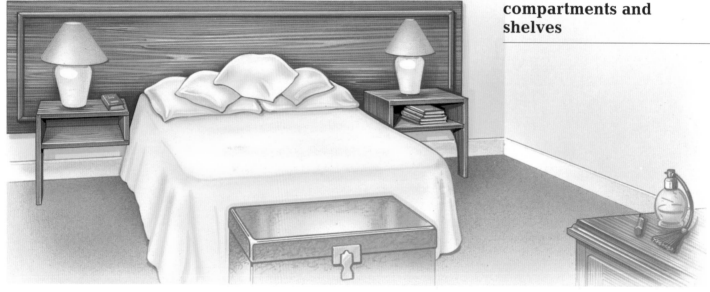

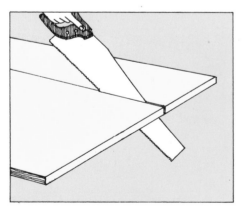

1 Make the headboard from veneered blockboard. Measure, mark, and cut it to suit the size of bed. The grain should run across bed width.

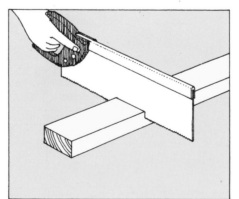

2 Cut the spacer rail at the top of the headboard from 50 x 25mm (2 x 1 in) hardwood timber to match the veneer of the blockboard.

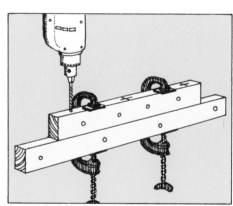

3 Cut a softwood support batten about 400mm (16 in) shorter than hardwood rail. Cramp edge-to-edge and drill three 8mm ($^5/_{16}$ in) holes. through both batten and rail.

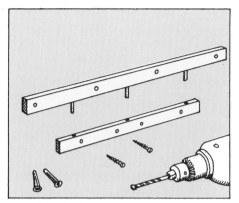

4 The holes go only halfway through hardwood rail. Glue 8mm ($^5/_{16}$ in) Dowels in holes in hardwood. Fix batten to wall with wall-plugs and screws.

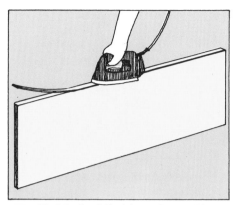

5 Finish the blockboard panel by ironing on edging strip. Trim flush with a block plane when completely cool.

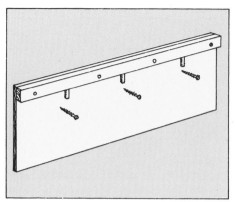

6 Glue and screw the hardwood rail to the rear of the headboard, flush with the top edge, with dowels pointing downwards. Cut a matching spacer batten for the bottom edge.

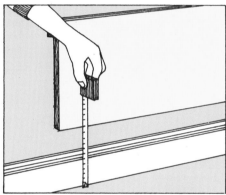

7 To fit the headboard, simply locate the dowels into holes in the support batten. Measure the height of bedside compartments.

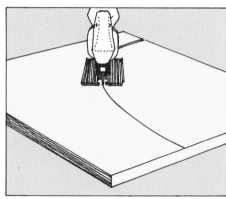

8 Cut blockboard for compartment pieces using a panel saw, and jigsaw for the curves. Trim edges with plane; apply edge veneer.

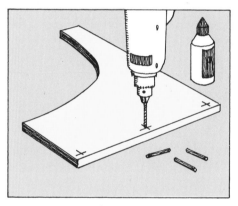

9 Use 8mm ($^5/_{16}$ in) dowels to join compartment components. Apply glue to edges and assemble the compartments; cramp together.

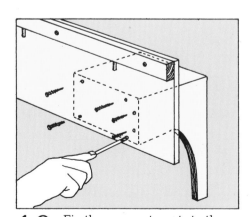

10 Fix the compartments to the headboard by drilling and screwing through from behind the headboard. Screw bottom spacer batten in position flush with bottom edge.

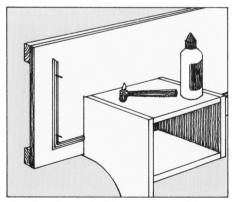

11 Cut suitable wood moulding, such as astragal or half-round, in a mitre box and fix to the headboard with glue and veneer pins.

12 Finish the headboard by sanding down, staining to a darker colour if required, and applying three coats of wood lacquer.

PROJECTS · STEP-BY-STEP ·

LOFT STORAGE

- **Easy and cheap to make**
- **Ideal for the storage of less frequently used items**
- **Adjustable shelves for big or small items**
- **Combine with flooring to make entire loft area usable**
- **Fit a loft ladder to make access easy**
- **Staggered units fit roof slope.**

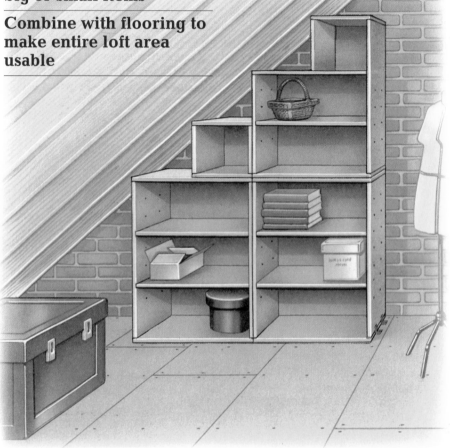

You can make use of loft storage space by installing a slide-away loft ladder and fitting a floor of chipboard sheets over the joists. Ceiling joists are not as strong as floor joists, so use the main loft floor area only for lightweight storage. Put heavier items on the storage units described here, and keep them to the sides of the loft.

For the floor use 2400 x 600mm (8 x 2 ft) sheets of 19mm ($^3/_4$ in) tongued and grooved chipboard and cut sheets in half lengthways so they will go through the loft hatch. Fix them to the joists with 50mm (2 in) countersunk screws and stagger the ends of the boards.

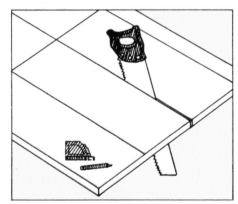

1 Make the basic rectangular shelf unit from 19mm ($^3/_4$ in) chipboard Cut the panels to give a maximum shelf width of 600mm (2 ft).

2 Cutting with a panel saw may produce rough edges, so smooth these with a block plane; work from the ends to the middle.

3 To produce an adjustable shelving system, drill two rows of 8mm ($^5/_{16}$ in) holes through the vertical panels, spaced 150mm (6 in) apart.

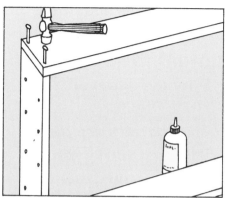

4 Assemble the main carcass of the unit in the loft by gluing and pinning the components using 50mm (2 in) oval nails.

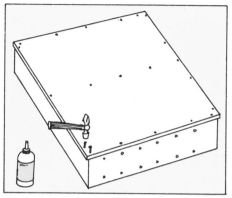

5 A rectangular back panel holds the unit square and rigid. Use hardboard, glued and pinned in place with 19mm ($^3/_4$ in) nails.

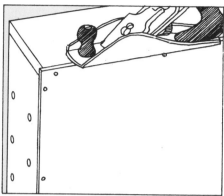

6 After the glue has set, trim the excess hardboard around the edges of the unit with a smoothing plane.

7 Use abrasive paper wrapped around a block of wood to remove sharp edges.

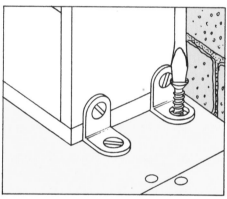

8 Fix the unit in position on the floor by screwing it down using metal angle brackets and chipboard screws.

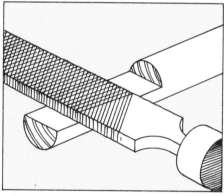

9 Cut the shelf supports from 50mm (2 in) long pieces of ramin (hardwood) dowels and file them flat on one side as shown.

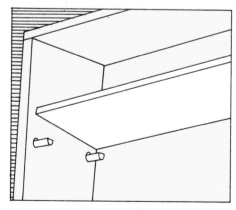

10 Leave 19mm ($^3/_4$ in) of each dowel round, to be inserted in the holes drilled in the vertical panels Rest shelving on dowels.

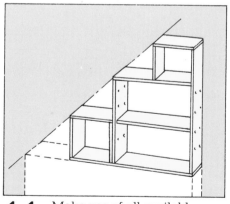

11 Make use of all available space by making small units to fit the slope under the rafters The method of construction is as above.

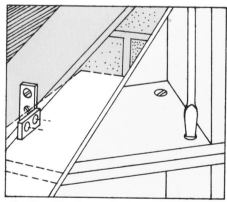

12 Fix the units to each other using 32mm ($1^1/_4$ in) screws. Fix to the rafters with metal L-plates bent through 90°.

FITTED WARDROBES

Probably the most important and effective job you will do in a house is to install fitted wardrobes in bedrooms. Although at a glance it may appear to be a mammoth undertaking it is actually a fairly straightforward exercise. As always with fitted furniture, there is the problem of uneven ceilings and out-of-true corners and floors to overcome, but this is done by first fixing a framework to the walls, using packing pieces of hardboard or plywood scraps to level out undulations, (see 'Techniques').

The advantage of this design, based around a typical situation of a chimney breast and two alcoves, is that the cupboards are constructed as a series of

- **Dimensions adaptable to suit any size**
- **Ample storage space**
- **Doors with panelled appearance**
- **Incorporates dressing table**
- **Can be varnished or painted**
- **Built around chimney breast**

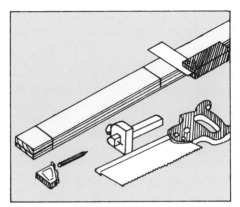

1 Cut to length 75 x 25mm (3 x 1 in) softwood for the fascia framework. Mark out T-halving and corner halving joints (see p. 149).

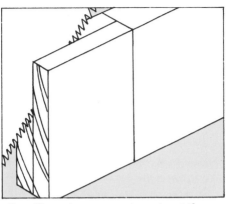

2 Use a tenon saw to cut out the halving joints at the ends of the framework rails.

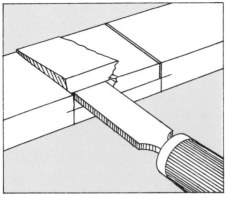

3 Cut down to the centre-line of the mid-rail joints with a tenon saw, then chop out the waste with a firmer chisel.

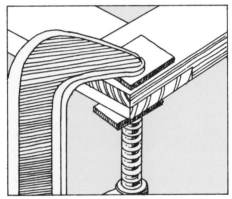

4 Use pva woodworking adhesive and cramps to complete the joints. Check with a try-square before final tightening.

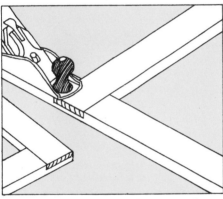

5 When the glue has set trim the joints neatly using a smoothing plane.

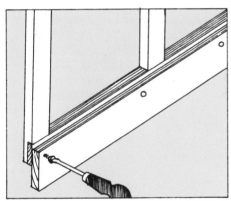

6 Mark out, then cut 150 x 25mm (6 x 1 in) softwood for the footboard. Screw it to rear of bottom frame member, 12mm ($\frac{1}{2}$ in) below the top edge.

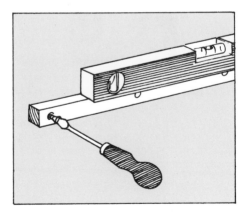

7 Cut 12mm ($\frac{1}{2}$ in) plywood shelves. Fix 25 x 25mm (1 x 1 in) battens to the wall using 63mm ($2\frac{1}{2}$ in) No 8 countersunk screws. Check battens are level.

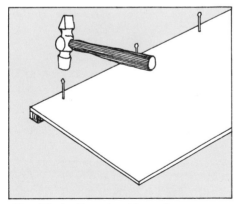

8 Fix battens to side and rear walls. Then fix the plywood to the battens with 30mm ($1\frac{1}{4}$ in) panel pins. Sink the heads below the surface with a nail punch.

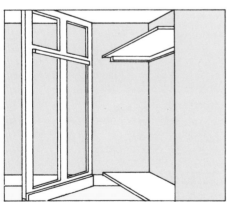

9 Fix a batten to the rear of the frame on the horizontal member. Offer frame into place. Pin top shelf to batten and lower shelf to footboard.

identical units, so you can have as many or as few as you want. An ideal width for the doors is 600mm (2 ft), although this might not prove to be convenient for the space you have available. You have to determine the number and width of the doors by measuring the distance from wall to wall and then calculating the number of same-size doors that will fit, allowing space for them to open.

The advantage of using 600mm (2 ft) doors is that you can cut them from a 1200mm (4 ft) sheet of blockboard without wastage. Although here we suggest blockboard, you could use purpose-made cupboard doors.

The central dressing table is not essential. If preferred you could simply have extra doors mounted on additional interior partitions. In this case you could dispense with the smaller upper doors and have floor-to-ceiling doors instead. This would reduce the work involved.

The interior arrangement is optional. Here we show hanging rails supported on proprietary brackets, but you could easily incorporate some shelves by adding an additional partition in each wardrobe section. Shelves can then be inserted using plastic joint blocks as supports. You can decorate the wall above the dressing table shelf with wallpaper to match the rest of the room, or you could fix mirror tiles as described on page 66.

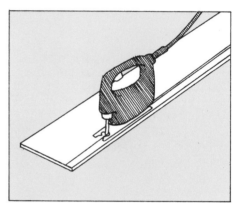

10 Cut out the top inner fascia board from 150 x 25mm (6 x 1 in) softwood.

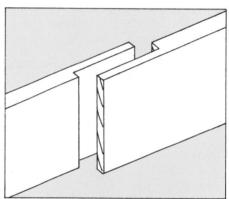

11 Depending on the length required for the fascia, you may have to join two pieces using a halving joint.

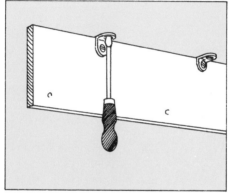

12 Screw angle brackets to rear of fascia board (with 18mm (^{3}/$_4$ in) No 6 screws). Then screw to ceiling with 50mm (2 in) No 8 screws and the appropriate fixings.

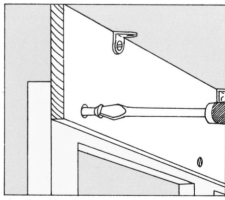

13 Fix the inner fascia board to the rear of the side frames using 37mm (1^1/$_2$ in) No 8 screws at 1200mm (4 ft) intervals.

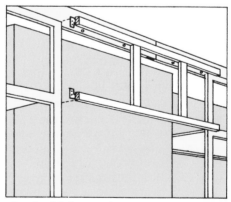

14 Make up the central cupboard frame from 75 x 25mm (3 x 1 in) softwood; fix it in between the side frames using brackets. Screw also to inner fascia.

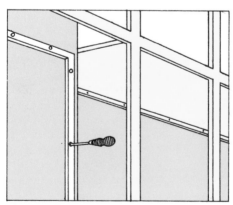

15 Fix 25mm x 25mm (1 x 1 in) battens to wall on chimney breast, with inner edges aligning with those of fascia.

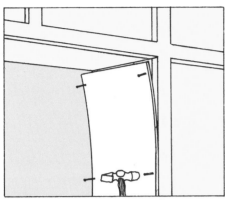

16 Cut and fix 18mm ($^3/_4$ in) blockboard to enclose each cupboard. Using 38mm (1$^1/_2$ in) panel pins, then side panels, fitting around skirting.

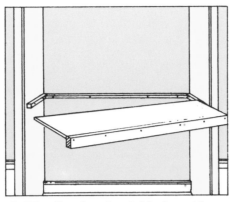

17 Cut dressing table from 18mm ($^3/_4$ in) blockboard. Fix 25 x 25mm (1 in) battens to sides of cupboards and rear wall. Fix 50 x 25mm (2 x 1 in) batten to front. Fix table in place.

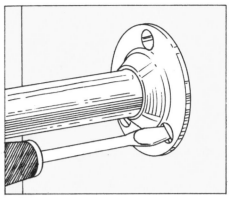

18 Fix chrome hanging rail brackets to the end wall and side of chimney breast. Slot the pole into one bracket before second one is fixed.

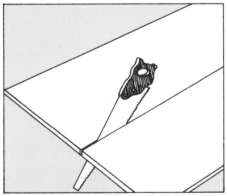

19 Cut 18mm ($^3/_4$ in) blockboard for the 600mm (2 ft) wide doors.

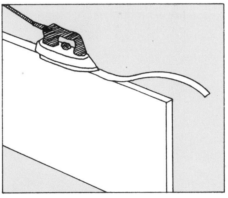

20 Trim all edges with a smoothing plane, then iron on edge veneer. Trim flush with a block plane when cool.

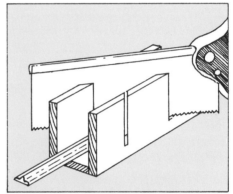

21 Cut and mitre astragal moulding with a tenon saw and mitre block.

22 Glue and pin moulding to the doors following pre-marked guidelines.

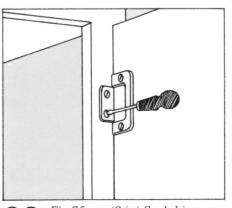

23 Fix 75mm (3 in) flush hinges to the doors – three per door – then fix the doors to the frame.

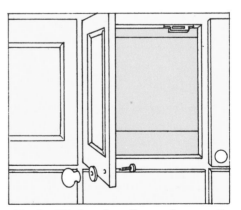

24 Fit door handles and magnetic catches. Sand down complete wardrobe for painting or varnishing.

BOXING PIPES

Nothing is more of an eyesore than pipework running down walls, in corners, or along skirting boards. Yet very little time, cost or effort is needed to box them in, and the carpentry skills involved are minimal. There are various ways you can fix the boxing-in. To cover pipes on the walls, we use steel angle plates to anchor the boards to the walls. To cover pipework at skirting-board level you fix 25 x 25mm (1 x 1 in) battens to the walls and floor, and screw the facing boards to them.

Boxing-in is not a feature in itself – it should be camouflaged by decorating it to match the walls. At skirting-board level you could take the floor-covering up and over the facing boards. However, this is not a good idea where access might be needed, as would certainly be the case where there is a stopcock on the pipes.

- **Easy to fix**
- **Hides an eyesore**
- **Can be camouflaged by decorating**
- **Effective on walls, in corners or along skirtings**

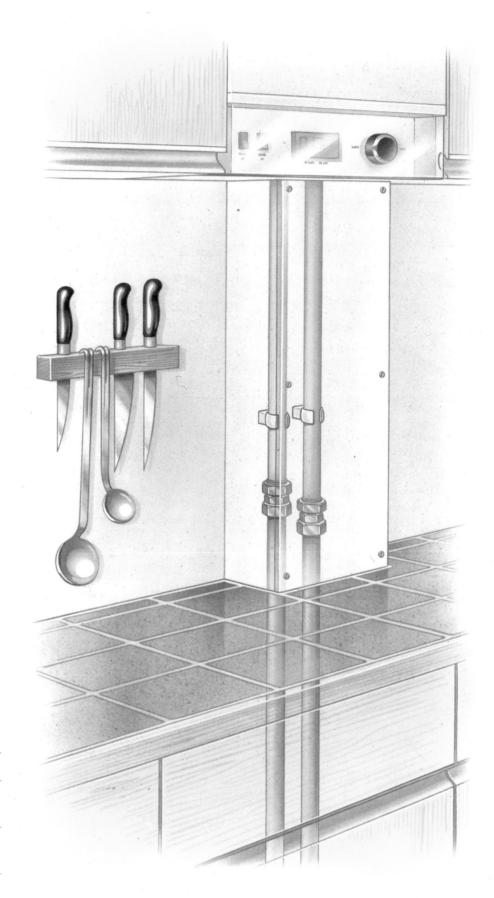

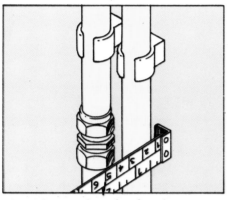

1 Measure how far the pipes project from the wall and cut side pieces from 25mm (1 in) thick board or softwood.

2 Use 12mm ($\frac{1}{2}$ in) screws to fix steel angle plates to the side pieces at 1m (3 ft) intervals.

3 Fix the plates to the wall using 37mm ($1\frac{1}{2}$ in) No 8 screws and the appropriate wallfixings.

4 Cut the front piece from 6mm ($\frac{1}{4}$ in) thick plywood.

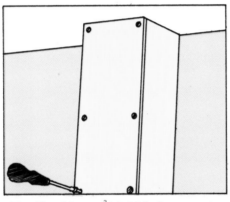

5 Use 19mm ($\frac{3}{4}$ in) No 6 screws to fix the front piece to the sides.

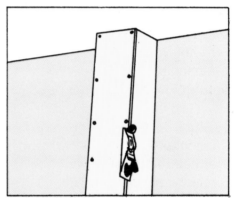

6 Trim the edges of the plywood flush with the sides using a plane.

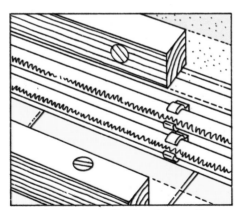

7 At skirtings fix 25 x 25mm (1 x 1 in) battens to the wall and floor using 37mm ($1\frac{1}{2}$ in) No 8 screws.

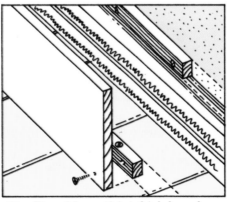

8 Fix a 25mm (1 in) thick board or softwood front piece using 25mm (1 in) No 8 screws. The top must be level with the wall batten.

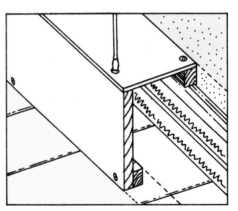

9 Finally fix 6mm ($\frac{1}{4}$ in) thick plywood to the wall batten and front piece using 19mm ($\frac{3}{4}$ in) No 6 screws. Trim plywood using a plane.

BLOCKING DOORWAY

Especially in larger, older properties, there may be a doorway that is not needed. Its presence can mean that otherwise useful wall and floor space is wasted. In a kitchen, for example, a run of wall cupboards may be interrrupted by a door.

Although the process of blocking a doorway is straightforward, creating a new doorway is a job that must be left to a professional, as you may have to add support to a loadbearing wall.

The skill in blocking a door is to ensure that afterwards you do not see its outline showing through the new decoration. It is important, therefore, to fix the timber framework and plasterboard as flush with the existing wall as possible. The join around the frame and wall should be filled carefully. If necessary, the plasterboard can be made flush with the wall using a coat of proprietary d-i-y plaster-skimming compound. Alternatively, you can cross-line the wall with lining paper (see Techniques) and finish with a thick, textured paper.

If you redecorate the wall on one or both sides of the opening with cladding or panelling, it will conceal evidence of an opening.

- **Helps re-shape a room**
- **Increases storage or living space**
- **Effective yet simple project**
- **Easy alternative to brickwork**
- **Requires accuracy rather than skill**

1 Remove the door from its hinges, then use a chisel to prise off the architraves and doorstop mouldings.

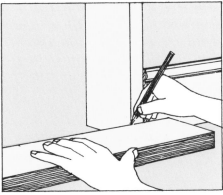

2 At the foot of the opening mark off the distance across the doorway on to a 25mm (1 in) thick batten of the same width as the frame. This is called a sole plate.

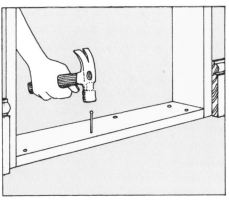

3 Cut the sole plate to length then nail to the floor flush with the front of the door frame.

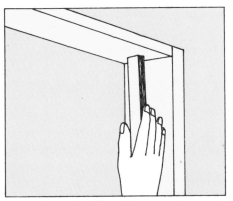

4 For each side of the opening, cut two 25 x 25mm (1 x 1 in) battens to the height of the frame.

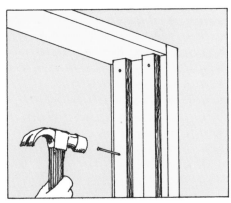

5 Nail the battens to the frame so that they are recessed from the edges of the frame by the thickness of the plasterboard – 12.7mm ($\frac{1}{2}$ in).

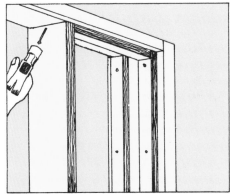

6 Skew nail a central support for the plasterboard to the head and sole plates. This should be 25mm (1 in) thick and 25mm (1 in) narrower than the sole plate, its width determined by the frame.

7 Fix twin battens – 25 x 25mm (1 x 1 in) – to the head and sole plates at each side of the central support and flush with the vertical battens.

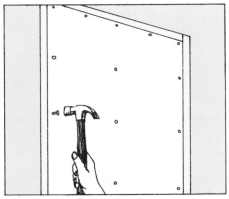

8 Cut the plasterboard to size and fix with plasterboard nails (grey side out if plastering) to the framework at 150mm (6 in) intervals.

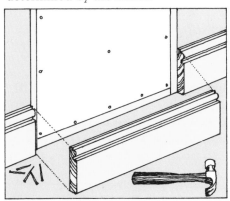

9 If you can obtain matching skirting board, cut a piece to length and nail in place. Fill the joins with wood filler. Alternatively, replace complete skirting.

KITCHEN TABLE

Although it is common in a modern kitchen to use worktops for food preparation, and breakfast bars for eating, many people prefer to have a traditional kitchen table where there is enough space for one.

The table shown here features two drawers and a plywood top. It is very straightforward to make from easily obtained materials – planed softwood and plywood.

By making it yourself, you have the great advantage of being able to ensure that the table exactly suits your particular requirements in terms of size and height.

TABLE HEIGHT

A common, but by no means standard height for table tops, is 760mm (30 in). For most people this is a good height for both sitting at and standing at, as will often be the case with a kitchen table used for food preparation.

If the table is going to be used by someone of above average height, it can be made higher, and if it is likely to be used mainly by people of shorter stature, it can be made lower.

- **Easily made from softwood.**

- **Money-saving two-layer plywood top.**

- **Features drawers at either end.**

- **Iron-on banding veneer hides plywood edge.**

- **Drawer fronts act as drawer stops.**

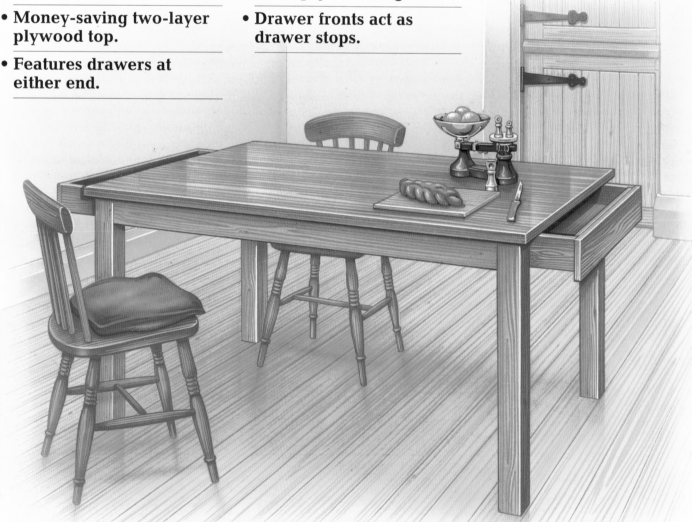

1 Use 75 x 75mm (3 x 3 in) planed softwood for the legs. Mark and cut to the length required: table height, less thickness of top.

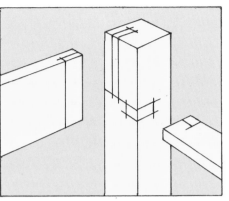

2 Mark out the joints in each leg for the cross braces (at the end of the table) and the side rails. Diagonally opposite legs will be alike.

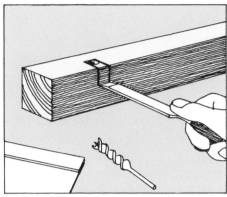

3 Cut a stopped housing for the cross brace by drilling to depth, cutting with a tenon saw (to width of brace) then chopping out to uniform depth with a firmer *chisel*.

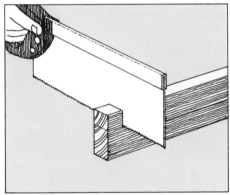

4 Cut the cross braces from 50 x 25mm (2 x 1 in) softwood allowing for the depth of the housing joint. Mark and cut haunch (notch).

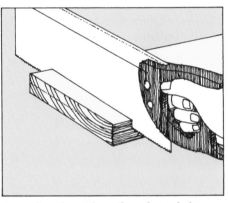

5 Cut the side rails to length from 100 x 25mm (4 x 1 in) planed softwood allowing for the depth of the joint. Mark and cut the offset tenon joint as shown.

6 Cut corresponding mortises (slots) in the legs. Bore a hole to width of the mortise at the end. Saw and chisel out the waste.

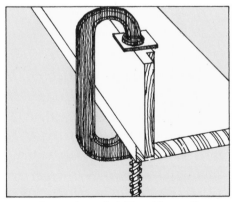

7 Cut to length 150 x 19mm (6 x ³/₄ in) planed softwood for the drawer runners. Glue to underside of rails. Hold with G-cramps.

8 When the glue has set, remove the cramps. Trim excess wood off the joint with a smoothing plane.

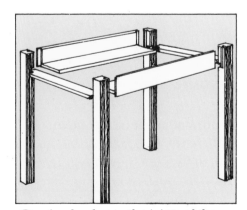

9 Apply glue to the joints of the table frame, then assemble it on a flat surface. Hold the assembly together with web cramps or rope.

However, in both cases, do not go to extremes if the table will also be used for dining.

The size of the top should suit the space available. If there will be chairs around the table, remember to allow extra room.

The sizes of timber chosen are intended for a table of modest proportions: approximately 1000 x 700mm (39 x 28 in). If you want a table much larger than this you should increase the sizes of timber proportionally.

THE DRAWERS

The drawer at each end is of simple box construction. The drawer runners are cut to fit between the legs along the length of the table. The wide bearing surface, supporting the drawer, spreads the load and keeps wear to a minimum. The runners are nailed and glued to the underside of the side rails and skew nailed to the cross rails (one nail at each end) to hold the top surfaces flush while the adhesive sets.

Each drawer consists of a butt-jointed framework with the base pinned to one edge. The false front is screwed and glued to one side of the framework. An offcut of wood loosely screwed to the back edge acts as a safety stop. In normal use it hangs down sufficiently to catch on the cross rail; to remove the drawer fully the stop must be held up. This type of drawer is simple to construct and gives the greatest internal depth. It may, however, require some effort to open and close if heavily loaded, for example with cutlery. If you have

this use in mind, the answer is to fit proprietary runners which roll on nylon bearings. In this case you would need to fit 25 x 25mm (1 x 1 in) supporting battens along the top of the timber runners, and the dimensions of the drawer would have to be adjusted to give the required clearances.

POSSIBLE MODIFICATIONS

If you are a competent woodworker, there are several ways in which you may wish to modify the design. For example, you could round the edges of the legs to smooth the sharp corners or you could taper the legs. In the latter case, increase the leg size to 100 x 100mm (4 x 4 in), so it can be tapered to 75 x 75mm (3 x 3 in) at the base.

METHOD OF ASSEMBLY

The suggested timber sizes and method of assembly are given in the diagrams and captions. The cross braces are joined to the legs with stopped housing joints. The housing, or slot, in the leg is cut out by boring, sawing with a tenon saw and then chiselling out the waste. To get the cross-brace to fit neatly into this housing, a haunch, or notch, has to be cut on the end of the rail. The length of the cross rails should be 50mm (2 in) longer than the distance between the legs. Each haunch is cut one third the width of the cross rail by 25mm (1 in) deep, and the leg housings are cut to accept the protruding portions.

The side rails fit into the legs by offset mortise and tenon joints. The offset tenon is cut on

the end of the rail, and the mortise, or slot, for this tenon is cut in the top of the leg. To cut the mortise, you bore a hole to the width of the tenon in the end of the mortise, then saw down each side of the mortise with a tenon saw and chisel out waste.

When all the joints have been cut, assemble the table frame on a flat surface. While the glue is setting, hold the frame tight and square with sash cramps (which can be hired), or a *web cramp*, which comprises seat-belt-type straps with a buckle fastening that can be drawn tight. Alternatively, loop rope or cord around the frame and then tighten it by twisting a stick round and round through it. This is also called a *Spanish windlass*.

The table top is cut from a sheet of 19mm ($^3/_4$ in) plywood, to overlap the table frame by about 12mm ($^1/_2$ in) all round. The corners should be rounded slightly, to help them withstand knocks and to reduce the risk of injury, especially to children.

The top is attached to the table frame with slotted angle brackets. The slotted portion (fixed to the top) allows for the natural expansion and contraction of the table with changing humidity. Slotted brackets are necessary with solid timber tops in which the amount of movement is greater than in plywood.

To finish the table, rub down all surfaces with abrasive paper and then apply three coats of clear lacquer to the frame, and four coats to the top, which will take more wear and tear.

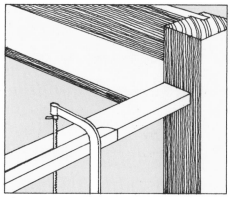

10 To avoid the need for drawer handles, cut a finger recess about 12mm ($\frac{1}{2}$ in) deep in the centre of each cross brace using a coping saw. Smooth with glasspaper wrapped round a cork block

11 Mark out the top squarely on a sheet of 19mm ($\frac{1}{2}$ in) plywood. Cut with a panel saw and plane the edges. Smooth with glasspaper.

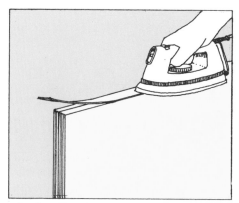

12 Finish the edges of the top by ironing on edge veneer. Allow to cool completely and trim flush with a block plane. Take off sharp corners with glasspaper.

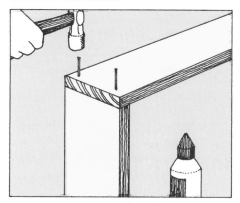

13 Cut 100 x 12mm (4 x $\frac{1}{2}$ in) planed softwood for the drawer frames. Plane 5mm ($\frac{1}{4}$ in) off width, and glue and pin together. Back and front fit between sides.

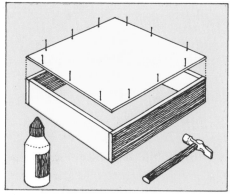

14 For drawer bottoms cut panels of 4mm ($\frac{3}{16}$ in) plywood about 2mm ($\frac{1}{16}$ in) oversize. Glue and pin to frame. Trim back edges with smoothing plane when glue has set.

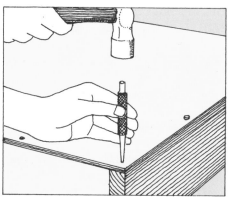

15 Punch all nail heads below the surface. Smooth base with glasspaper and apply wax polish to it and the drawer runners.

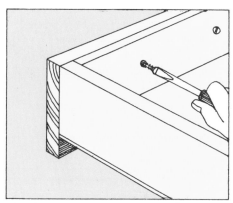

16 Cut 125 x 19mm (5 x $\frac{3}{4}$ in) planed softwood for the drawer fronts. Glue and screw to the drawer frame from the inside.

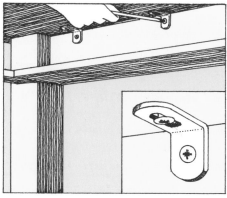

17 Slotted steel angle brackets allow for slight movement of the top. First screw through slot into top, then screw to side rails.

18 Sand down all surfaces first with medium, then with fine abrasive paper. Apply three coats of clear lacquer to frame (four to top).

BOOKCASE

Most homes have a collection of books to store and display. Open shelves are one solution, but if you have an attractive selection to present, then the best possible way is a quality bookcase. This piece of furniture is a simple yet robust construction using dowel joints for the main carcass and halving joints for the door frames. It is readily adaptable in size. If you have a special collection of books in mind – for example, a set of encyclopaedias – you can tailor the height and width of the bookcase to the precise dimensions of the volumes.

You don't have to build the complete unit; if space is at a premium, you can construct just half. On the other hand, you can build separate twin units and stand them in the bays on either side of a chimney breast.

Should you have no particular thoughts about size and you have a random collection of book shapes and sizes, the adjustable shelf system will appeal enormously. A series of holes drilled at 75mm (3 in) intervals in the sides of the unit allow the shelf supports to be moved up or down to accommodate any books purchased in the future. The overall size of the unit is 1050mm

(3 ft 6 in) high, 1500mm (5 ft) wide and 300mm (1 ft) deep.

Use 18mm (¾ in) hardwood-veneered blockboard or, if you prefer, white-finished blockboard for both the carcass and the frame. The central partition requires a double thickness so that the hinge screws can be fitted on either side. The doors can be glazed with a smoked glass, which gives an extra element of sophistication, or with plain glass.

You do not need to cut any intricate rebates in order to make glazed doors. The frame leaves a plain rectangular opening and you can order your glass to this size less a fraction to give a snug fit. Mitred quadrant moulding retains the glass in front, and butt-jointed square stripwood from behind. The latter allows easy replacement of the glass in the event of breakage.

To finish off the unit, rub it down smoothly with medium grade glasspaper before applying a wood stain followed

- **Attractive high quality appearance**

- **Can be tailored to any dimensions**

- **Fully adjustable shelving system**

- **Dowel joints used for strong construction**

- **Brass furniture for visual appeal**

- **Easy to construct glazed doors**

by coats of lacquer.

Brass door furniture – hinges and handles – complete the effect.

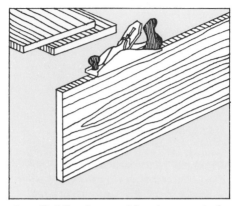

1 Cut the frame sides, two central partitions, base and top from 18mm ($^3/_4$ in) veneered blockboard. The top is 18mm ($^3/_4$ in) deeper than sides.

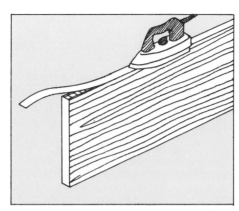

2 Iron-on matching veneer to all edges that will be exposed. Trim excess with smoothing plane when cool.

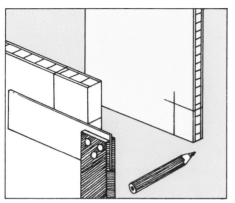

3 On the two sides at the bottom front corner mark out an L shape 50mm (2 in) deep and high. Use a try square for accuracy.

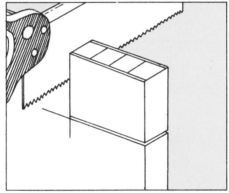

4 Cut out the L shape carefully with a tenon saw and apply iron-on edge veneer.

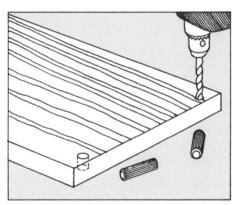

5 Mark out positions of all dowel joints, then drill holes 9mm ($^3/_8$ in) deep.

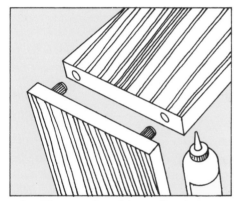

6 Use woodworking adhesive to assemble the cabinet. Check that the corners are square and allow joints to dry.

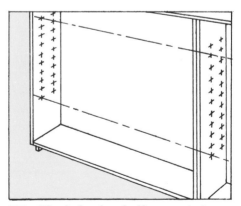

7 The holes for shelf supports in side pieces must be exactly aligned. A drilling template, made from 50 x 25mm (2 x 1 in) batten, ensures accuracy.

8 Mark out the hole positions on the batten and label the top. Drill the recommended size of holes for the shelf support studs right through the batten.

9 Clamp template, correct way up and with bottom on base of bookcase, to side panel. Drill through each hole using depth stop set to recommended depth.

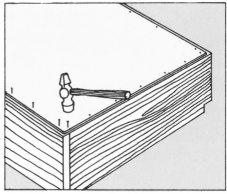

10 Cut out 6mm ($^1/_4$ in) plywood for the back. Glue and pin to the back, leaving it 9mm ($^3/_8$ in) short of all edges.

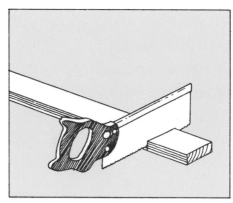

11 Cut out 50 x 25mm (2 x 1 in) hardwood for the plinth and fascia using a tenon saw.

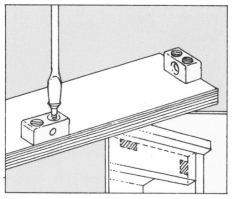

12 Use joint blocks to secure the fascia board to the top and sides, flush with the front edge of the sides.

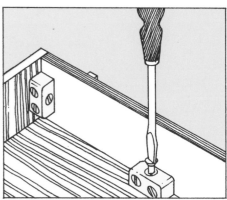

13 The plinth is also fitted with joint blocks. Here the cabinet is seen from its underside.

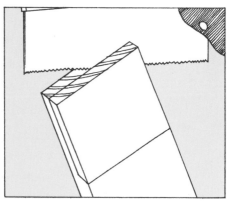

14 Cut corner halving joints for door frames. Overlap adjoining pieces and mark width of overlap on each. Cut half the depth of wood to the mark with tenon saw.

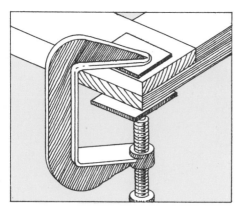

15 Use woodworking adhesive and cramps to assemble the doors. Leave to dry.

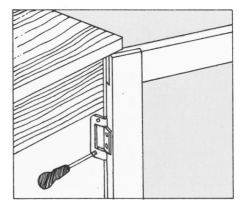

16 Fit 75mm (3 in) brass flush hinges to the doors, and fit the doors to the cabinet.

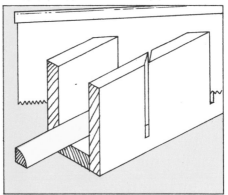

17 Have 4mm ($^3/_{16}$ in) thick glass cut to fit inside each door frame. Cut 9mm ($^3/_8$ in) quadrant moulding or glass bead to length using mitre box and tenon saw.

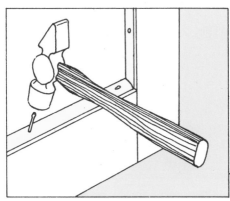

18 Pin the moulding to the front of the frame with 25mm (1 in) veneer pins.

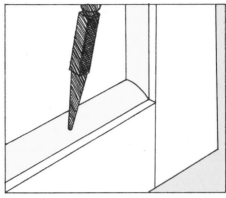

19 Use a punch to tap pinheads below surface. Fill with matching wood stopping.

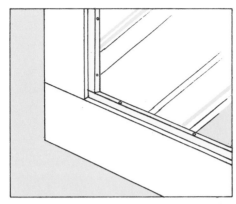

20 Retain the glass from behind with 9mm ($^3/_8$ in) square beading, cut square-ended. Pin the top and bottom lengths in position first, then fit the verticals between them.

21 Sand down the cabinet and stain to match the hardwood fascia and plinth. Apply three coats of wood lacquer.

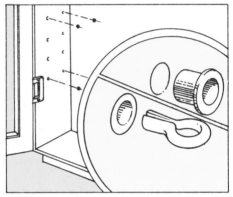

22 Tap a brass socket into each shelf support hole, using scrap timber to prevent damage. Insert shelf studs at the required height.

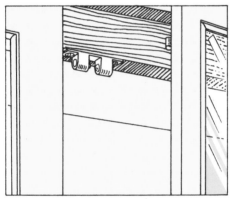

23 Fit double ball catches to secure each pair of doors. The catch body is screwed to the lower edge of the fascia.

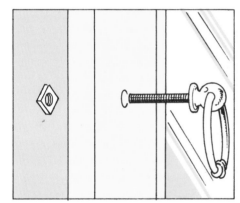

24 Fit brass drop handles by drilling hole through each door. Cut off surplus thread with a hacksaw after fitting and file smooth.

PROJECTS
STEP-BY-STEP

UNDER-BED STORAGE

In most houses there is a shortage of storage space, yet in many cases there is wasted space under the beds. Many divans are raised off the ground on legs about 175mm (9 in) tall, creating an ideal space to use for storage.

There is no need to alter or modify the bed. The storage unit is simply a drawer on castors that slides under the bed. The castors, should be non-swivelling; the shallower they are, the greater the storage depth.

Most beds that are suitable for this type of adaptation have six legs, and the drawer unit is made to a size that will slide between two pairs of legs. The drawer front should protrude at the sides so that when 'parked', it rests against the legs, which act as a drawer stop. The drawer unit for a single bed should be of such a length that when it is in the 'parked' position, with the front resting against the legs, the back is level with the legs on the other side For wider beds, it is better to make drawer units half the width of the bed to fit under each side.

The best material to make the drawer from is 18mm ($^3/_4$ in) blockboard, with 12mm ($^1/_2$ in) plywood for the drawer base.

- **Very easy to make**
- **Drawer units slide on castors**
- **No need to alter or modify the bed**

- **Ideal for blanket storage**
- **Made from blockboard and plywood**
- **Drawer front ensures unit 'parks' neatly against legs**

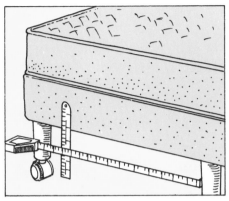

1 Measure the distance between the divan bed legs and between the base of the bed and the floor to enable you to work out drawer size.

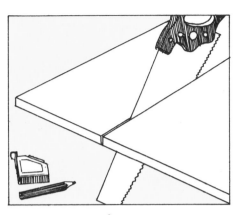

2 Use 18mm ($^3/_4$ in) blockboard for drawer frame, which should be not quite as deep as bed width. Mark and cut out the components.

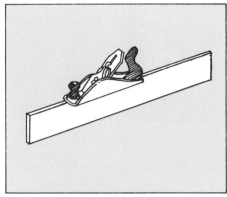

3 Cut slightly to the outside of the cutting lines and then use a plane to smooth the edges back to these lines.

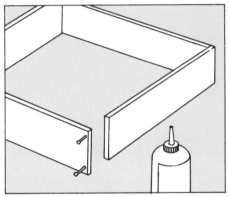

4 Assemble the drawer frame, gluing and pinning the corners, and holding the frame together with a *web cramp* or *Spanish windlass*.

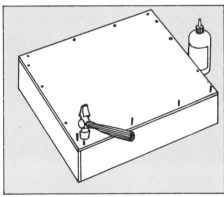

5 The drawer bottom needs to be substantial. Make it from 12mm ($^1/_2$ in) plywood. Mark and cut out so it is square. Glue and pin it in place.

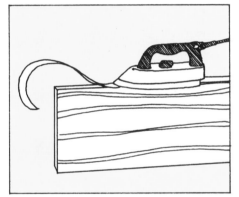

6 Mark a piece of blockboard for the drawer front. Cut it out and plane the edges true. Apply iron-on edge banding veneer.

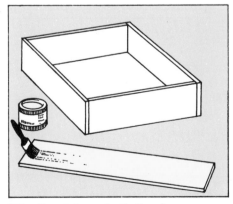

7 Sand down both the drawer unit and the front. Stain if a darker finish is required. Apply three coats of wood lacquer.

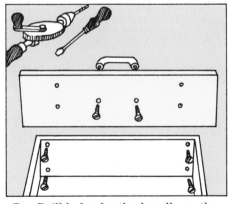

8 Drill holes for the handle on the drawer front. Fix the handle in place. From inside the drawer, screw the front to drawer unit.

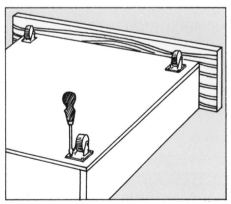

9 Complete the job by screwing four castors or rollers to the underside of the drawer unit, fixing them as close to the corners as possible.

PROJECTS
· STEP-BY-STEP ·

CONCEALED PLUMBING

There's nothing visually appealing about the pipework, pedestals and cisterns seen in a bathroom. That is why this project would benefit any home. Not only does it conceal plumbing, but it also gives a room a fully fitted look.

The L-shape formation of basin and toilet shown here is a classic bathroom arrangement. The instructions for constructing the framework are readily adaptable to any layout.

The uprights of the framework are of 50 x 50mm (2 x 2 in) softwood. This, combined with the 50 x 25mm (2 x 1 in) horizontal members, ensures a really solid base for the cladding.

Although pins and glue provide a perfectly sound joining method, increased strength is gained by using halving joints. The framework is screwed to both the wall and floor.

Full instructions for working with tongued-and-grooved cladding are given on page 66. Here it is worth reminding you that you must leave the cladding in the bathroom for a week before you use it so that it will become conditioned to the moisture content of the room. If you take it into the room and fix it immediately, there is a strong risk of it warping later – in bathrooms and kitchens, this risk is greater than in other rooms.

It is also important to seal the cladding thoroughly to keep out moisture afterwards, and we

- **Hides all plumbing pipework**
- **Adaptable construction for any situation**
- **Provides extra storage space**

- **Full access to all plumbing**
- **Gives room fully fitted appearance**
- **Cladding can be fixed vertically or horizontally**

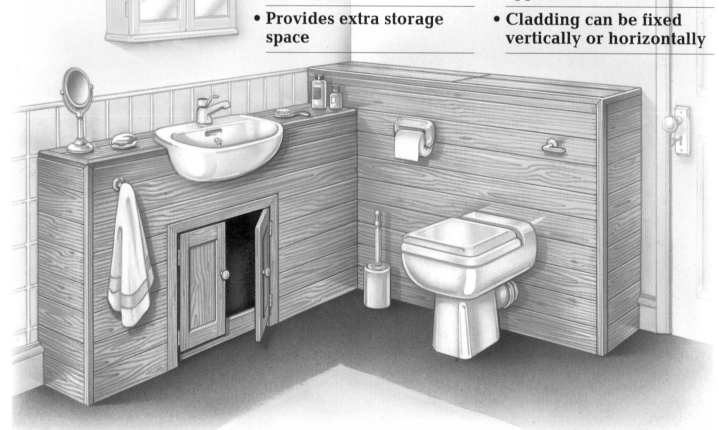

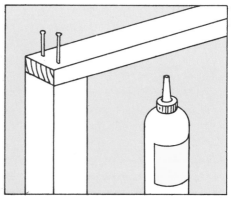

1 Measure and cut 50 x 25mm (2 x 1 in) and 50 x 50mm (2 x 2 in) softwood for framework. Join with pva woodworking adhesive and panel pins.

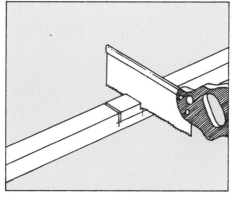

2 A stronger construction is made by cutting rebate joints. Use a tenon saw to cut down half the depth of the wood.

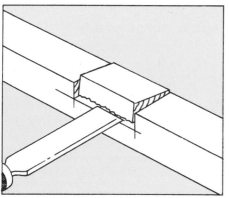

3 Chop out joint with a firmer chisel.

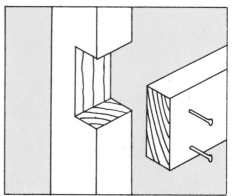

4 Use pva woodworking adhesive and 38mm (1½ in) panel pins to secure the joint.

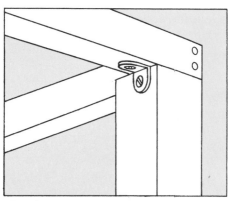

5 An easy way to make a join where three timbers meet is to use angle brackets.

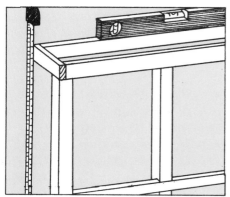

6 Mark out the position of the framework on the wall. Use a spirit level to find true horizontal and vertical.

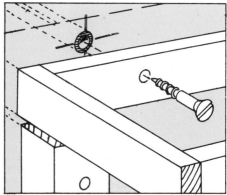

7 Fix framework to wall using 75mm (3 in) No 8 screws at 900mm (3 ft) intervals. Screw corner uprights direct to wall.

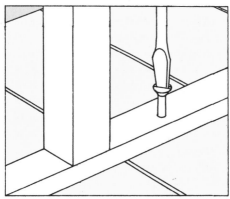

8 Screw the framework to the floor using 38mm (1½ in) No 8 screws at 900mm (3 ft) intervals.

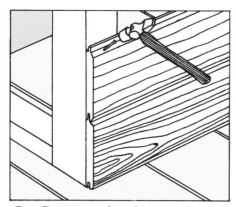

9 Cut tongued-and-grooved cladding to length. Fix by gluing and pinning through tongues (see p. 38). Leave opening under basin for doors.

recommend you use four coats of lacquer for this purpose.

The cladding is shown here being fixed horizontally, but you could equally well fix it vertically by adding a second horizontal 50 x 25mm (2 x 1 in) batten to the framework. Fix the two horizontal battens at equal distances between the top and bottom horizontal members.

Access to the plumbing is vital, of course, so here a door is built in to the front of the cladding to leave access to the pipes and basin hot- and cold-water stop-cocks. The toilet cistern is reached by removing the top, which is fixed with screws.

You could make a similar removable access point for the front of the basin, but making doors here enables you to use this invaluable storage space for cleaning utensils and household items.

The easiest time to install this construction is when a bathroom is being refitted. However, with careful measuring and cutting, it is not a great problem to cut out around existing pedestals and pipe outlets.

Apart from tongued-and-grooved cladding there are many other ways to cover the basic framework. You could, for example, use a system similar to the bath panel (p. 122), where plywood decorated with moulding is used to give a panelled look. You could also fit 18mm ($^3/_4$ in) plywood as a base for ceramic tiling. Even straightforward painting or varnishing over plywood is a possibility.

As can be seen in the final drawing, the system is readily adaptable to a straight run of appliances.

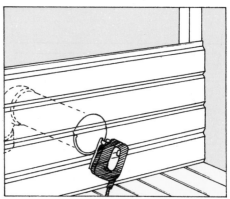

10 Mark out circle in panelling for the toilet waste outlet pipes. Drill a 10mm ($^3/_8$ in) diameter pilot hole and cut the opening with a jigsaw.

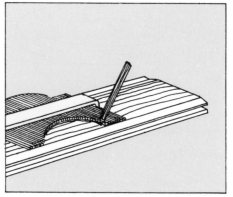

11 If the toilet is already connected, use profile gauge to trace outline of waste outlet pipe on to the cladding and cut out before fixing it to framework.

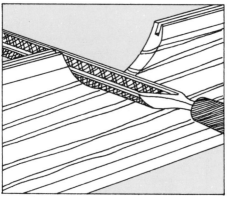

12 If necessary, trim the hole with a curved Surform. Use the same process for dealing with water inlet pipe.

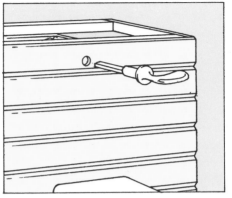

13 If the cistern is already in position, remove handle. Mark and drill a hole for the handle, using an auger bit in a swingbrace. Refit handle.

14 At the top, trim the cladding level with the framework using a smoothing plane.

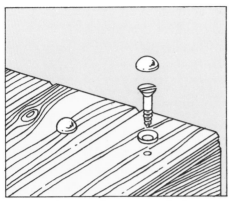

15 Secure the top panel above the cistern with screws fitted with cover caps.

16 At external corners fit L-shaped beading with adhesive and 25mm (1 in) panel pins.

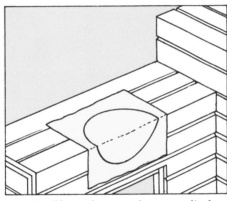

17 Place the template supplied with the basin in position and staple or glue in place. Scribe the outline, then cut out with a jigsaw.

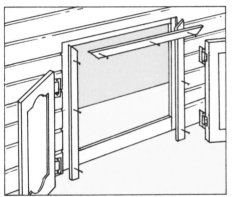

18 Fix mitred 50 x 12mm (2 x $\frac{1}{2}$ in) softwood to inner frame of opening. Add 75 x 25mm (3 x 1 in) softwood as footboard. Hang doors with 50mm (2 in) flush hinges. Allow 50mm (2 in) floor clearance.

19 Apply four coats of wood lacquer to the cladding.

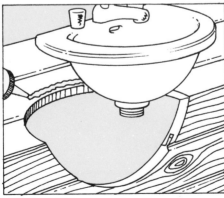

20 Fit basin on to silicone sealer at edge, then plumb in.

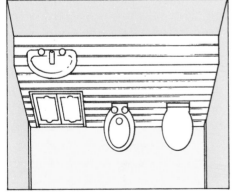

21 Use the same system of construction to incorporate a straight run of appliances.

ROOM DIVIDER

An extra room is always desirable, but it is not always possible to build an addition. A large room can be divided and the usual method is to erect a stud partition using timber framework and battening. This is not an enormous building job, but it entails including a door, perhaps adding a radiator and may be having to arrange window light which complicate the work and add greatly to the cost.

An alternative is to build a room divider such as the one shown here. This is ideal if you want to separate a dining area from a lounge. Since it is not a solid unit, the see-through effect means that it can be used even where space is limited. Ornaments and photographs on the shelves create sufficient screening without giving a claustrophic atmosphere.

The same system can be used to divide a children's bedroom so that each child has his or her own 'room' in effect.

This design is completely flexible, so that you can have as many partitions as you like and the distance between them is optional.

Use 25mm (1 in) m.d.f. for the partitions. The shelves can be of a thinner m.d.f. or glass.

- **Makes two 'rooms' from one**
- **Provides flexible living space**
- **Suitable for large or small rooms**
- **Ideal for children's bedrooms**
- **Adaptable design**
- **Requires simple skills**

1 Measure height of ceiling and cut partitions from 25mm thick m.d.f. Any width from 300mm (1 ft) is suitable.

2 Cut 50 x 25mm (2 x 1 in) softwood for foot and head *locaters*. The dimensions will be dictated by the partition width.

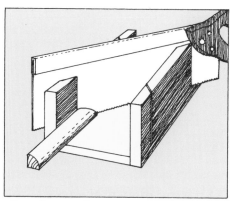

3 Cut quadrant moulding to length to fit on locaters. Use a tenon saw and mitre box to mitre the ends.

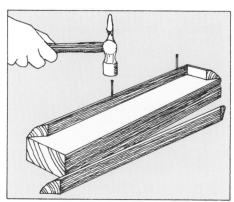

4 Glue and pin the moulding to the locater on three sides. Use 37mm (1½ in) panel pins. Sink heads below surface with a nail punch, then fill in.

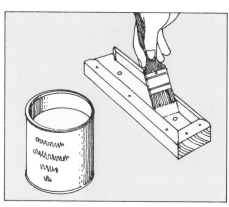

5 Paint or varnish the locaters.

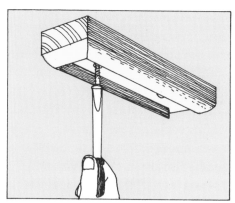

6 Screw the locaters to the ceiling joists using 75mm (3 in) No 8 screws – two to each locater.

7 Position locater on the floor. Temporarily insert a partition and use a spirit level to check for vertical. Screw locaters to floor using 75mm (3 in) No 8 screws.

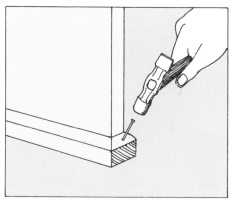

8 Slide partition into locaters and add the remaining piece of quadrant top and bottom.

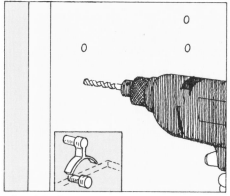

9 Mark out holes for shelf supports, drill partition then insert supports and rest shelves in place. Screw shelves to supports. Glass shelves should be retained with clips.

COFFEE TABLE

- **Combined table and magazine rack**
- **Straightforward assembly**
- **Sturdy framework**
- **Hidden dowel joint construction**
- **Make to any size required**
- **Finish with clear lacquer or paint**

If it is carefully made to ensure neat joints, this coffee table will be a very desirable piece of furniture.

Like any piece of furniture you make yourself, a great advantage of this table is that you can construct it to exactly the size required. A good size for a coffee table is about 600mm (24 in) wide, 750mm (30 in) long, and 450mm (18 in) high. You can reduce or increase these dimensions according to the floor space you have available.

Another influence on the size of table is the availability of 12mm ($\frac{1}{2}$ in) thick plywood for the top. Small panels, say about 900 x 600mm (36 x 24 in), should be available from your timber merchant or DIY store, which will save you having to buy an expensive, full size 2440 x 1220mm (8 x 4 ft) board. If you will be giving the table a clear finish, you may consider buying a veneered plywood top rather than using the ordinary birch plywood, which is more suitable for a paint finish.

The lower base assembly is made using 10mm ($\frac{3}{8}$ in) hardwood dowel rails as a rack for newspapers and magazines. If preferred, you could fit a sheet of safety glass over the dowels.

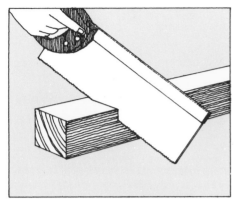

1 Mark and cut to length 50 x 50mm (2 x 2 in) planed softwood for end frames. Use a try square to ensure cutting lines are square.

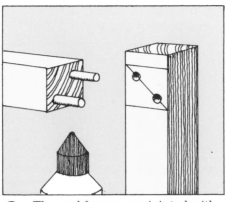

2 The end frames are jointed with hardwood dowels. Mark and drill dowel holes, then glue and assemble.

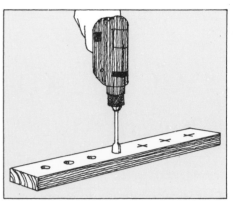

3 Measure and cut 50 x 25mm (2 x 1 in) softwood for side rails. Drill a series of 10mm ($^3/_8$ in) holes 50mm (2 in) apart in lower rails for magazine rack.

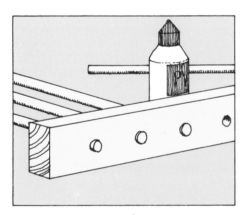

4 Cut the 10mm ($^3/_8$ in) dowels to length and glue into position in the lower rails. Check the rails are parallel and place on a flat surface.

5 To get a neat finish, use a plane to trim the dowel ends flush with the surface of the side rails after the glue has hardened.

6 Make the top from 12mm ($^1/_2$ in) thick plywood. Cut this out carefully, plane edges, and glue and pin upper side rails to long edges.

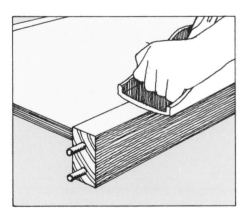

7 To get a neat, flush finish between the top and the upper side rails, after the glue has set, the tops of the rails are planed down.

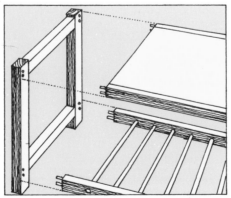

8 The rails of the top and lower assemblies are joined to the end frame with the dowel joints. Glue and assemble these units.

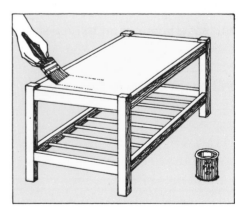

9 Carefully rub down with abrasive paper to remove sharp edges and leave a smooth surface. Apply three coats of wood lacquer.

OVERHEAD STORAGE

In most houses there is often a shortage of storage space. In older houses in particular, where ceilings are usually much higher than they are in newer homes, it is important not to forget the often wasted space above your head. As we show here, this area can be put to good use for long-term storage.

This storage unit can be built almost anywhere there are two facing walls not too far apart, and where the ceiling is fairly high. You can often find a suitable place for such a cupboard in a bedroom just above the door *architrave* or on an upstairs landing. If the walls are farther apart than shown, build a double width unit.

This project uses blockboard hinged doors mounted on a softwood frame, with a blockboard cupboard base finished off neatly on the underside with a sheet of plywood.

The design is enhanced by giving the doors a panelled effect using strips of decorative wood moulding, which are mitre-joined in the corners, like picture frames, and glued and pinned to the door surface. The cupboard will look best if it is decorated to blend in with the room. The

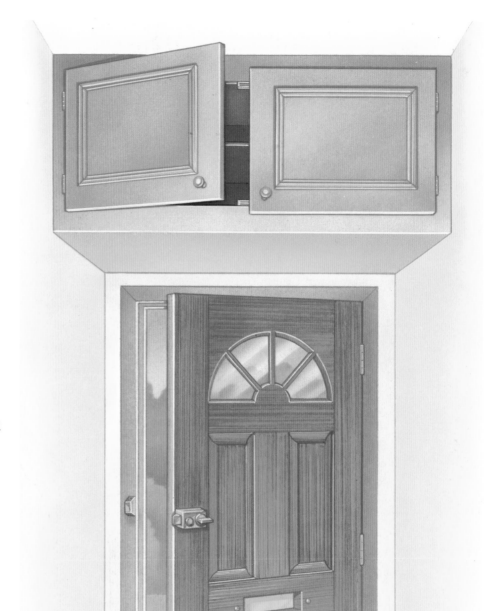

- **Useful storage cupboard for 'wasted' space**
- **Ideal for older houses with high ceilings**
- **Easily blended into room décor scheme**
- **Made from softwood, blockboard and plywood**
- **Blockboard doors have attractive panelled effect**
- **Fits between side walls**

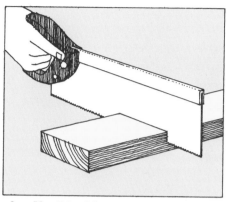

1 Use 75 x 25mm (3 x 1 in) planed softwood for the front frame. Measure the space and mark and cut the timber to sizes required.

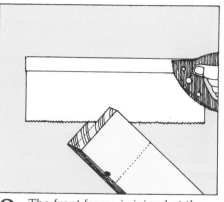

2 The front frame is joined at the corners with halving joints. Carefully mark these and cut them out with a tenon saw.

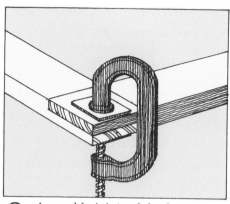

3 Assemble joints of the frame and check all are square. Apply woodworking glue and hold with G-cramps.

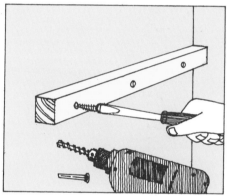

4 Cut 50 x 25mm (2 x 1 in) battens to the depth of the cupboard to support the shelf and base. Drill wall; insert wall-plugs and screw in battens.

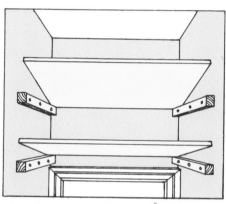

5 Cut sheets of 18mm ($^3/_4$ in) blockboard for the shelf base of the cupboard and glue and pin on top of the support battens.

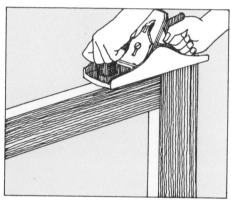

6 Trim edges of the frame until it fits neatly into the space, with the bottom edge flush with the underside of the lower battens.

7 Screw steel angle brackets flush with the top and sides of the frame and secure to the walls and ceiling using the appropriate fixings.

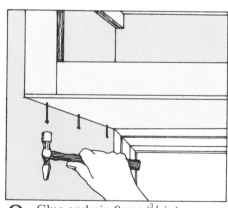

8 Glue and pin 9mm ($^3/_8$ in) plywood sheet to underside of the frame and lower battens. A rear batten will also be required if the back edge does not rest on the architrave.

9 Measure the front frame less 38mm ($1^1/_2$ in) all round and cut 18mm ($^3/_4$ in) blockboard for the doors. Plane the edges and apply iron-on edging veneer.

underside can be painted or papered to match the ceiling, and the central part of the door panels can be papered or painted to match the walls.

Inside, the cupboard can be finished with wood lacquer or painted in white or a light-coloured emulsion to reflect as much light as possible.

KEEPING ALL SQUARE
It is unlikely that the space between the walls where the cupboard will be built will be perfectly square. Therefore the first step is to make sure the front frame is square so that the doors will hang properly. Make this frame slightly oversize so that you can trim it to an exact fit after assembly.

Make sure the front frame, when fitted, is exactly vertical, and that the battens that support the cupboard base and underside panel are firmly fixed and perfectly horizontal.

The front frame is securely jointed at the corners by making halving joints. Mark the mid-point of the edge of the wood with a marking gauge, and then using a tenon saw, cut away half the thickness of the wood from each side. Glue the joint and hold together temporarily with a G-cramp while the glue is setting.

SAFETY NOTE
The door over which the unit is built should be lockable to prevent accidents when using the cupboards.

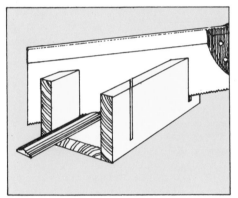

10 Use a suitable wood moulding, such as the astragal, to give a panelled effect. Mark this moulding to length and mitre cut the ends.

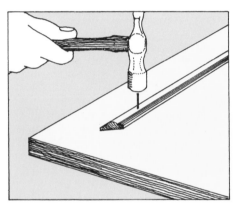

11 Glue and pin the lengths of moulding to the fronts of the doors. Make sure corners are tight and they are fixed parallel with edges.

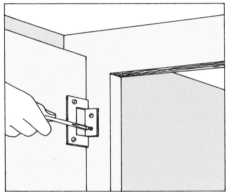

12 Flush hinges are the easiest type to use to fit the doors to the front frame. Fit the hinges to doors first, then hang doors on frame.

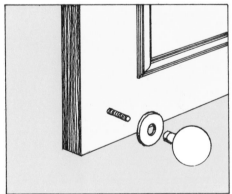

13 Fit the handles in the lower inside corners of the doors so they are easy to reach. Hold scrap wood behind door when drilling hole.

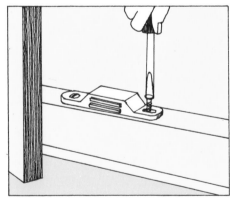

14 Magnetic catches are the easiest type to fit to hold doors closed. Fit the magnet part to frame and metal plate to door.

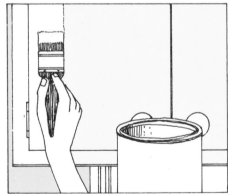

15 Finish the cupboard as required. The exterior is best sanded smooth, filled with fine surface filler, then painted.

BATHROOM CABINET

Every household is different when it comes to the number, size and shape of the toiletries kept in a bathroom. Ideally, you should be able to store everything you need in a cabinet, but too often those you can buy are not suited to your exact needs. This cabinet will solve nearly everyone's bathroom storage problem. It incorporates separate cabinets at either end with a shelf below on which a selection of items can be kept – probably those that are attractive or perhaps have ornamental appeal. This extra shelf can be increased in depth if you wish by increasing the depth of the sides. You could even add an extra shelf if you have a lot of items you would like to display.

The shelves inside the cabinets rest on shelf supports pushed into holes drilled in the sides. Additional or 'spare' holes allow for shelf height and spaces to be altered as and when required. The mirror and glass can be obtained cut to size from a local glazier – ask him to polish all the edges, not just the front one. You will need to take them out for occasional cleaning, so you don't want to be handling sharp edges.

In the middle section there is

shaped shelf. This is partly for decorative reasons, but primarily because the mirror is intended to pivot forward for applying make-up, shaving and so on. A full-depth shelf would encourage items to be left there, and they would always have to be removed to allow the mirror its full movement. The pivot brackets for the mirror are readily available from hardware stores and simply screw into place. To enable the mirror to be lifted into place it must be 30mm (1¼ in) shorter than the back of the cabinet. The gap at the top will be concealed by the

striplight at the front.

A striplight is especially useful if the cabinet is not situated on a wall where it would receive full benefit from the general room lighting. In any case, a mirror has to have front lighting for the user to see his or her face in the best possible light.

SAFETY NOTE:
If the striplight incorporates a shaver socket, it must be of the special type intended for bathroom use, with an isolating transformer to prevent electric shock.

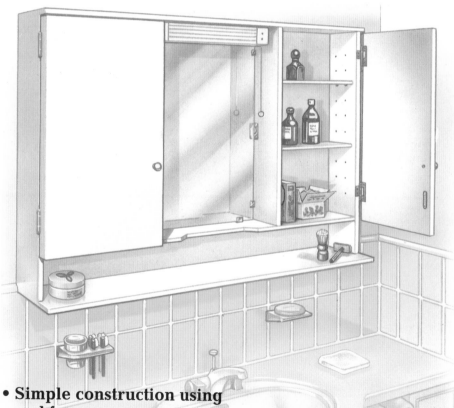

- **Simple construction using m.d.f.**
- **Ample storage space**
- **Incorporates display shelf**
- **Optional strip lighting**
- **Can be painted any colour**
- **Mirror can pivot forwards**

It is suggested that the cabinet is made from m.d.f. and is painted with a final coat of gloss. You then have the opportunity to colour it to complement the general décor in the room. Construction uses butt joints made with adhesive and pins.

Dimensions are optional, but we recommend 1050mm (3 ft 6 in) wide by 500mm (20 in) high and 150mm (6 in) deep.

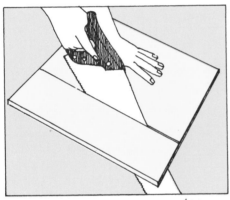

1 Mark out then cut 13mm ($^1/_2$ in) m.d.f. for the cabinet carcase.

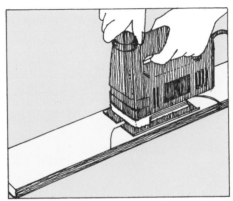

2 Mark out and cut the decorative indention for the middle shelf using a jigsaw or padsaw. Sand smooth the cut section using glasspaper.

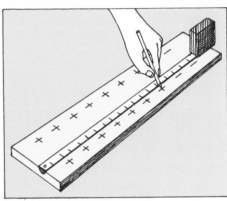

3 Mark out the positions of holes for adjustable shelves accurately on both sides of the cabinet.

4 Drill holes for adjustable shelf supports. See manufacturers instructions for depth and diameter of holes.

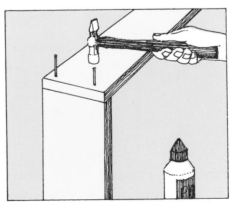

5 Using woodwork adhesive and 37mm ($1^1/_2$ in) panel pins assemble the carcase.

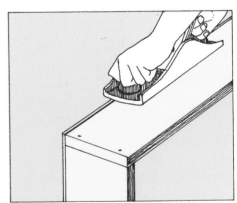

6 For the back use 6mm ($^1/_4$ in) m.d.f. Cut about 1mm ($^1/_{25}$ in) oversize. Use adhesive and 25mm (1 in) panel pins to secure it in place. When dry plane off excess.

7 Punch all pin heads below surface and fill holes with wood stopper.

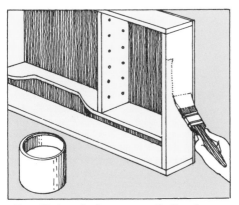

8 Cut and plane smooth the doors using 15mm ($^5/_8$ in) m.d.f. Sand down and paint the complete carcase.

9 Fix 50mm (2 in) flush hinges to the doors then hang the doors on the cabinet.

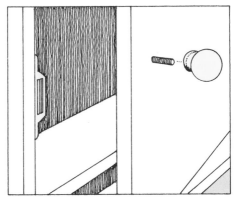

10 Fit door handles after drilling suitable size hole through each door. Fix magnetic catches.

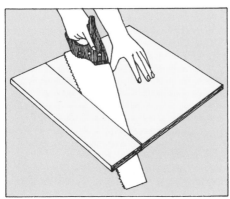

11 Cut out backing board for mirror from 15mm ($^5/_8$ in) m.d.f., allowing for thickness of pivots. Plane edges smooth then paint.

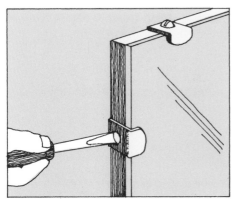

12 Use mirror clips to fix the mirror to the board. Use two clips top and bottom and one or two on each side, depending on height.

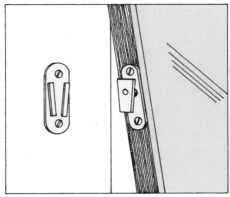

13 Fit the mirror pivot catches to the back board using screws supplied. Then screw a receiving plate to each side of the cabinet 75mm (3 in) from the back.

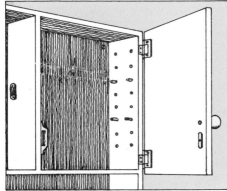

14 Fit cabinet to wall by screwing through corner brackets fitted in the top corners of both cupboards into the appropriate wall fixings. use 38mm ($^1/_2$ in) x No 8 screws.

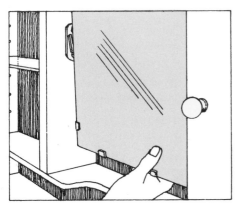

15 Lift mirror on to the receiving plate. Insert the 6mm ($^1/_4$ in) glass shelves on shelf supports pushed into selected holes in the cabinet sides.

LINEN STORAGE

Purpose-made storage units always prove to be the most successful in the long run. This project provides a home for linen, blankets, pillows and duvets. When it comes to changing the beds or making up a spare bed for a visitor, everything is at hand.

You can choose your own dimensions, but something around 900mm (3 ft) long by 600mm (2 ft) wide and 450mm (18 in) deep is convenient. It is a size that enables the unit to be tucked into a corner of a bedroom or an alcove on a landing without being too obtrusive.

The construction method calls for simply gluing and screwing the sides and base. Using butt joints, as shown, is more than adequate since the unit, although sizeable, is not intended to be moved around – it is supposed to remain in one place.

Simple triangular offcuts of blockboard are used for the feet and so provide an airflow around the unit.

Although a simple lift-on, lift-off lid could be used, it is well worth fitting a hinged lid with stays to support it in the open position when it is being used.

A piano hinge is used to

- **Ample storage space**
- **Dimensions easily adaptable**
- **Simple yet strong construction**
- **Can double as occasional seating**
- **Suitable for paint or varnish finish**

provide continuous support for what is a fairly heavy lid. Piano hinge is bought in lengths of 2m (6½ ft) and is cut to the required length with a hacksaw.

It is suggested that foam, covered with a preferred material, is used to cover the lid. This is not essential, but it does provide an opportunity to tie in the unit with curtains or other

cushions or furnishings in the room. Although not intended primarily as a seat, the unit is bound to be used as an occasional 'resting place', especially if situated in a bedroom, so 50mm (2 in) thick foam is recommended to make it more comfortable.

Since the unit is intended to remain in one place, handles

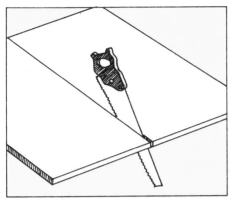

1 Measure, then cut out the sides and base of the carcass from 18mm ($\frac{3}{4}$ in) blockboard.

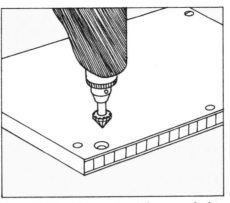

2 Drill and countersink screw holes at 225mm (9 in) intervals.

3 Assemble carcass using pva woodworking adhesive and 38mm ($1\frac{1}{2}$ in) No 8 screws.

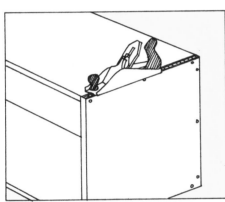

4 Use a smoothing plane to trim all edges.

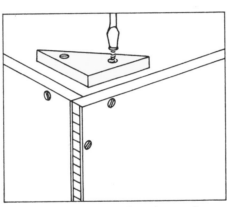

5 Cut four triangular pieces of blockboard for the feet and screw in place using 25mm (1 in) No 8 screws.

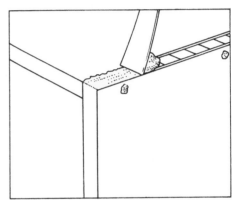

6 Fill all screw holes and end grain of blockboard with wood or cellulose filler, depending on intended finishing material.

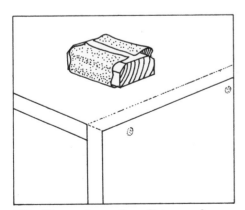

7 Use a piece of medium grade glasspaper or a purpose-made sanding block to smooth filler.

8 Apply paint or varnish to the outside of the carcass.

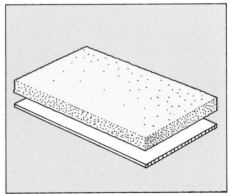

9 Cut out a piece of blockboard for the lid to overlap the front of the chest by 12mm ($\frac{1}{2}$ in), and a sheet of 50mm (2 in) thick foam for the top.

have not been incorporated to make it readily portable. It is likely to be moved only very rarely to a new position, or for decorating.

To decorate the sides use primer, undercoat and gloss top coat. Alternatively, you can use a varnish stain, perhaps to match other wood in the room. There is no need to paint the inside of the unit but do allow several days for the finish to dry and any smell to dissipate before using it.

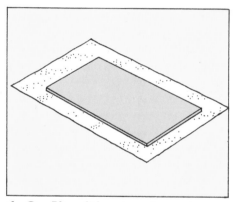

10 Place lid on top of covering material to measure required size. Allow 75mm (3 in) all round.

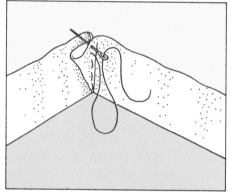

11 Pull two adjacent corners of material in at 45° and stitch with needle and cotton; trim excess material in corners with scissors.

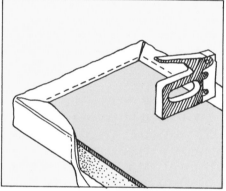

12 Remove lid, place foam in position. Fold material over the edge of the lid and staple down. Stitch and trim excess material at other two corners.

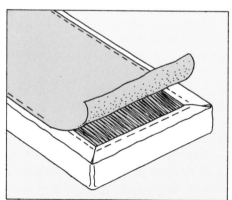

13 Cut another piece of material and double under the edges to finish 25mm (1 in) within perimeter of lid. Staple to underside of lid.

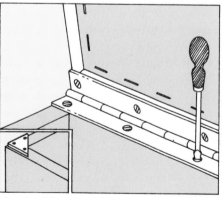

14 Fix piano hinge to the lid and chest. Use 25mm (1 in) No 4 countersunk screws. Cut two triangles of 4mm ($\frac{3}{16}$ in) hardboard 32 x 32mm ($1\frac{1}{4}$ x $1\frac{1}{4}$ in) and pin to front corners of chest to prevent strain on hinge.

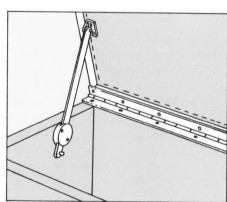

15 Fit a stay to either side of the lid. Use lift-up flap stays, which can be locked in the open position.

REFERENCE
SECTION

A knowledge of the proper tools and precise materials and fittings needed for a job plays a major part in successful d-i-y. Using a screwdriver that is too small, forcing a saw to cut a curve or drilling the wrong size hole in a wall are typical ways to frustrate yourself, create problems and produce poor results. This reference section is the cornerstone of the whole book. Before you start any decorating, repair or construction project, check to see that you have all the correct tools, and the right materials and accessories assembled and ready to use. Then read about the various processes and techniques involved and you can tackle that job with confidence.

TOOLS AND MATERIALS

TOOLS

Buy the best tools you can afford, look after them and they will last you a lifetime. It is very tempting to choose a cheap saw or a bargain screwdriver but, be warned, it will be harder to use the tools, you won't get such good results and sooner rather than later you will be spending more money on replacements.

Avoid buying a complete tool-kit in a box. There are three good reasons for this. First, you may never use some of the tools; second, you may not feel comfortable with a particular handle shape, length or balance; third, there is no need to spend money on an expensive box when a perfectly good tool-bag can be bought more cheaply.

For your tool-kit, you need a collection of all the items necessary to help you tackle all the basic jobs you will encounter in your home. Over the years, as your d-i-y aspirations grow and plumbing, electricity and sophisticated woodwork projects become part of your repertoire, you will gradually add to your kit. Initially, though, the items listed will be sufficient.

WOODWORKING AND GENERAL PURPOSE

Abrasive paper
This comes in sheets in different grades from coarse to fine and is chosen according to how rough the surface being smoothed. **Glasspaper** is commonly used to smooth wood, *aluminium oxide paper* is better for power sanders. **Emery cloth** is a harder abrasive for use on metals. **Wet** or **dry** abrasive paper is so-called because it can also be dipped in water before use, which lessens the dust produced. A **sanding block**, made of cork, rubber or wood, is used with abrasive paper. Wrap the paper around the block, making sure that it is unwrinkled. If you do not use a block, an uneven surface will result.

1 Firmer chisel
2 Abrasive – Sanding block
3 G-cramp
4 Dowelling jig
5 Pipe/cable detector
6 Sash cramp

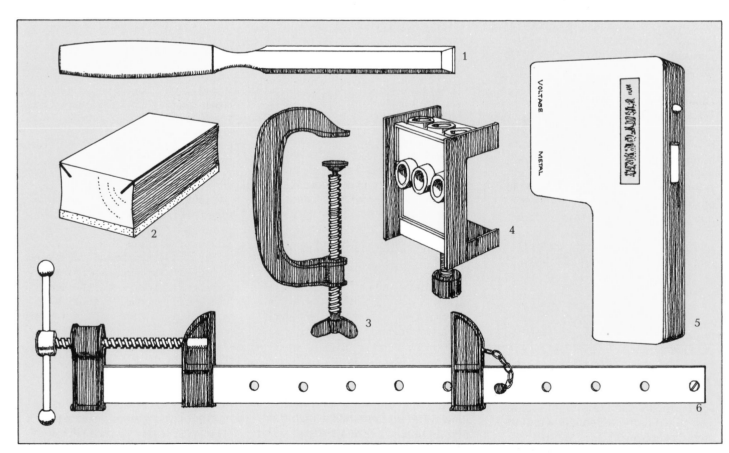

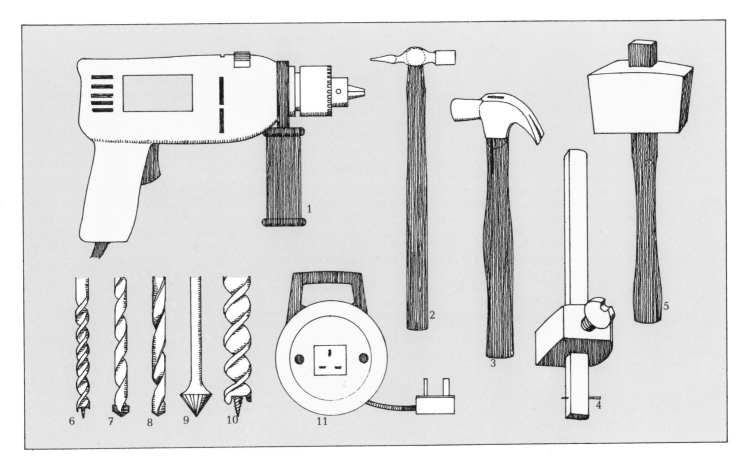

Purpose-made sanding blocks with abrasive on each face are also available.

Chisels

Used to cut joints in wood and to trim off thin slivers. Plastic-handled chisels can be used with a hammer; wooden handles must be struck only with a mallet. When bought, a chisel is not sharpened; it must be honed with an oilstone to sharpen it. For safety it must be kept sharp always. Firmer chisels are for general purpose work; two sizes 12 and 25mm ($\frac{1}{2}$ in and 1in) will cover all the jobs in this book.

Cramps

Sometimes called clamps, they are used mainly to secure glued joints while they are setting. The **G-cramp** comes in a vast range of jaw-opening sizes. **Sash cramps** or **web cramps** (a cheaper alternative) are indispensable for holding large frameworks, although you can improvise in some cases by making a **Spanish windlass** (see 'Techniques').

Detectors

Pin-point metal or wood objects, such as electric cables, water and gas pipes, or wood studs, hidden in walls and ceilings. Electronically operated, it will buzz or flash when an object is detected.

Drill stand

Used with a power drill to ensure absolute accuracy in straightness and depth of hole; for example, when making dowel joints. A spring-loaded lever lowers and raises the drill.

Drills

A **power drill** enables holes to be drilled into wood and walls. The variety of drills available ranges from a simple, single-speed model (which will make holes only in soft materials) to a multi-speed drill with forward and reverse action and electronic control. Initially, something in between, such as a two-speed drill with hammer action, is a good buy. Two speeds allow different materials to be drilled and the hammer action means you can make holes even in concrete.

1 Electric drill
2 Pin hammer
3 Claw hammer
4 Marking gauge
5 Mallet
6 Dowel bit
7 Masonry bit
8 Twist bit
9 Countersink bit
10 Auger bit
11 Extension lead

A selection of different size high-speed steel-type twist bits for both wood and metal are needed with a drill to make holes of varying diameters. A **countersink bit** is used to make a recess into which a screw head will fit. A **dowel bit** makes holes for dowels in wood. **Masonry bits** make holes in brick walls (not all are suitable for hammer action).

Extension lead

Most power tools are supplied with only a relatively short cable, so an extension lead is essential. Most useful are those supplied in a plastic drum with one or two socket outlets in it so that two tools can be

connected at once. Battery-operated power tools obviate the need for 'plugging-in', but they are really for occasional rather than constant use.

Hammers
Claw hammer The claw side of the head extracts nails and pins.

Pin hammer The head has a conventional hammer shape on one side and a wedge shape on the other. The wedge is useful for starting nails and pins held in the fingers. This hammer is for lighter jobs. A heavier version is the cross-pein hammer.

Mallet
Used to strike a wood or plastic-handled chisel. The tapered head ensures square contact with the chisel. A mallet is also used for tapping wood joints together.

Marking gauge
For accurately marking out woodworking joints. It makes only a light scratch mark. The steel pin(s) that makes the mark can be locked at

a precise point with a thumb screw.

Mitre block
A wood block with slots cut in the side at angles. When a tenon saw blade is placed in two opposing slots, the block serves as a guide to make a perfect mitre or square cut in the workpiece.

Nail and pin punches
Used with a hammer to drive nails and pins below the surface so they can be hidden below filler or stopping. The pointed end is 'cupped' so that it fits over a nail or pin head.

Oilstone and honing guide
Used to sharpen chisel and plane blades. An oilstone is a stone block with grit on the sides; oil is used as a lubricant while the blade is being sharpened. A honing guide provides an efficient method of holding the blade at the correct angle while sharpening.

Oribital sander
Also called a finishing sander, it leaves a fine, smooth finish on wood.

1 Mitre block
2 Honing guide and oilstone
3 Nail punch
4 Orbital sander
5 Pincers

A sheet of abrasive paper is fitted to the base plate. Various grades of paper from coarse to fine are available. Rougher grades are used on a coarse surface initially. A fine grade is used to finally smooth the surface.

A sander with its own dust collection bag is essential for indoor working since a lot of dust is produced.

Pincers
For removing nails and tacks from wood. The notched handle end is for levering out the nail head sufficiently for the pincers to grip.

Planes
A **smoothing plane** is used to smooth and straighten wood. It is a general-purpose plane and is about 250mm (10 in) long. Its blade is 50–60mm (2–2⅜ in) wide. It can be adjusted

according to how much wood you want to skim off.

A **block plane** is smaller – it can be held in the palm of your hand – and is useful for smaller jobs and for planing end grain.

A **power plane** makes it easy for the beginner to finish timber to precise dimensions. A one-hand model is lightweight and easy to use.

Pliers
As well as being used for cutting electrical wire, they are also useful for gripping things.

Portable workbench
Being light and portable, it can be carried to where you are working. It is like a giant vice – the worksurface can open in two halves. When closed, it grips the wood being worked on very tightly. It is particularly useful because it can also hold large and awkward shaped objects securely.

Profile gauge
Used to transfer awkward shapes on to the workpiece prior to cutting. It consists of tightly packed movable steel needles, which, when pressed against an object, reproduce its shape.

Putty knife
Specifically shaped flexible blade to smooth and angle putty around glass.

Saws
Power saws take the effort out of sawing wood or sheets of board, but they are dangerous and must be used carefully. A **jigsaw** is the best buy initially. It will cut all sorts of materials – wood, metal and plastic. It will also cut curves, shapes, angles and holes. The best models operate at variable speeds – slow for hard materials and fast for soft.

A **handsaw,** sometimes called a cross-cut or panel saw, is used for 'rough' cutting rather than fine work such as cutting joints. It has a blade up to 650mm (26 in) long and a wood or plastic handle. It will cut both wood and synthetic boards.

There are degrees of fineness in the teeth of a saw. Saws with smaller and closely spaced teeth give a finer cut.

A **tenon saw** has a stiffened 'spine' and is 250–300mm (10–12 in) long. It is used for cutting joints and other accurate work.

A **padsaw** is used to cut holes and shapes. When cutting in the middle of a board, a hole is first drilled through the wood so that the thin, tapered blade can be inserted and the cut started.

A **coping saw** has a fine-toothed blade and is used to make curved or circular cuts. The blade can be set at an angle to the frame too for greater manoeuvrability.

A **fretsaw** makes even more intricate cuts but has a fixed blade.

A **hacksaw** cuts metal. A small version – called a junior hacksaw – is ideal for small jobs.

In all frame saws the blade is inserted with the teeth pointing *away*

1 Power plane
2 Smoothing plane
3 Block plane
4 Profile gauge
5 Pliers
6 Putty knife
7 Portable workbench

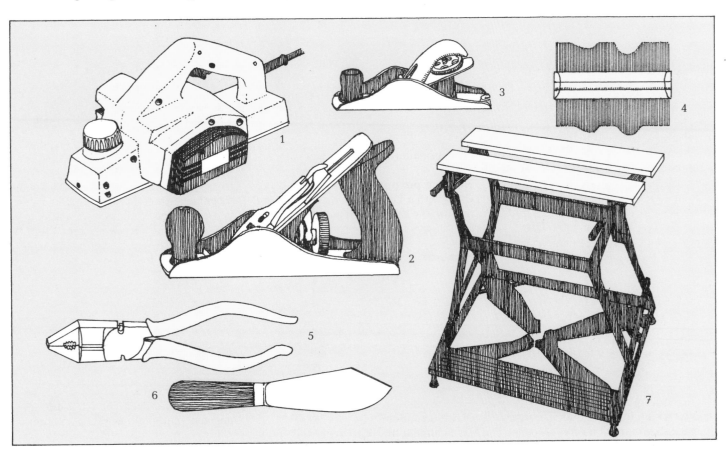

from the handle so that cutting is on the push stroke.

Screwdrivers

Screws have two types of head: **single slot** and star-shaped **cross-head**. Both types come in a variety of sizes, which means that you need several sizes and type of screwdriver.

You need three sizes of single-slot screwdriver (the size is the width of the tip): 5mm ($\frac{3}{16}$ in), 6mm ($\frac{1}{4}$ in) and 8mm ($\frac{5}{16}$ in). If you come across larger screws, add a 9mm ($\frac{3}{8}$ in) one to your list.

The pattern of cross-head screws varies. However, the Supadriv type will cope with all of them. You will need three sizes: 1, 2 and 3 point.

Screwdrivers have a vast array of handle shapes and colours in wood and plastic. The handle may be rounded, fluted, long and plain or rubber-covered. Buy whatever feels most comfortable to hold.

Blades vary in length according to the size of the tip – the wider the tip, the longer the blade and the bigger the screw it will handle.

A couple of **stubby screwdrivers** with really short blades are worth adding to your kit (one slot, one cross-head – both medium size) so that you can deal with screws in confined spaces.

Buy an **insulated screwdriver** – it has an insulating sleeve on the shaft – for electrical work.

Standard screwdrivers have fixed handles: you turn the handle and the blade turns with it. **Ratchet screwdrivers** allow you to drive in or remove a screw without altering your grip on the handle. You turn the handle to drive the screw a part turn, then turn the handle back to the starting position – the blade remains stationary – then you repeat the process, and so on until the screw is tight.

A **power screwdriver** takes the hard work out of screwdriving. It is supplied with interchangeable bits to drive different head shapes and sizes. It is battery operated and comes with a recharging unit – a bit of luxury but lovely to have. Screwdriver bits can also be fitted to some power drills.

Spanners

Used for tightening and loosening nuts, mostly in plumbing work. A range of sizes and an **adjustable wrench** – heavyduty model that can be made smaller or larger – are needed.

Spirit level

Used for checking that surfaces or lines are truly horizontal or vertical. A 1m (3 ft 3 in) long level is the most useful size. An aluminium or steel level will withstand more knocks than a wooden one.

Staple gun

Fires staples and is used as an alternative to pinning. Its advantages over conventional pinning with a hammer are that it is quick and is used one-handed, leaving the other hand free to hold the work.

1 Handsaw
2 Tenon saw
3 Padsaw
4 Fretsaw
5 Power jigsaw
6 Coping saw
7 Junior hacksaw

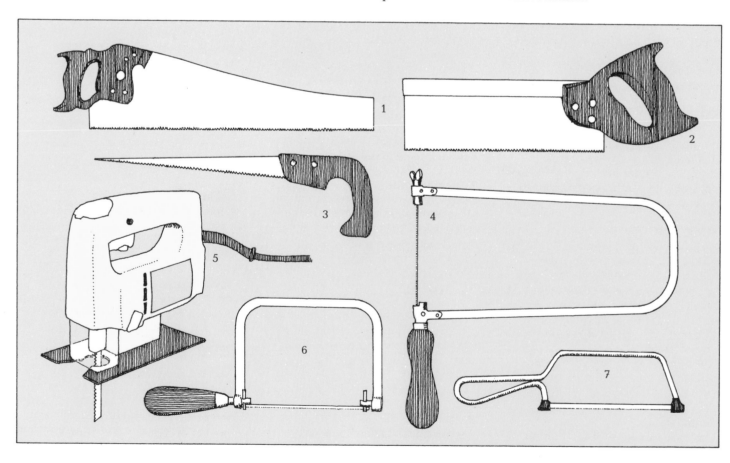

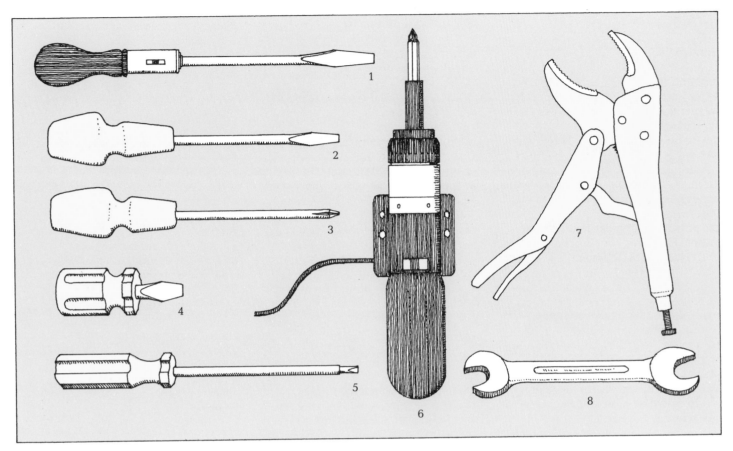

Steel measuring tape
A 3m (10 ft) or 5m (16 ft) long, lockable tape is best. Get one calibrated in both imperial and metric.

Steel rule
A rule that is graduated on either side in imperial and metric is most useful. It can also be used as a precise straight-edge for marking out cutting lines or when cutting soft materials, such as vinyl tiles.

SURFORM
Useful for rough-planing wood; further fine finishing is needed to obtain a smooth surface. The blade comprises a series of small teeth and holes, rather like a cheese grater, through which waste wood passes. The teeth do not get clogged up with wood. The blades, which are 150–250mm (6–10 in) long, are replaced when blunt. Curved blades are also available.

Swingbrace
Used with an **auger bit** for boring accurate holes of greater diameter than twist bits. The auger bit has a pointed screw thread at its tip to draw the bit into the wood. A brace with a 250mm (10 in) circular sweep is most popular and enables holes up to 50 or 75mm (2 or 3 in) to be drilled. Some swingbraces have a ratchet mechanism, which is particularly useful or even essential in confined spaces.

Trimming knife
Used with various blades for cutting all sorts of material. Safest are the retractable blade types, where the razor-sharp blade is drawn into the knife body when not in use.

Try square
An L-shaped tool comprising a steel blade and handle(or stock) set at a perfect right angle. Used for marking cut lines at right angles to an edge and for checking that corners are square.

WALLPAPERING EQUIPMENT

Paste brush
An old 125 or 150mm (5 or 6 in) wide paint brush is ideal for applying paste

1 Ratchet screwdriver
2 Single-slot screwdriver
3 Cross-head screwdriver
4 Stubby screwdriver
5 Insulated screwdriver
6 Power screwdriver
7 Adjustable wrench
8 Spanner

to wallpaper.

Pasting table
A fold-away pasting table about 1800 x 600mm (6 x 2 ft) is relatively inexpensive, light and portable, and very convenient.

Paste bucket
Any type will do. Tie a piece of string across the middle to provide a resting place for the brush. Lining the bucket with polythene saves having to clean it out; just throw away the liner.

Pencil and straight-edge rule
For measuring and marking. A folding boxwood rule is equally handy, as it can be used to measure long and short distances.

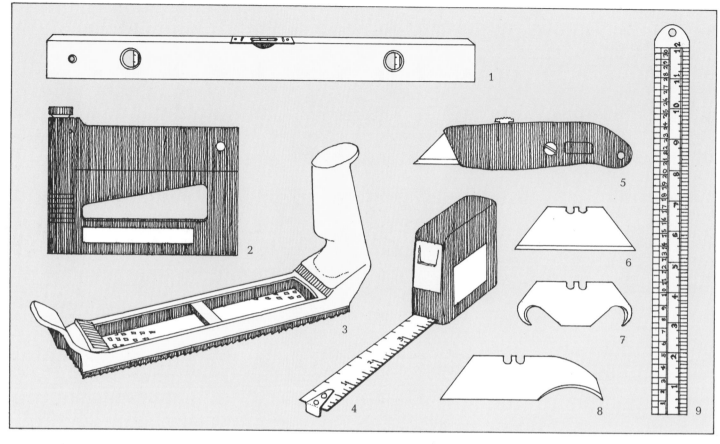

Plumb bob

An alternative to a spirit level for marking true verticals on the wall as a guide to hanging the lengths. Shop-bought types are inexpensive. Otherwise just tie a weight to a length of string and ensure that it hangs freely.

Shears

A pair of paperhanger's shears about 200mm (8 in) long are important to make long, clean cuts. A smaller pair of household scissors are useful for making intricate cuts.

Wallpaper hanging brush

For smoothing out lengths of paper.

Wooden seam roller

For smoothing down the edges of lengths. It **must not** be used on embossed papers or the raised areas will be flattened.

PAINTING EQUIPMENT

Brushes and rollers

Brushes come in a range of sizes. A kit consisting of a 25, 50, 75 and 100 or 125mm (1, 2, 3 and 4 or 5 in) sizes will cover most jobs. Basically, you choose the width to suit the job: a **narrow brush** for fiddly work, such as painting glazing bars on windows; a **broad** one for flat, uninterrupted surfaces, such as walls or flush doors; an **angled bristle brush** for window frames.

Most paint brushes consist of natural animal bristle. Brushes with synthetic fibre 'bristles' are suitable only for rough work; the fibres do not hold paint as well as natural bristle.

Buy the best brushes you can afford and look after them well.

Paint rollers are used mainly for decorating walls and ceilings with emulsion paint. You get a roller cage and handle, on to which you slip the sleeve that applies the paint.

Most **sleeves** are about 180mm (7 in) wide, but you can use larger ones if you are prepared for the extra effort involved in 'driving' them.

Plastic foam sleeves are cheapest, but absorb a lot of paint that won't come out again and are splashy to use.

Fibre sleeves may be natural or

1 Spirit level
2 Staple gun
3 Surform
4 Steel measuring tape
5 Trimming knife
6 Straight blade
7 Hooked blade
8 Concave blade
9 Steel rule

synthetic, and have short, medium or long pile. Fibre type is less important than the right pile length – short for flat surfaces, medium for slightly textured surfaces, and long for heavily embossed or indented surfaces.

You need a special **roller tray** into which to pour your paint so you can load the roller evenly.

Chemical stripper

Liquid and paste paint-strippers are sold under various brand names. They are brushed on to loosen and lift old paint. Not economical for large jobs, but handy for careful stripping of intricate mouldings and around window frames.

Electric heat gun

Used for paint-stripping. It looks and works like a hair-dryer but is vastly more powerful. (Never use it on hair.)

Filling knife

Has a flexible blade and is used for smoothing filler or stopping into holes and cracks. Wide and narrow versions are available.

Paint or wallpaper scraper

Has a stiff blade; used for stripping paint and wallpaper from flat surfaces.

Sanding equipment

Needed for rubbing down surfaces to provide a key for new paint, and for smoothing over cracks that have been filled. *See* Abrasive paper and Orbital sanders.

Shavehooks

Used to scrape paint from mouldings and tight corners. There are two types: triangular and multishaped, for dealing with curved surfaces.

Sponge

For washing surfaces prior to painting.

CERAMIC TILING EQUIPMENT

Adhesive spreader

A notched plastic tool used to spread a bed of tile adhesive correctly.

Grout spreader

A squeegee-like rubber blade for spreading grout cement into spaces between tiles.

Sponge

For cleaning away adhesive and grout from the tile surface.

Tile cutter

There are various types. One looks like a pencil with a tungsten-carbide tip, which is used to score the surface where the tile is to be broken. Better is a pincer-like cutter with a wheel to score a cut line; the tile is placed between the jaws and the handles are squeezed to make the cut. A **heavy-duty cutter** is a combined jig and cutting lever.

Tile file

Used to clean up sharp and uneven edges of a cut tile.

Tile nippers

Pincer-like tool for nibbling off narrow strips and shapes that cannot be cut by a conventional cutter.

Tile saw

Tungsten-carbide rod saw blade fitted into a frame will cut L-shapes or curves. The tile must be clamped in a vice while being cut.

1 Broad brush
2 Narrow brush
3 Angled brush
4 Paint roller
5 Shears
6 Pincer-type tile cutter
7 Paste brush
8 Seam roller
9 Multishaped shavehook
10 Triangular shavehook
11 Filling knife
12 Swingbrace
13 Try square

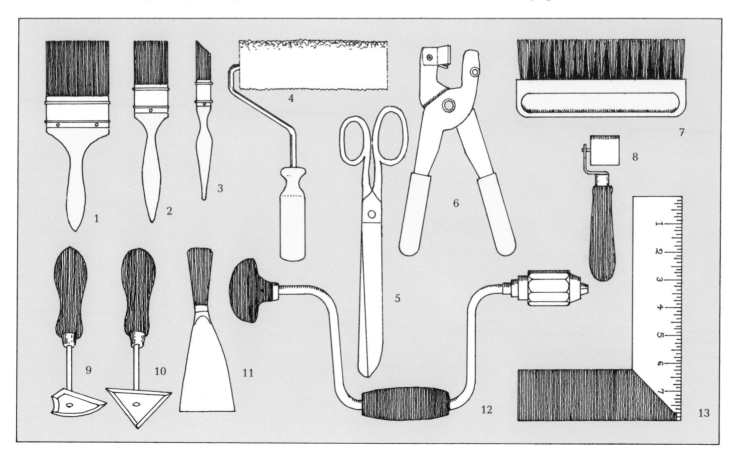

TOOLS AND MATERIALS

MATERIALS

WOOD

Battens

The usual sizes of battens are 25 x 25mm (1 x 1 in) or 50 x 25mm (2 x 1 in), although the term is used to describe any fairly narrow piece of wood.

Battens are used mostly either as wall-fixed bearers for shelves or to make a level framework against a wall to which boards or cladding is fixed. Planed battens are used if they are to be seen, but sawn battens are used for economy when building frameworks. Appearance is usually an important criteria with shelf battens, so planed wood is the usual choice.

Blockboard

Made by sandwiching wood strips between two outer veneers. Common thicknesses are 12, 18 and 25mm ($\frac{1}{2}$, $\frac{3}{4}$ and 1 in). More expensive boards have a double facing veneer, such as plywood and an exotic wood. Blockboard has excellent strength, but leaves an ugly sawn edge (gaps often appear between the core strips), which must be covered.

Chipboard

Chipboard is available plain or covered with natural wood veneers, pvc or melamine coatings, or plastic laminate. There is also a selection of imitation wood-grain effects and a limited range of colours. Thicknesses range from 6 to 40mm ($\frac{1}{4}$ to $1\frac{1}{2}$ in), 12, 18 and 25mm ($\frac{1}{2}$, $\frac{3}{4}$ and 1 in) are the commonest for plain chipboard.

It is rigid, dense, fairly heavy and strong if well supported. A sawn edge can be crumbly, and ordinary screws do not always hold well – special chipboard screws should be used. Most grades are not moisture resistant and will swell up if they get wet. The better quality laminate-faced boards are far stronger than a plain chipboard, which needs a lot more support if used for shelving.

Fibreboards

This group includes **hardboard** and **medium-density fibreboard (m.d.f.)**. Common thicknesses of hardboard are 3, 4, and 6mm ($\frac{1}{8}$, $\frac{5}{32}$ and $\frac{1}{4}$ in). As it is weak, hardboard is used mainly for panelling over a supporting framework. M.d.f., from 15 to 35mm ($\frac{5}{8}$ to $1\frac{3}{8}$ in) thick, is highly compressed and does not flake or splinter when sawn or drilled. A clean, hard sawn edge remains, which doesn't need to be filled or covered up by moulding or edging.

1 Square moulding
2 Scotia moulding
3 Quadrant moulding
4 Corner moulding
5 Half round moulding
6 Hockey stick moulding
7 Astragal moulding
8 Fluted and chamfered dowel

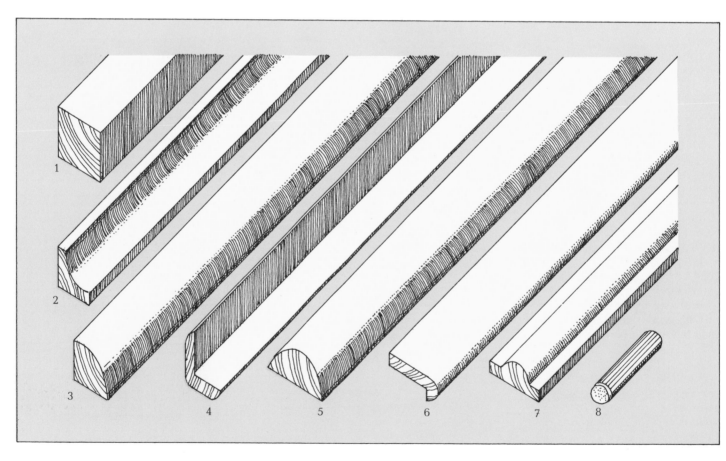

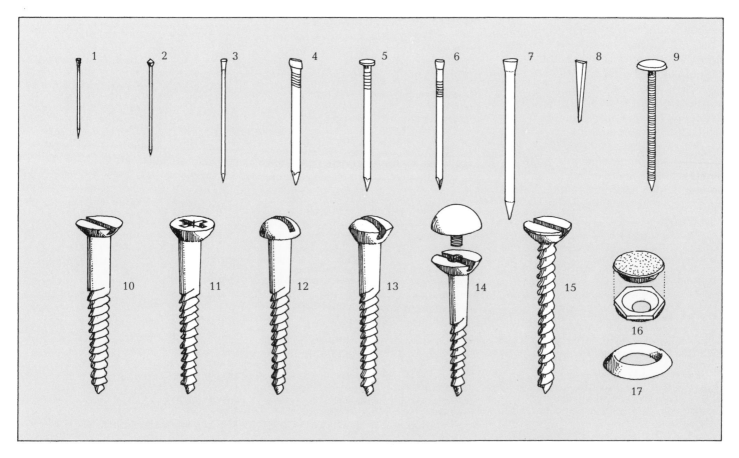

Mouldings

Mouldings are used to cover sawn edges or gaps, or as ornamentation. There is a huge range of shapes and sizes from square thin bead up to door architraves. Scotia, quadrant and corner mouldings are the most commonly used.

Mouldings are usually made from redwood or ramin. More exotic and expensive hardwoods are stocked by specialist timber merchants but many of the colours can be matched using cheaper wood stain.

Moulding is available in standard lengths of 2 or 3m (7 or 10 ft), and must be perfectly straight, so check it before buying. If you need to buy several lengths for a job, then make sure the colour and grain formation of each length is a good match.

Plywood

Made by gluing thin wood veneers together in layers (called plies), with the grain in each layer running at right angles to its neighbours. The most common boards have three, five or seven plies. There is a range of veneer finishes, such as teak, oak or mahogany, or a decorative plastic finish. Usual board thicknesses are 3, 6, 12 and 19mm ($\frac{1}{8}$, $\frac{1}{4}$, $\frac{1}{2}$ and $\frac{3}{4}$ in). Moisture resistant (MR) board is made for internal jobs where conditions may be damp.

Timber

Timber is classified as either softwood or hardwood. **Softwoods** come from evergreen trees and hardwoods from deciduous trees. Most, but not all, softwoods are softer than hardwoods. Softwood is cheaper and so is used in all general work. It is available in a range of standard metric sizes. Although you can buy an imperial length – for example, 6 ft – you will be charged for the next metric size up – 2.1m (6 ft 10$\frac{5}{8}$ in). Lengths start at 1.8m and rise in increments of 300mm (12 in) to 6.3m (20 ft 8 in). Standard thicknesses range from 12mm ($\frac{1}{2}$ in) up to 75mm (3 in), and widths from 25mm (1 in) to 225mm (9 in).

Standard sizes are sawn sizes – that is how the timber is delivered from the sawmill to the timber merchant.

1 Panel pin
2 Hardboard pin
3 Veneer pin
4 Oval brad
5 Round wire nail
6 Round lost-head nail
7 Masonry nail
8 Glazing sprig
9 Plasterboard nail
10 Countersunk single-slot-head screw
11 Countersunk cross-slot-head screw
12 Round head screw
13 Raised head screw
14 Mirror screw
15 Twin thread screw
16 Screw cap
17 Screw cup

Since the size is nominal, only sawn wood is used for rough work, floor joists, frameworks, and so on. However, where appearance and accuracy are important, smooth, planed wood is used. Since planing takes a little off each face, planed softwood will be about 5mm ($\frac{3}{16}$ in) smaller in width and thickness than its stated size. Planed timber is referred to as p.a.r., or planed all round.

Don't buy wood that is badly cracked, split or warped; it is difficult, if not impossible, to work with it. You can see if a length is warped by looking along its length for any bowing or twisting.

Hardwoods are very expensive and often you have to order them or find a specialist timber merchant. In d-i-y work hardwood is used mostly only for beading and mouldings in order to make exposed sawn edges attractive. Ramin, which has a pale colour, is the hardwood most frequently used for this purpose.

All wood must be conditioned or dried out for a week or two before it is used. This lowers its moisture content from 17 to 10 per cent. Wood is usually stored outside at timber yards and so will be 'wet'. As it dries indoors, it shrinks slightly. Boards should be stacked in a pile with pieces of wood between to allow air to circulate.

This way the boards will not warp as they dry. If wood is not conditioned before use, problems may occur later as it dries out.

FIXINGS

Adhesives
A pva (polyvinyl acetate) woodworking glue – there are various brands – is strong and used for all indoor jobs. Use the waterproof type where joints might be splashed.

Catches
Magnetic catches comprise a magnet, fixed to the carcass of a cupboard, and a striker plate, which is fixed to the door. The two must be aligned perfectly when the door is closed. The pulling power of the magnet is important – for small cabinet doors a magnet with a 'pull' of 2–3 kg (4$\frac{1}{2}$–6 lb) is sufficient; wardrobe doors need a 5–6kg (11–13 lb) 'pull'.

Common mechanical catches are the **spring-loaded ball catch** and the **roller catch**. Some are adjustable. This type is best, as accurate alignment is vital.

Dowels
Dowels are used to make strong framework joints. Made of hardwood, dowels are sold in diameters of 6, 9 and 12mm ($\frac{1}{4}$, $\frac{3}{8}$ and $\frac{1}{2}$ in). You can buy them 25 or 38mm (1 or 1$\frac{1}{2}$ in) long or you can buy long lengths and cut your own to size.

Buy dowels with **fluted** (finely grooved) sides and **chamfered** ends, which allow excess adhesive used in a joint to escape. If you have plain dowel, then you have to saw the flutes and chamfer the ends yourself.

Hinges
Flush hinges are the easiest type to fix, as they do not have to be recessed into the door or frame. For lightweight doors, use flush or **decorative flush** hinges; for cupboard doors, choose **cranked** hinges, which allow the doors to open through 180°. When fitting flush hinges, the inner leaf is screwed to the edge of the door or cabinet panel, and the outer leaf is screwed to the face of the other part. Both these

1 Cavity-wall fixing
2 Roller catch
3 Magnetic catch
4 Spring-loaded ball catch

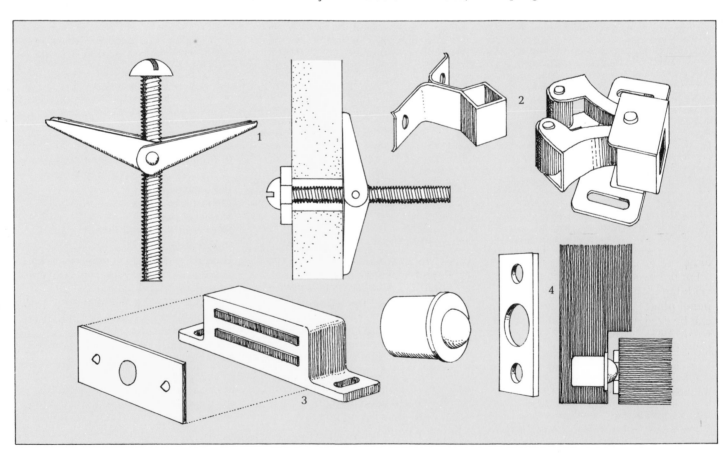

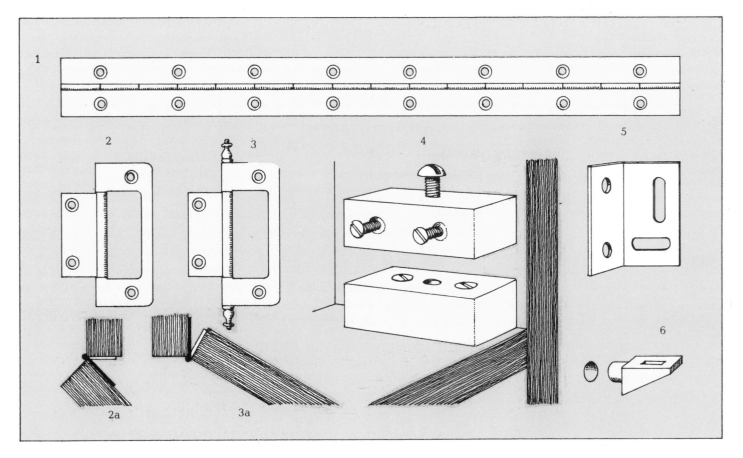

1 Piano hinge
2 Flush hinge, 2a plan view from above
3 Decorative flush hinge, 3a view from above
4 Plastic knock-down joint block
5 Adjustable fixing plate
6 Stud shelf support

hinges are available in 50mm (2 in) and 75mm (3 in) lengths.

Use **piano hinges** for fixing flaps. They are sold in 2 m (6 ft) lengths and are cut to the required size with a hacksaw.

Nails

Round wire nails with large, flat circular heads are used for general-purpose work. Lengths are 20–150mm ($^3/_4$–6 in). Use **round lost-head** nails or **oval brads** (oval wire nails) where appearance is important. Their heads are driven below surface with a nail punch. Both are 25–150mm (1–6 in) long.

For lightweight work, such as fixing cladding, panels or moulding, use **panel pins**. They have tiny heads that can be driven below the surface of the wood. **Veneer pins** are similar, but even thinner. **Hardboard pins** are copper-plated and square in cross-section. They have diamond-shaped heads that readily sink below surface. These three types are 15–50mm ($^5/_8$–2 in) long.

Use hardened steel **masonry nails** for wall fixings. Lengths are 15–100mm ($^5/_8$–4 in). Wear eye protection when hammering them.

Glazing sprigs, used for fixing glass, are 13–20mm ($^1/_2$–$^3/_4$ in) long. **Plaster-board nails** have large heads and are 30 or 40mm ($1^1/_4$ or $1^1/_2$ in) long.

Screws

A modern **twin-thread** screw is the best choice in almost all cases. Except the longest type, these screws are threaded for their entire length, which gives an excellent grip in all woods and boards. They are also quicker to drive than ordinary screws. The best types are zinc-plated (no rusting) and hardened, which means they are stronger and the head is less likely to be damaged from the wrong size screwdriver.

Countersunk-head screws are mostly used, since the head lies flush with or below the surface after fixing. Screws with **round heads** are for fixing metal shelf brackets and similar jobs. Where neatness is important, **raised countersunk-head** screws are used alone or with **metal screw cups**.

Ordinary **wood screws** have a smooth piece of shank just below the head.

All types of screw are available with single-slot heads or cross-heads. The latter give a better grip, especially when an electric screwdriver is used. **Screw cups** or **screw caps,** which completely cover the screw head, are used for a neat finish where screws need to be accessible – the side of a bath panel, for example.

Screws come in many lengths and diameters. The ones most often used are 12mm ($^1/_2$ in) to 100mm (4 in), and diameters from Nos 6 to 10 .

Wall-fixings

Traditional fibre plugs have largely been superseded by plastic versions, which can be used with a range of screw sizes.

Hollow walls – plasterboard partition and lath-and-plaster – need special **cavity-wall fixings**. There are many types and virtually all operate in the same way: expanding wings open up to grip securely across the back of the plasterboard or laths.

Wallpaper paste
A universal paste, which can cope with a variety of paper types, is most common. Follow the instructions for mixing with water.

Vinyl wallcoverings require a paste that contains a fungicide to inhibit mould growth.

PREPARATORY MATERIALS

Filler
Cellulose filler is sold under various brand names in powder form for mixing with water. Use it to fill cracks in walls and ceilings, and to fill cracks in wood. Filler can be bought in ready-to-use forms; this is not economical but it is handy to have a tube around for small, quick repairs. For large cracks and holes (such as those left after removing picture rails), use a **plaster filler**.

Knotting
Shellac knotting is a liquid sealer dabbed over knots in bare wood to prevent resin bleeding out and showing through newly done paintwork.

Size
This is brushed on to porous walls before papering. It helps ensure that the paper will adhere firmly to the wall. Most modern wallpaper pastes can be used to make size – just dilute the powder according to the instructions.

Stabilizing solution and aluminium primer sealer
Use on bare plaster ceilings and walls to seal in dried water stains, nicotine stains, old distemper and areas where flaking paint has been scraped off. Brush on the sealer with a wide brush.

Sugar soap
Use to wash down walls, ceilings and woodwork before decorating.

White spirit
Use to clean gloss paint from brushes, and to thin some paints.

WALLCOVERINGS

Lining paper
Thin, white paper used in certain circumstances to cover walls before painting or hanging wallcoverings.

Standard wallpaper
Comes in a variety of weights and patterns. If not handled gently, the lighter papers tend to tear after pasting and when being hung. For the beginner, a medium-weight paper, which will withstand a fair amount of pulling about, is best.

Vinyl
A plastic coating is fused to a strong backing paper. Available in many patterns, including textured vinyls, which simulate brickwork and ceramic tiles. A tough wallcovering that is easy to handle and can be scrubbed clean, making it particularly advantageous in kitchens, though it can be used anywhere in the home. Vinyls are also available in a ready-pasted form; the paste is in a dried state on the backing and is activated by immersing each length in water.

Washable paper
Available in many patterns. The paper has a coating that can be wiped clean, making it ideal for kitchens and bathrooms.

Novamura
Made from foamed polyethylene, it is very light in weight. Its insulating property helps to reduce condensation. The wall is pasted, not the wallcovering.

Anaglypta
Thick patterned paper suitable for covering walls and ceilings that are structurally sound but not in good condition. Can be painted with emulsion after hanging.

Woodchip
A paper with a finer textured surface than anaglypta, made from woodchips and sold in various designs. Intended for painting with emulsion.

PAINT

Primer
Use on bare woodwork to seal the wood and as a base for the other paint coats.

Undercoat
Has good covering power and provides a key for the top coat of gloss. Where applied over old gloss, one or two coats should be used to obliterate the old paint.

Gloss
Provides a hard-wearing, shiny finish. Available in liquid or non-drip (jelly) form.

Emulsion
Available in various degrees of finish from matt to satin. Normally used on walls and ceilings, but the 'glossy' emulsions also can be used on woodwork.

OTHER FINISHES

Lacquer
Quick-drying cellulose lacquer is an excellent, glossy, finishing treatment for furniture. It is very resistant to heat, scratches and solvents.

Varnish
Clear and tinted polyurethane varnishes can be applied to bare wood as a finish instead of paint. They should always be applied with a clean brush.

REPAIRS & PREPARATION

CEILINGS & WALLS

Plaster

Leave **new plaster** until completely dry (at least four weeks). Prime with a building adhesive (1 part to 5 parts water). Allow to dry thoroughly.

Bare plaster means that the wall or ceiling has never been painted. If, while rubbing the surface with your hand or a dry brush, a good deal of dust comes off, you must first cover the plaster with a coat of stabilizing solution. Brushed on like a normal paint and allowed to dry overnight, it seals loose, powdery surfaces so that the emulsion paint sticks well to the wall or ceiling. If you don't use a stabilizer, the emulsion paint will start to flake off the wall after a few months.

If the plaster is not dusty, apply a diluted coat of the emulsion paint first. Usually the instructions on the can will advise using 1 part of water to 9 parts of emulsion.

A clean plastic bucket makes a handy container for mixing diluted paint. Stir it well for a minute before using it. Allow four hours drying time before applying further coats of emulsion paint.

Paint new plasterboard with a couple of coats of plasterboard primer sealer before painting or wallpapering.

Previously painted surface

If the old paint is sound – that is, not flaking – then wash it with diluted sugar soap and rinse with clean water. You can then apply undiluted coats of emulsion paint. Old paint may be flaking off because it was applied over a dusty surface (see Bare plaster) or a dirty or greasy surface (usually in a kitchen), or because the wall is damp – in this case you have to establish the cause and cure for the damp, which might mean calling in expert advice.

Do not try to paint or wallpaper over flaking paint, as the new decoration will not stick to the flaky surface. Scrape off all the flaking paint until only sound paint remains. There is no short cut here – it is a straightforward job using a paint scraper and energy!

Now examine the surface for dust or grease and clean it as necessary. Apply a coat of stabilizing solution before decorating. Then paint or hang the wallcovering.

Textured painted surface

Provided it is clean, it can be given one or more full coats of emulsion.

A papered wall or ceiling

You can apply one or more full coats of emulsion to paper that has previously been painted, provided that it is well stuck down all over. Otherwise, strip off the paper and treat the wall as bare plaster.

Textured papers (such as woodchip or Analgypta) can be repainted if well stuck down. Use full coats of emulsion.

The safest thing to do with ordinary wallpaper is strip it off. If you choose to paint it (use full coats) and it is well stuck down, you may get away with it. The risk is that the paint will loosen the paper, producing large bubbles where it has lost contact with the wall. You can get some idea of what might happen if you test a 'hidden' area behind a large piece of furniture first. It is not a foolproof test, but it is better than nothing. If the paper is spoiled by painting, it will have cost you the price of the paint and your time – and you will have to strip the paper, of course.

Where a ceiling has become badly discoloured, first apply a coat of aluminium primer sealer.

A dried water stain, caused by a leaking roof or plumbing problem, will not be hidden by coats of emulsion. It must also first be coated with an aluminium primer sealer. For small patches, you can buy a special sealer, sold under brand names, which comes in a spray can.

Stripping wallpaper

Ordinary wallpaper (which includes papered ceilings) is removed by soaking and scraping. You must allow at least ten or fifteen minutes for the water to soak through and loosen the paste. The soaking process can be speeded up by adding a proprietary wallpaper stripper solution to the warm water, though, generally, adding a little liquid detergent plus a handful of wallpaper paste (to make the water cling to the paper rather than run down the wall) is sufficient.

Many wallcoverings are specially made to be easy to strip. To see if that is what you are faced with, just raise the bottom edge and pull upwards; you should be able to remove the paper in complete strips, completing a room in minutes. A thin backing paper might remain on the wall; if this is sound, hang the new paper over it. If it is loose, even in small areas, strip it off by soaking and scraping.

Emulsion-painted papers can be problematic. It is possible to break down the surface by scraping or wire brushing to allow soaking water through to loosen the old paste, but this can be tough going. The simple alternative is to use a steam stripper, which loosens the paper quickly and effectively so that it can be scraped off as normal.

After stripping the paper, go over the surface with a sanding block to remove small nibs, then wash down with diluted sugar soap to remove all traces of the old adhesive.

The amount of further preparation needed will depend on whether the ceiling or wall is to be papered or painted. If it is to be painted, even slight hairline cracks must be filled and smoothed carefully, otherwise they will show through the new paint. If there are many slight cracks in an otherwise sound wall, cover the wall with lining paper or a wallcovering made for painting.

Fill any superficial cracks with a cellulose filler. Use the edge of a filling knife to 'undercut' the crack – that is, to make it wider below surface. Force the filler into the cavity, where it will set and form a strong repair. Leave the filler to set, then sand it smooth with glasspaper.

If there are cracks in the joint between the ceiling and wall, cover them with ceiling cove.

Larger holes should be filled with a

plaster filler, which is much more economical to use. If the hole is deep, apply the plaster in a layer no more than about 12mm ($\frac{1}{2}$ in) deep. Wait an hour for it to set, then apply another layer. You can use a wide filling knife, but for a flat finish, draw a long straight-edged piece of wood across the surface.

Gaps between the tops of skirtings and the wall or alongside door and window frames can be filled with filler, but first squeeze strips of newspaper into the gaps to provide a solid backing. A speedier alternative is to use a strip of mastic sealant applied from a cartridge. Even if the gap expands or contracts slightly, the sealant will keep it covered.

It is always worth brushing size on to the wall before hanging wallpaper. This seals porous walls, which means the paste won't sink into the surface and cause some loss of adhesion between it and the paper. It also leaves the surface slippery so that the paper will be easier to push into place. Apply the size with a large brush – just 'paint' the wall with it and leave it to dry for an hour before papering.

Make sure all fittings such as wall lights and roller blinds are removed, because you can't paper around them. Into each screw hole pop a matchstick, leaving about 12mm ($\frac{1}{2}$ in) protruding. This will be forced through the paper as it is brushed on to the wall, so that you will know where the screw holes

are when you replace the fittings later. Make sure that the electricity is switched off before removing wall lights and that the power to any bare wires is cut off until wallpapering is complete and the lights are back in position.

Woodwork
All woodwork – doors, skirtings, window frames, and so on – is prepared for painting in exactly the same way. First remove all fixtures such as door handles and clothes hooks, and put them, together with the screws, in a safe place for replacement later.

Examine the paintwork closely. If it is smooth and sound, **do not** strip it off

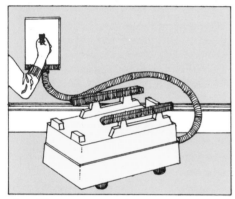

1 Use a steam stripper to remove stubborn wallcoverings. Steam delivered through the hand plate softens the old paste quickly.

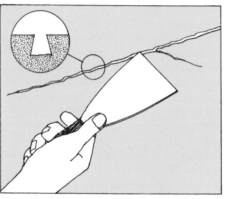

2 Undercut cracks so that they are wider below surface. The filler will be well anchored in place.

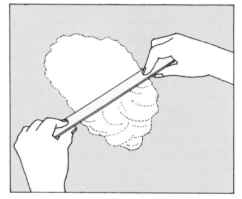

3 To smooth plaster, use a straight-edged batten wider than the patch. Press the ends against the wall and draw it down the plaster.

4 Gaps between the top of a skirting and the wall can be filled with flexible mastic sealant.

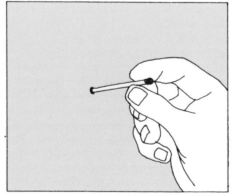

5 To find screw holes for fixtures after papering, put a matchstick in each one, leaving about 12mm ($\frac{1}{2}$ in) to pop through the new paper.

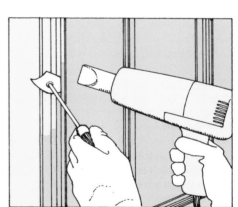

6 A shavehook is needed to get paint out of mouldings. Keep the heat gun moving to avoid scorching the wood.

– it serves as an ideal base for the new paint. The only time to remove sound paint is when a door or window is not closing properly because the paint is too thick.

Rub down lightly with medium glasspaper to take the shine off the old paint and leave a surface to which the new paint will grip. Wash it with sugar soap, rinse with clean water and leave it to dry. It's worth cleaning out keyholes and the top edges of doors and window frames because any dirt trapped there can be picked up on the brush bristles and spread on to the new paint. About ten minutes before painting use a lint-free rag moistened with white spirit to wipe the surface and pick up any dust that has settled – especially in corners. This dust is the cause of a 'speckled' effect you sometimes see spoiling finished paintwork.

If there are signs of the previous paint having run down the surface – most likely to be seen around door handles or below mouldings – rub them flat with medium glasspaper. The same applies to any small areas of wrinkled paint.

Where paint has chipped or there are hairline cracks – usually found in the joints of a door or window – apply cellulose filler with a filling knife. Allow the filler to dry, then rub smooth.

If the wood is to be varnished rather than painted, use a wood stopping of a shade to match the wood. Cellulose filler cannot be used because it dries white and would be seen through the varnish.

Paint that is in a poor state – peeling or flaking or with lots of chips in it – as is sometimes the case with door frames or skirtings, should be removed back to bare wood.

The easiest way to remove paint is by using a hot-air gun. Rather like a hair-dryer, this directs a blast of hot air, which softens the old paint so that it can be stripped off with a flat scraper or a shavehook in mouldings. Play the gun back and forth across the surface so that it is not directed at one spot, which could scorch the wood. If that does happen, use glasspaper to sand down to fresh wood.

There are various chemical paste and liquid strippers sold under brand names. They are much more expensive to use than a heat gun, especially on really thick paint, where more than one application is needed, so for speed and economy, use a heat gun where possible. However, heat can cause glass to crack, so you might prefer to use a chemical stripper here. Chemicals are also useful in clearing intricate mouldings because of the possibility of the wood being scorched. Dab or brush the chemicals on, following the instructions, and when the paint wrinkles, strip it off with the appropriate shavehook.

When the paint is removed and the wood is bare, clean the surface where chemical stripper was used. This is done with white spirit or whatever the instructions on the container advise – the object is to completely neutralize any remnants of the stripper, which could adversely affect the new paint.

Next, fill any holes or cracks as before, sand down the surface by using glasspaper or an orbital sander and you are ready to paint. Use a lint-free rag to dab shellac knotting on to any wood knots on the surface and allow to dry. Follow with primer, undercoat and gloss paint, allowing each to dry for the recommended period before applying the next coat. Always use the undercoat recommended for the top coat of gloss. If necessary, especially where the old paint was a dark colour, you might have to use two layers of undercoat to completely obliterate the old colour. Allow the first undercoat sufficient drying time before applying the second coat.

Metal work
Where metal window frames are being painted, follow the same procedure as for woodwork. If in good condition, lightly rub down, wash with sugar soap, rinse with clean water and apply undercoat and gloss. If there is flaking paint on a window, strip it off, apply metal primer, undercoat and gloss. Any rust spots should be rubbed clean with emery cloth before applying a metal primer.

Paint radiators only when they are cold and keep the heat turned off for twenty-four hours after the final coat of gloss. An undercoat followed by gloss is sufficient.

Ceramic tiles
One of the advantages of tiles is that they can be applied to almost any surface, provided it is dry and level. Preparation may take as long as the actual tiling, but is essential for a good finish. If you attempt to work on an uneven surface, the tiles will quickly start to run out of true and will be impossible to align.

Old tiles
Ensure they are firmly fixed and remove grease and dirt. The odd loose tile can be refixed with tile adhesive.

Timber, chipboard
Absorbent surfaces should be primed with building adhesive (see under Plaster).

If the surface is generally uneven, you have two choices. First, get a professional plasterer to re-plaster the wall. Second, line the wall with plasterboard.

FLOORS

Examine the surface carefully to see if there are any protruding nail or pin heads. If so, drive them below the surface with a hammer and nail punch. Remove any old carpet tacks with a claw hammer or pincers. Fill small gaps between boards with mastic. Block off larger gaps by planing a strip of wood to a wedge shape, smearing its sides with woodwork adhesive and tapping it down into the gap. Leave it to dry, then plane it smooth with the surface. If there are lots of gaps, cover the floor with sheets of hardboard.

A floorboard that squeaks when trodden on is irritating and is impossible to cure easily once a floorcovering has been laid. So, faced with a bare room, walk all over the floor, especially in those areas that get most use, and listen for a squeak. The noise is caused either by the edges of two boards rubbing together or by loose boards. If it is the former, puffing some talcum powder down between the edges of the offending boards should do the trick.

If a board is loose, refix it. Originally, the boards will have been nailed to the joists below. You will notice pairs of nails at the ends of the boards, and possibly in the middle. Find the point of the squeaking noise and you will have found the loose nail. Although a board can be re-nailed, it is better to take out the loose nail with pincers or a claw hammer and insert a screw in exactly the same place. This way you will know you are putting the screw directly into the joist and not into a cable or pipe below the boards. Use a screw such as a 50mm (2 in) long No 8 or 10, which will give a really firm fixing.

Laying hardboard

If you are going to lay a vinyl floor, lino or cork tiles, you must first cover the floorboards with sheets of hardboard. This will provide a perfectly flat, smooth surface and ensure that the floorcovering wears well. Even those floorboards that are flat and have no gaps between them are not suitable as a sub-floor for the

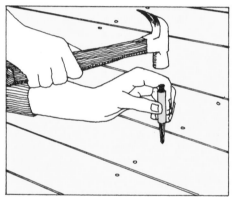

1 Punch any protruding nails below the surface. Extract carpet tacks.

2 Fill wide gaps by glueing a wood wedge in place and planing it smooth. Hammer on to scrap wood to prevent damage.

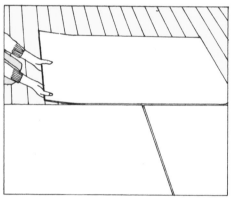

3 Lay sheets of hardboard so that the joints are staggered.

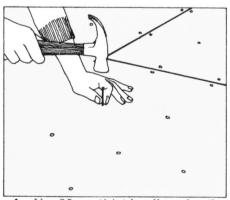

4 Use 25mm (1 in) hardboard nails to fix the sheets. Punch all heads below the surface. Using pliers to hold the nails saves many a bruise.

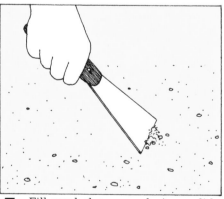

5 Fill any holes or cracks in a solid floor with mortar.

6 Use a self-smoothing screeding compound to level undulations in a solid floor.

floorcoverings mentioned. After a while, their outline will tend to show through the floorcovering in the areas of heaviest use, causing premature wearing.

Before laying, you should condition hardboard to the moisture content of the room in which it is to be used. All rooms have different moisture contents – kitchens and bathrooms obviously having the highest – and to prevent any new timber warping later, it must be brought to the same moisture content as the room.

Brush or spray cold water on to the rough side of the hardboard. Use about 1 litre ($1\frac{3}{4}$ pt) for each 2440 x 1220mm (8 x 4 ft) board, then stack the boards flat on the floor, back to back, for 48 hours in the room in which they are to be used.

You will find the boards easiest to handle if you cut them into 1220 x 1220mm (4 x 4 ft) sheets first. By drawing chalk lines across the room from the mid-point of opposite walls you will find the centre of the room. It is important to start laying here. Don't start from a wall, since few are perfectly true and you will soon find it difficult to line up the edges of the hardboard. The boards should be laid with the joints staggered in brickwork fashion. This makes sure that edges of the boards will not coincide completely with the edges of floor tiles laid later, which would leave a weak spot.

Fix the hardboard sheets (rough side uppermost for tiles, smooth side uppermost for sheet vinyls), with 25mm (1 in) long hardboard nails inserted at 150mm (6 in) intervals, starting near the middle and working out to the edge of the sheet. At the edges insert the nails at 100mm (4 in) intervals and 12mm ($\frac{1}{2}$ in) from the edge itself. Use a nail punch with the hammer to sink the nail heads below the surface of the hardboard.

Butt up the edges of the sheets as you work outwards towards the skirtings. Cut pieces to fit odd gaps at the skirtings and around obstacles such as door frames. You don't need to cut these pieces to an exact fit – within 6mm ($\frac{1}{4}$ in) is acceptable. You might even find convenient gaps below skirting boards under which the hardboard can be slipped.

Chipboard floors
These rarely give problems, but if a squeak develops, deal with it in the same way as floorboards. If a section is softened by a water leak, prise it up and lay a new piece of flooring-grade chipboard of the same size and thickness. Nail or screw it to the joists below.

Levelling a solid floor
If you have a solid concrete ground floor that is cracked and uneven, you can create a new smooth floor surface by putting down a self-smoothing compound. This is a powder you mix with water and pour on to the floor surface, where it dries to give a smooth hard, level surface, about 3mm ($\frac{1}{8}$ in) thick. Fill holes and cracks beforehand with a mortar mix. Buy a bag of dry mortar mix for small jobs such as this. Mix the ingredients with water according to the instructions and then smooth it into place with a flexible filling knife.

TECHNIQUES

MEASURING & MARKING

Using a try square
Before use, test a try square for accuracy by holding the stock (handle) firmly against a straight-edged piece of wood and marking a line on the wood against the blade. Then turn the try square over and check that the blade exactly coincides with the drawn line.

To accurately mark timber to length for cutting, first measure and mark the cutting-line position on one face of the wood. Use a sharp pencil or trimming knife for this, depending on the accuracy required. With the stock of the try square held against the wood, and the blade aligned with the length mark on the face side of the timber, pencil or score a cutting-line across the timber. Then mark each edge, using the try square blade as a guide, working from each end of the originally marked line. Finally, use the try square on the side to link the two lines drawn down the remaining edges of the timber. If the lines do not join exactly, either your square is not accurate (check as described above) or the wood is not planed or sawn square.

Using a spirit level
Spirit levels are used to position battens, shelving and other fixtures truly horizontally or vertically on a wall. Vials (glass tubes) containing air bubbles in liquid are used to give horizontal and vertical readings. The reading is correct when the bubble is exactly between the two lines etched on the vial.

Using a sliding bevel
This marking tool has a blade that can be locked at any angle. It is useful when fitting an item to a slope, such as the boards in the under-stairs workshop (p. 142). With the stock held vertically, the blade can be set to the particular slope by tightening the blade locking lever. This angle can then be transferred to the item to be shaped.

Making templates
Templates are patterns used to reproduce shapes. They can be used to ensure that an item with a complicated shape will fit an opening, such as when fitting floor tiles against a doorway, or they can be used to check that shaped items, such as the tops of the screen on p. 145, both look attractive and are uniform.

With a large item like the screen top, first make a pattern from stiff paper. Fold the paper in half across the width to cut out the shape, so you can be sure sides are identical. When you like the shape, trace round it on to a sheet of hardboard, and cut this out with a jigsaw or coping saw to produce a template that can be used several times.

Using a profile gauge
This is an adjustable, reusable template that enables you to reproduce fairly small but complicated shapes, such as the intricate decorative timber moulding around a door frame, and the moulded top of a skirting-board. When the profile gauge is pressed against a shape, the pins adopt the outline of the shape. You can then draw around the gauge with a pencil to transfer the shape of the moulding on to the item to be shaped to fit against it.

Using a marking gauge
This tool is used to mark a fine line parallel to an edge, and is useful for finding the centre of a batten. To set the marking pin to the width required, loosen the thumb screw on the stock and tap the beam on the end to move the stock in the direction required.

When making a halving joint (see p. 224), it is necessary to scribe a line at exactly the mid-point of the rail. To find this point with a marking gauge, set the pin to about the mid-point of the rail. With the stock held against the rail, prick the rail with the pin.

Move the gauge to the opposite face of the rail, and pin-prick the rail again. Make slight adjustments to the pin position until the two pin-pricks coincide exactly from each side of the rail.

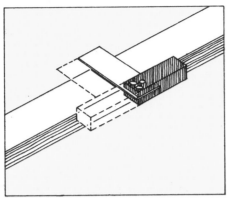

1 Test the accuracy of a try square by marking a line to a straight edge. Then turn the stock over to see if the blade touches the line.

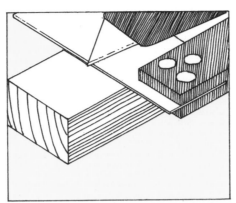

2 To square a line on a length of wood to be cut, first mark across the wood with a pencil or, ideally, a knife against the blade.

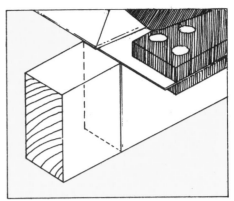

3 From each end of this line mark down the edges of the wood, then square across on the remaining side to join up the lines.

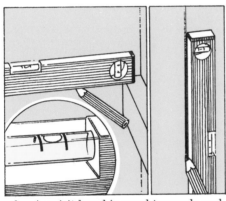

4 A spirit level is used to mark and check horizontals and verticals. The bubble must be exactly in the middle of the glass vial.

5 Use a sliding bevel when you have to mark angles, such as when working under the slope of a staircase. A lever locks the blade.

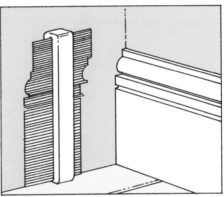

6 A profile gauge has a central portion that holds a row of movable pins. The pins reproduce a shape they are pressed against.

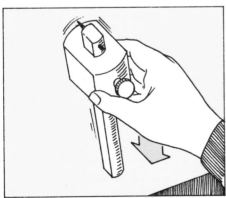

7 To adjust a marking gauge, slightly loosen the screw that locks the stock on the beam, then tap the end of the beam. Check setting after tightening.

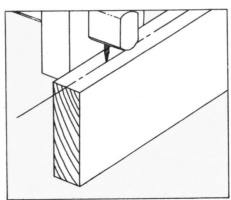

8 For a halving joint, you must mark the exact centre of the wood. Move the stock on the beam until the pin position is same from each side.

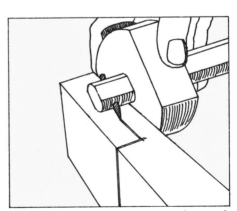

9 To use the gauge, press the stock against the side of the wood, then push the gauge away from you so the trailing pin marks the wood.

USING HAND & POWER TOOLS

Smoothing sawn edges

When edges need to be smooth to look good or to have an iron-on edging veneer applied, clamp the board in a vice or portable workbench with the edge to be smoothed uppermost, and plane down to the cutting line with a sharp smoothing plane. You can safely plane solid timber from one end of a length to the other (called planing with the grain – if it leaves a rough surface, plane in the opposite direction), but with blockboard or other composite or synthetic board, or with a piece of timber where you are planing across the grain, it is most important to plane from each edge to the middle to prevent the corners from splitting.

Where it is vital to get the edge absolutely square, it is best to make a **shooting board**. This is made from two lengths of wide board screwed together as shown in the diagram, with a batten acting as a stop screwed across the upper board at 90° to its edge. The board to be trimmed is held against the stop and the plane is run along the shooting board, leaving the edge perfectly flat and true. A shooting board is ideal for trimming end grain because it prevents the edge from splintering.

It is also worth making a mitre shooting board, with battens screwed to the shooting board at 45°, so that you can plane mitred mouldings (see p. 228) to fit.

Using a block plane

A block plane is a small plane specifically for trimming end grain.

Hold the body of the plane as shown in the diagram. Plane from the ends to the middle to prevent splitting of the edge, or support the edge with scrap wood to prevent it from splitting.

Using an auger bit

Auger bits are used for drilling broad, shallow holes in timber. By using the auger in a brace, you can control the depth of the hole (it may be important not to bore right through the wood). You should also choose a bit that cuts exactly to the width required when making a housing or mortise.

Cutting with a handsaw

Stand comfortably, holding the saw as shown in the diagram. Hold the board steady, with the cutting line overlapping the edge of your workbench, and, with a helper supporting the offcut, saw steadily along the waste side of the cutting line. Trim back to the line with a plane.

If you have difficulty in sawing straight, clamp a batten beside the cutting line so that when the saw cuts alongside the batten, it cuts on the waste side of the board.

Sawing with a power saw

If you are making a straight cut and the cut is parallel with, and close to, a straight edge, you can use the rip fence on the saw to achieve a straight cut. If the cut is some distance from the edge, or if the edge is not straight, you can use a batten to guide the saw, as for hand sawing.

Using a padsaw

Drill a hole in the waste part of the cut-out, insert the tip of the padsaw and saw round the cut-out on the waste side of the line.

Making cut-outs with a jigsaw

Drill a hole on the waste side of the cut-out so the blade can be inserted. Switch on and carefully cut on the inside of the line. To make a right-angle corner, cut into the corner from each side.

Mitre cutting with a circular saw

To make a mitre cut with a circular saw, adjust the sole plate of the saw (the base of the saw through which the blade protrudes) to tilt at 45°.

On a wide skirting-board, it is important to cut across the board at right angles (but with the blade set at 45°). Make this easier by cutting against a thin board clamped at right angles to the edge.

Making a shaped cut

A coping saw is ideal for making complicated cuts on the edge of a board, such as when butt-joining skirting-boards to form an internal corner. Fit the blade so the saw cuts on the down stroke if working with the board held flat.

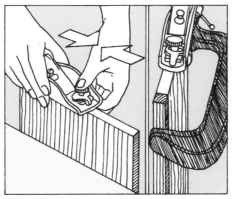

1 A shooting board is easy to make from a couple of wide, square-edged boards, overlapped to form a step. A batten restrains the work. Use a stop on the bench to hold the board steady.

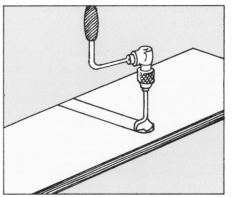

2 A block plane is ideal for smoothing end grain. Hold the body of the plane as shown while applying pressure to the front. Clamp scrapwood against far edge to prevent break-away.

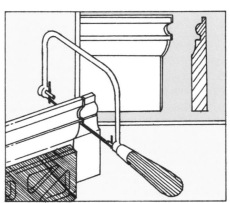

3 Use an auger bit in a brace to bore out the end of a stopped housing joint. The bit should be the same width as the slot.

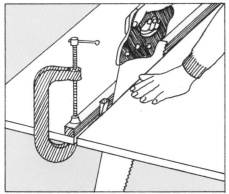

4 A batten clamped to the board makes it easy to make a straight cut with a handsaw. Push a wedge in the cut if it closes on the saw blade.

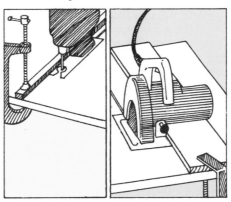

5 A batten can also be used to guide a power saw for straight cuts. Use a wide, thin batten with a circular saw to clear body of saw.

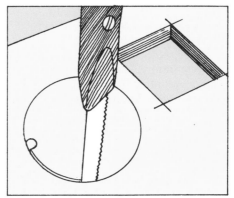

6 A padsaw is ideal for making square and circular cut-outs. Padsaw blades are available for fitting in trimming-knife handles.

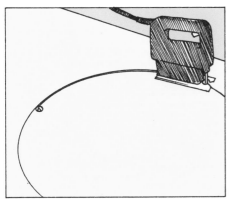

7 To make as large cut-out, it is best to use an electric jigsaw. Drill a start hole in the cut-out on the waste side for the blade to pass through.

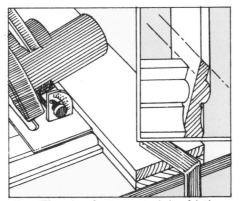

8 The simplest way to join skirting-boards at external corners is with mitre cuts. Set a circular saw to cut precisely at 45°. Cut over scrap piece of board.

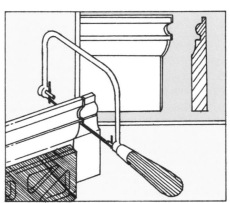

9 Skirtings can be joined at internal corners with mitre cuts, but it is better to shape with coping saw and butt-join.

WOOD-WORKING JOINTS

Butt joints

Butt joints are simple to make, but need to be carefully prepared in order to be strong and look professional.

The square-ended butt joint involves joining two pieces of wood or board together, usually end to side, to form a right-angle corner or a T-joint. The joint is usually reinforced by gluing it and then fixing with either nails or screws. The secret of success with this joint is in ensuring the joining surfaces are perfectly flat and square. Both accurate marking out and cutting are important, although poorly cut edges can be trimmed square with a plane if necessary (see p. 222).

Butt joints can be glued and pinned or screwed, as in the projects on pps. 154 and 182, or they can be held with reinforcing blocks, as in the project on p. 148. Gluing and screwing square battens on the outside of the joints considerably strengthens them and automatically squares up the frame.

Dowel joints

Dowels (hardwood pegs) are a good means of strengthening butt joints without using screws or nails, both of which are visible on the surface.

Use pre-cut, fluted dowels with chamfered ends, which make a strong joint by allowing glue to escape from the dowel hole, coating the surface of the dowel as the joint is assembled.

After preparing a good butt joint, drill aligning holes in the mating surfaces of the joint, and insert dowels in these holes before assembling the joint. One way of doing this is to drill holes in one piece for centre points that mark the other piece for drilling when the joint is assembled. There are also various dowelling jigs (drill-aligning gadgets) available to make it easy to drill holes that align in both parts of the joint.

Halving joints

These joints are ideal for joining wood of identical thickness at corners (corner halvings) or at cross rails (T halvings).

The joints are formed by cutting each piece to exactly half its thickness. First overlap the two pieces of wood and mark the exact width of each piece on the other one. Use a try square to accurately and squarely mark the width of the cut-outs on each piece, and a marking gauge set to exactly half the thickness of the wood to mark the depth of the joints (see p. 220).

Cut out a corner halving joint using a tenon saw. First clamp the wood almost upright, but sloping slightly away from yourself, and cut down to the shoulder line. Turn the wood around and cut down to the shoulder line on the other side. Move the wood upright and cut straight down to the shoulder. Finally, hold the wood flat and saw across the shoulder to complete the cut.

To form a T halving, cut one piece as above. Cut the other, which needs a central cut-out, down to the centre line on the shoulder line at each side of the cut-out, and chisel out the waste wood.

Stopped housing joints

A housing joint is a slot into which a rail fits, as in the kitchen table on p. 174. In a stopped housing joint the slot is taken only part way across the joint so it does not show at the front. Drill out the end of the slot (or housing) as described on p. 223. Saw the sides of the slot with a tenon saw, and then chisel out the waste wood.

To complete this joint, cut a **haunch**, or notch, out of the rail so it fits in the housing slot and butts tightly at the front.

Offset mortise-and-tenon joint

This joint is also used in the kitchen table, to join the side rails to the legs. The tenon on the rail is set to one side and is cut with a tenon saw in the same way as a corner halving joint. The mortise slot, cut to the same width as the tenon, is made with an auger bit, tenon saw and chisel in exactly the same way as a housing joint.

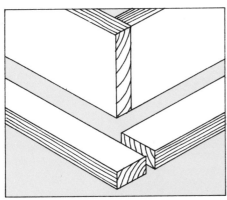

1 To be successful a butt joint must be cut squarely and accurately. Trim with a plane if necessary, then glue and pin.

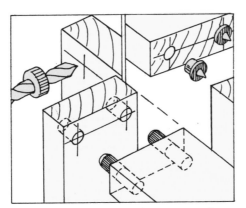

2 Hardwood dowels are a good means of strengthening a butt joint without having nails or screws showing. Centre points help align holes.

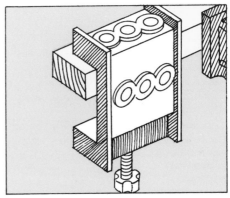

3 To make it easy to align dowel holes, various dowelling jigs are available. These also help to keep the drill bit square to the surface.

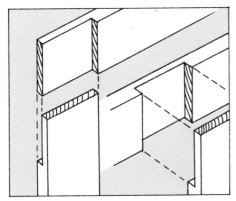

4 Many of the projects use corner halving and T halving joints to join components of similar thickness.

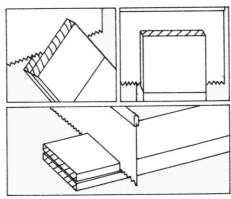

5 Form a corner halving by sawing rail with tenon saw. First saw down to shoulder at each side, then saw square to shoulder, then across.

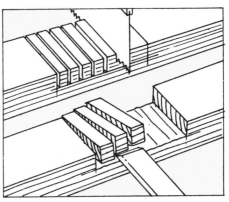

6 A T halving is used to join a cross rail. To make cut-out, saw down to shoulder line, and then chisel out the waste wood.

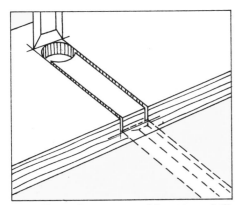

7 To make a stopped housing, drill out end (p. 222), then saw down each side of housing slot and chisel out the waste.

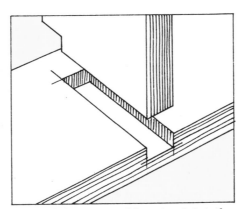

8 With a stopped housing joint, the rail that fits in the housing must have a haunch, or notch, cut in the front so it fits neatly.

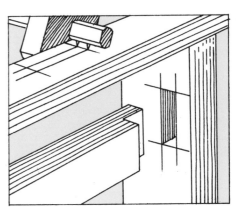

9 An offset mortise-and-tenon joint is used to join side rails to legs in the kitchen table project. The rail tenon is made like a halving joint.

FIXINGS

Using woodworking adhesive
Modern woodworking adhesives tend to be so strong that often they will hold a joint together on their own, although it is usual to reinforce the joint by nailing.

For most of the projects in this book, it is sufficient to use a ready-to-use pva (polyvinyl-acetate) adhesive, the well-known white glue.

Apply the glue to one of the surfaces, bring them together and hold them in position for at least 12 hours for the glue to set.

Using nails and pins
Usually it is best to reinforce a joint by nailing or pinning.

For neatness, use lost-head or oval nails, which have small heads that look unobtrusive when driven flush or below the surface. If small sections of timber are being used, fix them with pins, such as panel pins or veneer pins, which are fine nails that are less likely to split the wood.

The correct length of nail to use is about three times the thickness of the piece being fixed. Rather than driving nails straight in, drive them at an angle (called skew nailing) and drive alternate nails at an opposing angle so they dovetail.

For a neat finish, drive the nail head below the surface of the wood with a nail punch.

Using plastic joint blocks
Plastic joint blocks make it very easy to join timber at right angles. The ends of the timber are sawn square and the joint block is screwed in place to hold them together.

Fixing timber with screws
Always screw a thinner piece of timber to a thicker one. With the thinner piece uppermost, first drill a pilot hole slightly narrower than the width of the screw, excluding the threaded part, and to the depth of the screw. Then drill a clearance hole about the same diameter as the screw shank to about one-third the depth of the hole. Finally, with a countersink bit, **countersink** the top of the hole to take the screw head when the screw is driven home.

Using wall fixings
Wall fixings are used to join fittings such as shelf brackets and timber battens to a wall. Wall fixings fall into two groups: those for solid walls and those for hollow walls. Solid walls sound solid when tapped and produce grey or red dust when drilled (using a **masonry** drill bit). Hollow walls sound hollow when tapped and, after drilling through the plaster layer, the drill bit either disappears into a void or drills into wood if it hits the timber framing.

For solid walls choose a wall-plug that is correct for the size of screw you will be using (the details are printed on the plastic moulding of the plugs). For most uses the screw should be No 8 or 10 in thickness and should be long enough to go through the fitting and the plaster layer, and into the masonry for about 25mm (1 in). The plaster is usually about 10mm ($^3/_8$ in) thick. The plug will also specify what thickness masonry drill to use to make the hole for the plug. Before drilling, check the wall at the drilling position with a battery-operated cable and pipe detector to ensure that there are no unpleasant surprises hidden under the surface of the wall.

Hollow walls are usually made of a sturdy timber framework covered with plasterboard, or lath and plaster. For a strong fixing, it is best to screw straight into the main timbers, called studs, which can be located by using a metal or stud detector (similar to a cable and pipe detector) or by probing with a sharp pointed tool. A metal detector shows up the fixing nails, which will show where the studs are.

Lighter fixings can be made on to plasterboard and lath and plaster by using a fixing designed for that wall.

Aligning holes
When drilling holes in panels for adjustable shelving supports, make a template from hardboard or plywood drilled with accurately spaced holes. If you mark an end 'top' and place it in the same position on each panel, you can be sure the holes will align.

Drilling to a constant depth
When it is important to drill to a certain depth, mark the drill shank with plastic insulation tape as shown.

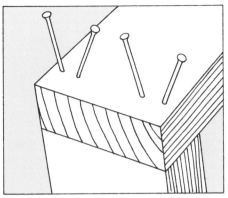

1 Glue and pin a butt joint for strength. Drive the pins in at opposing angles to form a dovetail effect that is difficult to pull apart.

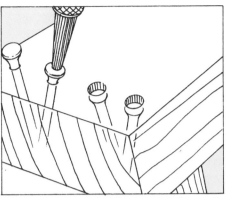

2 For a neat finish use a nail punch to push nail heads below the surface. Fill the indentation with wood-coloured 'stopping' (filler).

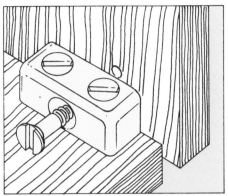

3 Plastic joint blocks are an easy means of forming butt joints. They produce accurate right angles and allow a joint to be dismantled.

4 These are the stages to follow when inserting a screw. Make a full depth pilot hole, then a clearance hole and, finally, countersink.

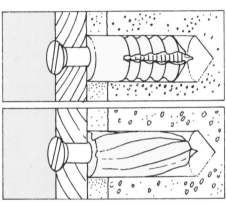

5 These are typical wall fixings for solid walls. Top is a conventional wall-plug and below is plug for softer building blocks.

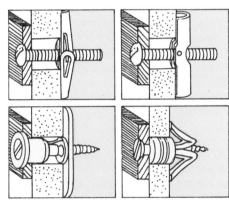

6 There are many types of fixings for cavity walls. None are particularly strong, so for firm fixing screw into main timbers.

7 This home-made drilled hardboard template will ensure that holes for adjustable shelf supports are evenly spaced.

8 Often it is important not to drill too deep, for example when drilling a panel for shelf supports. Simply wrap self-adhesive insulating tape around the drill bit.

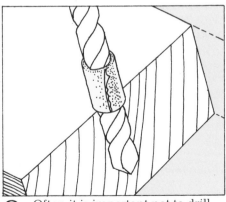

9 Before drilling into a wall, use a metal detector to ascertain that there are no buried water pipes or electric cables there.

FITTING & FINISHING

Applying edge veneer

The sawn exposed edges of blockboard should be covered in some way. The easiest method is to use an iron-on edge veneer.

Make sure the edge is planed smooth (see p. 222), hold the veneer in place at one end, slightly overlapping the end, then apply a hot iron to the veneer (over brown paper, to prevent scorching) to activate the glue. Finish when cool by trimming the edges with a knife or plane, and smooth with abrasive paper.

A more substantial way of finishing an edge is to glue or pin on a strip of hardwood. This should be slightly wider than the blockboard so it can be planed to width after the glue hardens.

Cutting and mitring mouldings

To give a panelled door effect, glue and pin a rectangle of wood moulding (decorative wood strip) on the front.

Make the moulding like a picture frame, cutting the ends at an angle of 45° in a mitre block. After cutting, plane on a mitred shooting board to ensure that the moulding fits together neatly at the corners.

Fitting a flush hinge

Flush hinges are ideal for doors that lie on the surface of the framework, but they can also be used with doors set within a frame. There is no need to cut a recess because one of the hinge flaps closes within the other.

For surface mounting, screw the leaves to the face of the framework (or carcass) and door. The narrower inner leaf is the one to attach to edges.

Fitting flap stays

Stays for pull-down flaps should be chosen carefully. There must be room in the cupboard for the stay to be accommodated when the flap is closed. Most flaps require two stays to be fitted: often these are 'handed', so you need a left-hand and a right-hand stay.

The majority of stays are supplied with fitting instructions, which vary according to the type of stay. Basically, the stay slider fits to the side of the cabinet and the stay pivoting anchor screws to the flap. Fit the slider first, then, with the stay pulled right out and the flap held level, screw the stay anchor to the flap.

Fitting a magnetic catch

Screw the magnet part of the catch to the side of the cabinet, place the metal catch plate over the magnet, then close the door firmly. The plate will mark the door and should be screwed to the door at this position.

It is best to fit a catch as close as possible to the handle, to minimize strain on the hinges.

Using cramps

Very many types of cramps are available for a variety of holding jobs. G-cramps are the most common type and are useful for holding items such as halving joints together while the glue sets. Use scraps of wood between the workpiece and the jaws of the cramp to prevent the cramp from marking the surface. Never over-tighten a cramp or you will squeeze all the glue out of the joint and weaken it.

For holding frames together while glue sets, use either a proprietary web cramp, which is like an adjustable strap that goes round the unit, or make a Spanish windlass from a loop of rope which can be tightened by winding a stick around. Use scraps of wood to prevent the rope from digging into the surface.

Fitting frames against a wall

When you make a frame, it should be perfectly square, but when you come to fit it against a wall you will probably find the wall is out of true. Therefore the edge of the frame will have to 'scribed' to fit.

Hold the frame against the wall as close to its final position as possible. Where the gap against the wall is widest, pull the frame away by about 25mm (1 in). Then, while holding a pencil against a block of wood 25mm (1 in) wide, move the block along the wall while drawing a pencil line on the frame to follow the contour of the wall.

Finally, cut or plane the frame back to this line, and the frame will fit tightly against the wall.

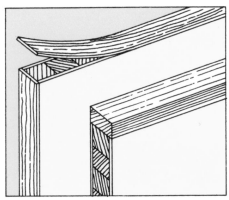

1 Exposed edges of blockboard should be covered. The easiest way is to apply an iron-on veneer. Use a strip of hardwood if the edge takes wear.

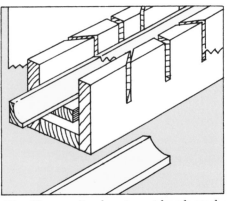

2 Use a mitre box to cut hardwood mouldings to 45° when forming a panel effect. Note that moulding rests on scrap wood in mitre box.

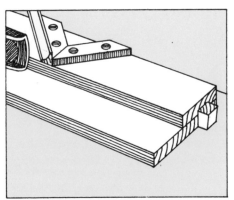

3 An excellent way to clean up the ends of the mitres is with a mitre shooting board, which is used in conjunction with a smoothing plane.

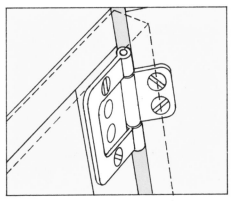

4 It is easiest to use flush hinges when fitting doors. One hinge flap fits inside the other so there is no need to recess the hinge.

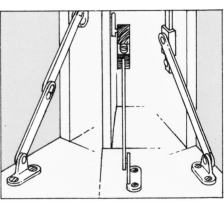

5 There are many types of flap stays and choice depends mainly on how much room there is in the cabinet for the stay arm to retract.

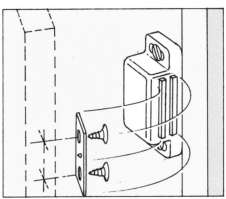

6 A magnetic catch is easy to fit. Screw the main part to the cabinet, with plate on magnet, close door on to plate to mark position, and screw plate to door.

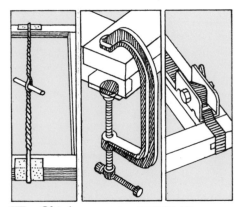

7 Obtain as many cramps as possible – they act as extra hands. A **Spanish windlass** can be made, G- and web cramps must be bought.

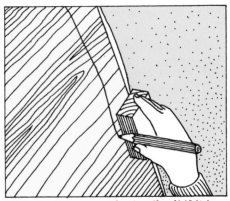

8 An item must be 'scribed' if it is to fit tightly against a wall. Use a small block of wood and a pencil to trace a line on the panel.

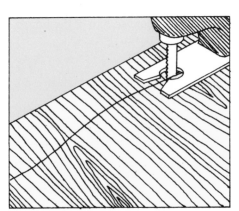

9 Scribing reproduces the undulations of the wall on the panel. Cut or plane to this line and the panel will fit close to the wall.

YEAR-ROUND WORKPLAN

No two houses are the same, but you will ensure your home is kept in tip-top condition and runs smoothly with as few emergencies as possible if you follow our year-round workplan. It covers the important features of the majority of homes, and suggests the optimum time of year for doing a wide range of jobs. Where a task is essential at a particular time it is marked*. Tasks not so marked are best tackled at about the time recommended. Of course, emergencies should be dealt with as and when they occur.

JANUARY/FEBRUARY

Dripping taps* Fix dripping taps at the earliest opportunity. If you ignore them in freezing weather, you could end up with a sinkful of dirty water as a result of a frozen drainpipe. If the drip is severe, the basin could overflow, ruining decorations and carpets.

Check electric plugs Unplug each electric appliance, take off the plug cover by loosening the screw on the underside and check that all the terminal screws are tight on the bared ends of the wires. There should be no stray strands of wire nor any bare wire showing. At the same time you can double check that the plug is wired properly, that the flex grip is clamped on to the *outer* insulation of the flex, and that the correct size fuse is fitted (the appliance instructions specify this).

Check plumbed-in appliances Pull out the washing machine and dishwasher, and check that the water supply pipes (hoses) and drainpipes are not cracked or perished. They hold water at high pressure, so get old pipes replaced in case they burst and cause a flood.

MARCH/APRIL

Interior decorating This is a good time to start interior decorating. Do one room at a time, starting with a small, plain room if this is the first time you have decorated.

Paint Touch-up chipped areas using fine-surface filler. When dry, smooth down with fine abrasive paper, and follow with a dab of paint.

Cracks/dents/holes Go round and fill damaged areas with a ready-mixed wall filler. Just press it in place with a flat-bladed filling knife.

Frozen pipes Have a good look at the pipes for splits and burst joints before attempting to thaw them. It is best to turn off water at the mains and call a plumber if in doubt.

Damp patches There are many reasons for damp patches at this time of year. Structural damp (such as rain coming through the roof or walls, or from leaking pipes) needs the attention of a builder to cure the fault. To cure condensation requires improved heating, insulation and ventilation. If you are not sure of the nature of your damp problem, tape a piece of cooking foil over the damp patch and leave it for a couple of days. Moisture on the surface of the foil indicates condensation; moisture on the underside is a sign of structural damp.

Wallpaper troubles If edges and corners have lifted, glue them down with a smear of heavy-duty wallpaper paste. Use a latex adhesive (used to bind carpets and fabrics) on vinyl and other plastic 'papers'.

Electrical tool kit Keep a small tool kit ready to deal with those electrical problems that involve no more than changing a fuse. It should contain an electrician's insulated screwdriver, torch, trimming knife and a pair of pliers, a selection of plug fuses (3, 5 and 13 amp) and fuses or fuse wire for the main fuseboard near the electricity meter. Make a note alongside the unit which fuse controls which part of the electricity system, or get an electrician to show you.

MAY/JUNE

Fit a circuit breaker* Even though plugs are fused, there is a risk of electrocution with any power tools if things go wrong, especially when used outdoors or in damp areas. A circuit breaker, technically called a residual current device (RCD) or earth-leakage circuit breaker (ELCB), will switch off the current in a fraction of a second if the cable gets cut, etc. The simplest type to fit plugs into an ordinary socket like an adaptor, and you plug your tool or extension cable into this.

Woodworm* Although woodworm can be burrowing under the surface of wood almost all the year round, they are seen in spring, when they become active and emerge as small beetles, leaving the tell-tale holes in the surface of the wood. Keep a watch for the holes, and beetles, and either inject woodworm fluid into the holes if there are not many of them, or call in a specialist eradication company if the problem seems widespread.

Airbricks These are found on outside walls just above ground level and keep ground-floor timbers well aired and rot-free. Make sure airbricks are kept clear of growing plants, and rake away soil that may be piled round them.

JULY/AUGUST

Exterior decorating By now, wet wood will have dried out. Start decorating at the top of the house and work downwards, preparing surfaces first and then painting them. Where possible, work in the shade in areas that have been dried off by the sun. If you are working at a height, work from a scaffold tower if possible; otherwise work from a securely tied ladder.

Exterior woodwork Even if not exterior decorating, check over outdoor timber and repair or replace sections that are affected by rot.

Metal windows Scrape off any rust, wire brush the frame and apply a rust-killing primer, an undercoat and a top coat of paint.

Window putty Rake out dried old loose putty, paint the frame with primer, then press in new putty, smoothing the surface with a smooth-bladed tool, such as a filling knife.

Service heating system* It is important to have heating systems professionally serviced once a year. In summer, turn on the system once a month to keep the pump in working order.

Home security With annual holidays approaching, take steps to improve home security. Fit extra door and window locks. Consider having a burglar alarm system fitted.

SEPTEMBER/OCTOBER

Insulation Check over home insulation. In the loft, insulation should be at least up to the tops of the rafters, and doors and windows should be draught-proof. Self-adhesive draught strips are easy to fit on clean, dry surfaces of door and window frames.

Lag pipes and tanks* When insulation is fitted, lofts become colder, so make sure all water pipes and tanks in the loft are wrapped in insulation (lagging). Never insulate beneath a tank.

Water-tank check Make sure an insulated tank (cistern) is fitted with a water-resistant (but not air-tight) lid to keep out insects. Metal cisterns should be free from brown rust scale. If necessary, have a plumber fit a plastic replacement.

Gutters and rainwater downpipes On a wet day, check gutters and rainwater downpipes for leaks. Joints between sections are prone to trouble, and sometimes sections develop cracks. Sticking waterproof repair tape across the affected part (after drying off) will act as a temporary repair until you have the system renewed. If gutters are overflowing, clean out fallen leaves and other debris blocking them.

NOVEMBER/DECEMBER

Radiator care If central heating radiators do not get sufficiently hot, air may be trapped in them and they need 'bleeding'. First turn off the central heating. Buy a special key for turning the small bleed nut at the top of the radiator at one end. Loosen this nut and listen for the hiss of escaping air. When water trickles out, tighten the nut (turn clockwise).

Locate and test stopcocks Before an emergency like a burst pipe occurs, locate the water supply stopcocks so the water can be turned off. Make sure they are not too stiff to turn; if necessary get a plumber to free them.

Winter holdiay precautions Avoid frozen pipes by leaving central heating on a very low level with internal doors and the loft hatch open, or have the heating come on for short periods night and morning. If this seems wasteful, have the system drained down by a plumber, but be sure to refill again before turning on the heating system.

Burst pipe repair kit Keep a torch and a roll of waterproof repair tape handy so that you can make temporary repairs to a burst pipe or leaking joint.

GENERAL REPAIRS

DEAL WITH THESE AS SOON AS THEY OCCUR

Broken windows Not only dangerous, but a real security risk; they let in water, too. Replace with a new pane at the first opportunity.

Leaking pipes Keep a constant watch for damp patches, indicating leaking pipes. If left unattended, they can ruin decorations and start wood rot.

Dripping overflow pipes A sign of faulty ball valve in a toilet cistern or water tank. Must be repaired or replaced before a complete failure allows the water to overflow and flood.

Difficult to flush WC A flap valve in the flushing mechanism needs to be renewed. Call in a plumber.

Slow to clear sink/basin Grease or dirt build-up in the waste pipe. Try de-greasing with washing soda crystals and boiling water, or use a proprietary drain cleaner.

Blocked sink/basin Block the overflow outlet, with a wet rag, for example, and work a rubber plunger up and down to clear the blockage. Alternatively, poke a flexible wire drain cleaner down the outlet (plug hole).

Blocked WC/drains Well worth calling in a specialist drain clearer to tackle this job!

Storm damage After a storm, look for broken slates or tiles on the ground, and examine the house roof and chimneys through binoculars. Have any damage repaired by a builder and claim on the household insurance.

Smoke alarm: Install one of these essential safety devices on each floor level. Only a few pounds to buy and easy to fit by screwing to a ceiling.

GLOSSARY

All purpose
Used in all situations and with all materials; for example, all-purpose wallpaper paste can be used to hang vinyls, woodchip, lightweight paper and so on. Sometimes it is called universal.

Analglypta
The brand name of a heavyweight, textured wall-covering that is intended to be painted with emulsion.

Architrave
The plain or ornate wood frame around a window or door.

Balusters
The vertical posts or pillars supporting the handrail on stairs.

Banister
Sometimes called the balustrade, it refers to the complete barrier (balusters and handrail) on a staircase or landing.

Batten
A narrow strip of wood, for example, 25 x 25mm (1 x 1 in), 50 x 25mm (2 x 1 in) or 75 x 25mm (3 x 1 in) in section.

Beading
Thin section of wood, usually square or rectangular, used to cover gaps or end grain of wood.

Bed down
To place tiles, for example, firmly into mortar or adhesive.

Bevel
A slanting edge, for example, on a piece of wood or glass, or on a bevel-edged chisel.

Bitumen felt
Roofing material impregnated with bitumen.

Bleeding through
When paint or resin in wood seeps through a top coat of paint or a wall-covering, staining the surface.

Bolster chisel
A chisel having a blade 75–100mm (3–4 in) wide which is struck with a club hammer to cut bricks.

Bonded
One material being joined to another with adhesive.

Bradawl
Tool which is twisted on the surface of wood to make a slight indentation to serve as a starter hole for a screw to be driven into.

Buttering
Putting on a generous layer of adhesive.

Butting up
Two pieces of material meeting right against each other.

Cable
Carries electricity from the consumer unit around the power and lighting circuits to switches, socket outlets and ceiling roses. Modern cable is called twin core and earth and the greater the current flowing through it, the thicker is the cable.

Cantilever
A structure – for example, a shelf – fixed to a wall and overhanging its support.

Cartridge and applicator gun
All types of mastic and panel adhesive are supplied in a tube container. This is fitted into a device which, by squeezing its trigger, applies pressure to the base of the tube and forces the material out through the nozzle.

Casement
A hinged-opening window.

Centres
The distance or spacing between the centre lines of objects. For example, nails can be fixed at 300mm (12 in) centres across a workpiece. Battens 50mm (2 in) wide placed at 400mm (16 in) centres would have a gap of 350mm (14 in) between them.

Chamfer
A corner or edge at a 45° angle. If the angle is other than 45°, it is called a bevel (q.v.).

Chinagraph pencil
Used to draw cutting guide lines on glass; it leaves a crayon-like mark.

Conditioning
Acclimatizing wood, cork tiles or

other material to the moisture content of a room before fixing it in place.

Consumer unit
The central control box of a domestic electricity system. It is from here that all the power and lighting circuits are fed around the house and controlled by fuses and a main on/off switch.

Cornice
Sometimes called coving, it is the continuous horizontal moulding that covers the join between wall and ceiling. It can be plain or ornate and be made of plaster, expanded polystyrene or wood.

Countersink
To insert a screw so that its head lies below surface in a cone-shaped recess.

Cutting-in
Painting accurately into an angle without smudging an adjacent surface; for example, painting window frames without getting paint on the glass.

Dado rail
A wooden rail that is fixed horizontally and roughly at chair-back height along a wall as a decorative feature.

Decorative seal
A coat of liquid used to both decorate and protect a wood surface.

Detector
Electronic device used to trace cables, pipes or timber uprights in walls.

Disposable blade
A cheap blade that is thrown away when blunt. More expensive blades are normally resharpened for use.

Double-sided tape
Tape with adhesive on both surfaces.

Dried edge
The line where the paint has dried when work has been halted before the entire surface has been painted. It is clearly seen when the surface has been fully painted.

Dry
The method of fixing, laying or mounting material without an adhesive being used.

Dry stripping
Removing old paintwork by scraping or sanding without the aid of heat or chemicals.

Dusting
A solid wall or floor which has a coating of dust on the surface.

Escutcheon
The protective plate around a keyhole or door handle.

Expansion gap
A space left between a material and a wall for the material to expand into and so prevent it from buckling; for example, round the perimeter of wood-block flooring.

Expansion strip
A strip of material used to fill an expansion gap where

appearance is important. The strip would be flexible enough to contract under pressure from expanding material.

Face nailing
Nails driven directly into the centre of boards and not into the tongues.

Feather
To draw a sponge across a surface so that the material being applied is left with the thinnest possible edge.

Flex
Thinner and more flexible than cable, it connects electrical appliances or lighting to the cable carrying the power from the consumer unit. Flex is round, white, and can be of rubber or pvc. Flex used for outdoor appliances is normally orange. Two-core and three-core versions are available – the latter being needed for metal light fittings and appliances requiring an earth conductor.

Float
A flat, rectangular steel sheet with a handle. It is used to smooth over plaster.

Float glass
Floating is the method of manufacturing glass to create a perfectly flat surface. A mirror made of float glass will have no distortion in the reflection.

Flush
A single level or flat surface, or surfaces that adjoin at the same level.

Framework
An arrangement of battens built to receive a covering of some kind, such as cladding.

Full coat
Paint applied undiluted.

Galvanized
Metal that has been coated with zinc to prevent it from.rusting.

Gate valve
A tap fitted into a general distribution water pipe which can control the water flowing through it. General distribution pipes run at low pressure. The valve is usually operated with a wheel rather than a conventional tap handle.

Gauge
The number indicating the thickness or diameter of a screw, for example, No. 6. Also refers to tools for measuring.

Gauging rod
A piece of wood used in brickwork and tiling which is marked off in brick or tile increments. It is used for checking the alignment of courses during bricklaying or tiling.

Grommet
A ring of plastic or rubber lining a hole in an electrical fitting which protects cable entering the hole from wearing.

Grouting
Filler used in the joint lines between ceramic tiles. It can be purchased as a powder to be mixed with water or in ready-to-use form.

Hollow wall
An internal wall made by nailing plasterboard to both sides of a timber framework.

Housing
An enclosed aperture containing another object.

Joists
The horizontal beams of wood that support the floorboards and/or ceilings.

Key
Abrasions or score marks made on a surface so that paint, plaster or adhesive will get a better grip.

Laying-off
Brushing out paint to spread it across the surface without reloading the brush.

Line
A length of string used as a guide to ensure you work to a vertical or horizontal line.

Locator
Small block fixed to one part of a workpiece to ensure its correct alignment with another.

Loose lay
Flooring material which is not fixed in any way.

Masking
Protecting a surface from splashes or defining the boundary of a surface to be painted.

Mastic
A compound which is used to seal tiny gaps and joints. It dries firm but never sets completely, thereby remaining flexible and able to cope with any surface movement.

Mating surfaces
Those faces of two pieces of wood that meet when a joint is made.

MCB
A miniature circuit breaker, which is a modern substitute for a circuit fuse in the electric consumer unit or fusebox.

Mitre
To cut two mating surfaces, each to a 45° angle, so that the components form a right angle when joined.

Mortar
A mixture of sand and cement used in building walls or for rendering, or for filling large cracks.

Mortise
A recess cut in a piece of wood to receive the projecting tongue (tenon) of a mating piece.

Moulding
Ornamental patterns in wood found on door panels, balusters, etc. Also narrow strips of wood used to cover gaps between meeting parts of a structure; for examples of different types of moulding see p. 210.

Mullions
The vertical strips of wood used

to divide a window into smaller sections. *See also* transoms.

Nosing
The front rounded edge of a stair tread.

Offcuts
Pieces of wood discarded after sawing a main piece.

Offering
To hold an object in its intended position on the wall or framework.

Ovolo moulding
A narrow, shaped length of wood. (*See* 'materials').

Packing pieces
Small scrap pieces of wood or board used behind a batten to compensate for an undulation in the wall surface.

Paint pads
Used mostly for applying emulsion paint. Consists of short mohair bristles fixed to a foam pad and mounted on a handle. Various sizes are made.

Pilot hole
A hole drilled in wood to accept the complete length of a screw. This makes it easier to drive in the screw.

Plinth
A length of wood, usually about 50 to 150mm (2 to 6 in) wide used as a skirting to cover the gap between the floor and the bottom of doors in a piece of furniture. Can also be called a footboard.

Plumb
Perfectly vertical.

Plumb-bob
A line of string with a weight on one end (called a bob) which is used to check that something is vertical. The string will automatically hang down at a true vertical.

Pointing tool
An implement used to shape the mortar in between courses of bricks.

Porous surface
Brickwork or other material that allows water or paint to soak into it easily.

Pre-drilled
Screw holes factory made in material for convenience when assembling or fixing an item.

Pre-sealed
Something – for example, cork tiles or wood flooring – that has been treated in the factory with a coating of sealer.

Primer-sealer
An oil-based coating that is used to seal a surface and provide a stable background for paint.

RCD
A residual current device, also known as an ELCB (earth-leakage circuit breaker) or RCCB (residual current-operated earth-leakage circuit breaker). It detects a broken flex or cable or a fault in an appliance and instantly switches off the power.

Runs
A trickle of paint, usually coming from a fixture or a corner, caused by applying an excessive amount.

Sash
The part of a window that can be opened.

Score
To scratch or abrade a surface. *See also* Key.

Screed
A layer of cement-based material used to cover a floor.

Scribe
To shape the edge of a piece of wood; for example, to fit exactly the contours of a wall.

Secret nailing
Using one of different methods to hide evidence of nails used in fixing.

Setting
Drying of paint, adhesive, filler, and so on.

Shading
Checking that the colours in two rolls of wallpaper are an exact match – sometimes there are slight differences, which may be noticeable after the paper is on the wall.

Shoulder
See Techniques, cutting joints in wood.

Skim coat
A very thin coat of plaster.

Skirting
The horizontal board fixed at the base of a wall.

Soak wallpaper
To leave a length of wallpaper that has been pasted for a few minutes in order that the paste can soak in. Medium-weight paper needs a couple of minutes and heavyweight papers need up to ten minutes to become supple. If paper is not soaked, it will not stick properly. Not all wall-coverings need to be soaked – read the instruction label.

Sound condition
In good structural order, needing no repair work.

Spacer washers
Plastic washers, about 3mm (1/8 in) thick, which are placed between a screw head and the wall to ensure a gap is left behind a mirror and the wall.

Spanish windlass
Improvised cramps with thick string or cord; used to secure frameworks while adhesive is setting.

Spreading rate
The area that a given quantity of paint will cover.

Stopcock
A tap fitted into a water pipe which enables the water supply to be turned off or on. Normally used in mains supply pipe where the water is running at high pressure.

Structural movement
Movement of part of a house; this can be normal seasonal movement or be due to a building fault, such as failed foundations.

Sub-floor
The floor – timber or concrete – found below the floor-covering.

Swing-brace
A tool with a bit to make large diameter holes in wood. The handle can be turned in a complete circle. The term 'swing' is not always used.

Tacking
Fixing using tacks.

Tees and cross tees
The metal sections used to form a supporting grid for suspended ceiling tiles.

Template
A pattern made of a shape, particularly an awkward one, which is transferred to another material to be cut.

Textured compound
A thick paint-like compound which provides a textured finish for ceilings and walls.

Thinning
Diluting paint to use as a primer coat or to make it more liquid. Water, white spirit or a thinner recommended by the manufacturer is used.

Tile file
Flat strip of metal having a tungsten carbide abrasive surface. It is used to smooth the rough cut edges of tiles.

Tongued-and-grooved
Timber cladding that is meant to lock closely. One edge of the board has a tongue, or projection, on it; the other has a groove, or slot. The tongue of one board slides into the groove of its neighbour.

Touch-in
Put a dab of paint on to a small area.

Transoms
The horizontal strips of wood used to divide a window into smaller sections. *See also* mullions.

Undercut
A crack made wider below the surface so that an inverted V-shape is formed. This holds the filler in place.

Unfinished
Usually applied to a material (eg parquet floor tiles) which are supplied without a protective coating.

Universal
See all-purpose.

Unstable surface
Not suitable for redecoration before remedial work is done. The problem can be a very minor one, such as dust or dirt, or major, for example, like structural instability.

Veneer
A thin layer of attractive timber fixed to a thick core of a less appealing wood.

Waterproof building paper
Available in rolls from builder's merchants, it comprises a sandwich of two sheets of strong paper with a filling of bituminised fibre netting.

Woodchip
A thick, textured wallpaper, which is intended to be painted with emulsion.

Work
To apply movement or pressure to a tool, material or workpiece.

Workable
Any liquid that is at the right consistency for easy application.

Working with the grain
Painting, polishing or sanding wood in the direction of the grain.

CALCULATING THE NUMBER OF ROLLS

Measurement round walls in metres, including doors and windows	Height from skirting in metres							Ceilings
	2.1-2.3	2.3-2.4	2.4-2.6	2.6-2.7	2.7-2.9	2.9-3.0	3.0-3.2	
9.1	4	5	5	5	6	6	6	2
10.4	5	5	5	5	6	6	7	2
11.6	5	6	6	6	7	7	8	2
11.6	6	6	7	7	7	8	8	3
12.8	6	7	7	7	8	8	9	3
14.0	7	8	9	9	9	10	10	4
16.5	8	8	9	9	10	10	11	4
17.7	8	9	10	10	10	11	12	5
18.9	9	9	10	10	11	12	13	5
20.1	9	10	11	11	12	12	13	6
21.3	10	10	12	12	12	13	14	7
23.8	10	11	12	12	13	14	15	7

NUMBER OF ROLLS REQUIRED

WALLPAPER CALCULATING CHART

To calculate the number of rolls you require take (a) the measurement round your walls in metres (including doors and windows) and find the nearest appropriate measurement in Column 1.

Then (b) work out the height, in metres, from the skirting to the ceiling. Find the appropriate category in the large central column. The number of rolls of wallpaper you require will be the number located where your (a) and (b) points meet. The number of rolls for your ceiling is located in the right hand column on the same line as the number of rolls required.

INDEX